A Guide to
Reading & Writing
JAPANESE

Third Edition

A Comprehensive Guide to the Japanese Writing System

first edition compiled by
Florence Sakade

third edition revised by
Kenneth Henshall, Christopher Seeley & Henk de Groot

TUTTLE PUBLISHING
Tokyo • Rutland, Vermont • Singapore

Published by Tuttle Publishing, an imprint of Periplus Editions (HK) Ltd., with editorial offices at 364 Innovation Drive, North Clarendon, VT 05759 and 61 Tai Seng Avenue, #02-12, Singapore 534167.

Original edition © 1959 by Charles E. Tuttle Co., Inc.
Third edition © 2003 Periplus Editions (HK) Ltd.

LCC Card No. 59-10412
ISBN-10: 0-8048-3365-6
ISBN-13: 978-0-8048-3365-3

Distributed by:

Japan
Tuttle Publishing
Yaekari Building, 3rd Floor
5-4-12 Osaki, Shinagawa-ku
Tokyo 141-0032, Japan
Tel: (81) 3 5437 0171; Fax: (81) 3 5437 0755
Email: tuttle-sales@gol.com

North America, Latin America & Europe
Tuttle Publishing
364 Innovation Drive
North Clarendon, VT 05759-9436, USA
Tel: 1 (802) 773 8930; Fax: 1 (802) 773 6993
Email: info@tuttlepublishing.com
www.tuttlepublishing.com

Asia Pacific
Berkeley Books Pte Ltd
61 Tai Seng Ave, #02-12
Singapore 534167
Tel: (65) 6280 1330; Fax: (65) 6280 6290
Email: inquiries@periplus.com.sg
www.periplus.com

10 09 08   10 9 8 7 6

Printed in Singapore

TUTTLE PUBLISHING® is a registered trademark of Tuttle Publishing,
a division of Periplus Editions (HK) Ltd.

CONTENTS

INTRODUCTION

1 Aim

This newly revised edition is designed for students and others who have at least an elementary knowledge of spoken Japanese and are wanting to acquaint themselves with the Japanese writing system. To this end, this book sets out the 1,945 Chinese characters contained in the officially approved character list—the *Jōyō kanji* (General-Use Characters) List—which in 1981 replaced the earlier list approved in 1946.

2 This Book and the Modern Japanese Writing System

2.1 About the Characters Selected

While the *Jōyō kanji* List (hereafter abbreviated to JK List) does not represent an exhaustive list of Chinese characters which the student will encounter in modern Japanese texts, in combination with the two syllabaries (hiragana and katakana) it does nevertheless provide a very sound basis for reading and writing modern Japanese. In Japanese schools, 1,006 of the more commonly used JK List characters are taught in the six years of elementary school, the balance of 939 characters being spread out over the intermediate and high school curriculum. The JK List characters also form the basis of character usage in modern newspapers, though sometimes the Japan Newspaper Association chooses to deviate from the List in some ways. At the end of 2001 the following 39 characters in addition to those in the JK List were adopted by the Association for active use in newspapers: 闇鍋 牙瓦鶴玩磯臼脇錦駒詣拳鍵虎虹尻柿餌腫袖腎須誰腺曽酎枕賭瞳 頓丼汎斑釜謎妖嵐呂. We simply list these here for readers' possible future reference, and do not go into readings or meanings.

For writing the names of their children, Japanese today can choose from a corpus of characters consisting of the JK List together with a supplementary list of characters for use in given names. The first such name character list, approved in 1951, consisted of 92 characters, but that has been expanded on repeated occasions (and not without some controversy) to 285. We do not list these here.

This book is divided into two main sections. Section One presents the 1,006 characters designated by the Japanese Ministry of Education to be taught during the six years of elementary school—termed here 'Essential Characters'. The choice of these characters is the result of extensive research and deliberation by the Ministry. For these characters, the editors of this volume have endeavored to give illustrative character compounds that are in common use.

Section Two of this book sets out the 1,945 characters designated for general everyday use (including the 1,006 characters taught at elementary school). In 1946 the Japanese writing system underwent fairly radical reform in the direction of simplification, but the 1970s onwards saw some movement away from what some saw as an over-simplification, and the trend towards use of a bigger range of Chinese characters has been encouraged by the development and popularity from the mid-1980s of word-processors and computers that can handle conventional Japanese text. Despite this trend, the major impact of the orthographic reforms of the late 1940s has meant that the Japanese writing system of today still remains much simpler than it was before 1946.

2.2 How Characters are Read in Japanese

Typically, each Chinese character has two types of readings—*on-yomi* and *kun-yomi*. The *on-yomi* (on reading, i.e. Sino-Japanese reading) is a reading originally based on the Chinese pronunciation associated with each character, and reflects the fact that the Chinese script was adopted from China the best part of 2,000 years ago, when the Japanese themselves did not have a writing system. Contrasting with the *on-yomi* is the *kun-yomi* (*kun* reading, i.e. native Japanese reading). In some cases, a given Chinese character has several *on* readings, reflecting different forms of underlying Chinese pronunciation. A given character may also have more than one associated *kun* reading. Context and the use or absence of accompanying kana (*okurigana*) are the pointers as to which reading is appropriate in a given case.

In this book, the majority of the readings set out in the JK List as it appeared in the *Kanpō* (Official Gazette) of 1 October 1981 have been included, but some readings have been excluded, bearing in mind the aim of this book, because they are archaic, obsolescent, or not common (e.g. *nagomu* [to soften] for 和). Also excluded from among the formal readings listed in this book are the sort of common minor—or relatively minor—variations in character readings which are found only in certain environments in compounds. For instance, the character 学 has the on reading GAKU, which is truncated to GAK- in the compound 学校 *gakkō* [school, college], the *kun* reading *ame* [rain] of 雨 changes to *ama-* as the first element in compounds such as 雨戸 *amado* [rain-shutters], and the character 合 GŌ is read GAT- in the compound 合点 *gatten* [understanding, consent]. It was considered best for readers of this book to learn such changes gradually as they progress.

In modern Japanese usage there are quite a number of characters which lack either an *on* reading or a *kun* reading. For instance, nowadays the character 糖 [sugar] is employed only for its on reading TŌ, while the character 箱 [box] is used only for its *kun* reading *hako*.

2.3 Writing Characters

Firstly, the student should make every effort to practice so as to keep the characters of uniform size in relation to one another. Thus, the 2-stroke character 刀 *katana* should be written within the equal-sized imaginary square or circle as the 15-stroke 論 RON [argument, opinion], and by the same token the element 言 should be written larger when used as an independent character (read GEN, GON, [speech, word]) than when used as a radical / component in a more complex character such as 論 RON above.

Secondly, bear in mind that Chinese characters sometimes consist of just a few strokes, sometimes many, but the characters are always written according to a set stroke order. Listed below are some principles that will be of assistance with regard to priority in the order of strokes.

1. Top to bottom:

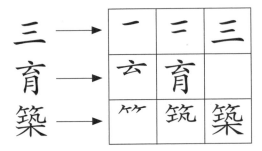

2. Left to right:

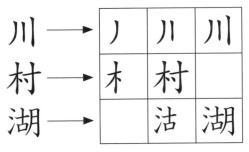

INTRODUCTION

Other rules are:

3. When two or more strokes cross, horizontal strokes usually precede perpendicular ones:

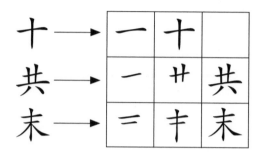

4. Sometimes perpendicular strokes precede horizontal ones:

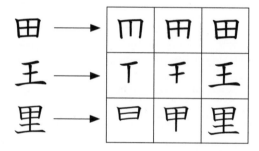

5. Center first, then left and right:

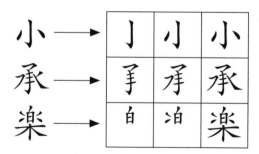

6. Perpendicular line running through center written last:

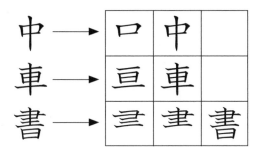

7. Right-to-left diagonal stroke precedes left-to-right:

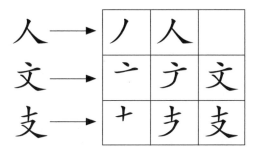

While the above may all seem rather complicated, the student might find solace in the fact that, as noted above, the writing system has been simplified to a considerable extent compared with the past, and has been mastered by many thousands of students having neither native speaker competence in Japanese nor prior background knowledge of the Chinese script.

2.4 Romanization

There are several different systems of representing Japanese using the Roman alphabet. This book employs a slightly modified form of the Hepburn system, this being a system which is widely used and which is based on conventions associated with the spelling of English. The minor modification involves using the letter n rather than *m* to represent the syllabic nasal ん when the latter occurs immediately before the consonants *m*, *b* or *p* (thus, for instance, *shinbun* [newspaper], not shimbun, and *kenpō* [constitution], not *kempō*). Other points to note are:

1. use of a macron to indicate vowel lengthening for *o* and *u*, e.g. *gakkō* [school], *renshū* [practice];

2. use of a hyphen in cases where it is considered that this might facilitate understanding of boundaries between constituent elements in a Japanese word, e.g. *sara-arai* [dishwashing], rather than *saraarai*; and

3. use of the apostrophe ' instead of a hyphen after a syllabic nasal ん, such as *tan'i* [unit] (a word of three short syllables, which in kana would be written たんい) as opposed to *tani* [valley] (a word of two short syllables, written たに in kana).

2.5 Kana Signs and Combinations

The two main sections of this book are followed by a section setting out individual symbols in the hiragana and katakana syllabaries, and illustrations of stroke order for each of those symbols. Each of the two syllabaries evolved and became established over a period of many centuries, thereby becoming cemented as integral components in the modern writing system.

Katakana, which are more angular in appearance than hiragana, are today used first and foremost to represent loanwords of European origin, e.g. パン *pan* [bread] and ビール *biiru* [beer]. Hiragana are used widely and variously elsewhere to represent such elements as grammatical particles, inflectional endings of verbs, and frequently to represent in writing words which would otherwise need to be written with intricate or uncommon characters such as those for *ōmu* [parrot] (鸚鵡) or for the *ken* of *sekken* [soap] (石鹸).

For the convenience of users of this book, the final part consists of an alphabetical index of readings for the 1,945 JK List characters.

3 Layout Details

The 1,006 most essential characters are set out in Section One in accordance with the Education Ministry's division into six grades. These are in running sequence, but note that the grade divisions are:

1–80	= Grade One		81–240	= Grade Two
241–440	= Grade Three		441–640	= Grade Four
641–825	= Grade Five		826–1,006	= Grade Six

Characters within each grade are set out in the traditional '50 sounds' (*gojūon*) order which is commonly used for reference-type works in Japanese, except that the characters in Grade One alone are ordered on the basis of semantic groupings. Each character is typically accompanied by the *on* reading, then the *kun* reading and English meaning(s). The context is the best guide as to which reading is appropriate in a given case.

Also included for each of the 1,006 characters is information regarding the total number of strokes (the stroke count) and the set order to be followed in writing individual strokes. In most cases, three examples of character compounds are provided for each of these Essential characters.

Section Two, which presents the total 1,945 General-Use characters, gives them with their on and / or *kun* readings, and English meanings, but without illustrative compounds. In many cases, however, compounds containing characters which are among the 939 'non-essential' characters may be found among the compounds given for each of the 1,006 characters in Section One. The order adopted for listing the corpus of 1,945 characters is that of stroke count (and, within a given stroke count, by radical). So as to avoid undue repetition, each of the 1,006 Essential characters appearing in Section Two is given with the corresponding reference to Section One, to which the reader can refer for details.

With regard to the typographical conventions employed in giving readings and meanings for characters, these are explained by means of the example below.

見 KEN[1]; *mi(ru)*[2], to see, look[3]

[1] *On* reading in upper case.

[2] *Kun* reading in lower case italics. Parentheses used to indicate end-syllable(s) to be written in kana (thus, *mi(ru)*, since this word is conventionally written 見る).]

[3] English meaning(s) given in regular lower case.

Also note the use of a comma after a single on-reading to indicate that it can be used as a stand-alone word, e.g. "ZA, seat..." (i.e. 'za' exists as a word meaning 'seat'), as opposed to "U canopy..." (i.e. 'u' does not exist as an independent word).

4 Final Notes

Good luck with your study. For aspects of the modern Japanese language such as grammar, vocabulary, or style, you should refer to other appropriate textbooks and reference works, a variety of which are now available from Tuttle Publishing.

5 Select Bibliography of Main Works Consulted for this Edition

Note: All the books in Japanese listed below have been published in Tokyo.

Haig, J.H. et al. (ed.), *The New Nelson Japanese-English Character Dictionary*. Charles E. Tuttle, Tokyo, 1997.

Henshall, K. G., *A Guide to Remembering Japanese Characters*. Charles E. Tuttle, Tokyo, 1988.

Masuda, K., et al. (ed.), *Kenkyusha's New Japanese-English Dictionary*, Kenkyusha, 4th ed., 1974.

Morohashi T., *Dai kanwa jiten*. 13 vols. Taishukan, 1955-60.

Sanseido henshūho (ed.), *Atarashii kokugo hyōi handobukku*. Sanseido, 1991.

Satō K. (ed.), *Kanji hyakka daijiten*. Meiji shoin, 1996.

Seeley, C. *A History of Writing in Japan*. Paperback edition: University of Hawai'i Press, 2000.

Shirakawa S., *Jitō*. Heibonsha, 2nd ed., 1992.

ACKNOWLEDGEMENTS

The editors of the Newly Revised Edition respectfully acknowledge the work of the earlier editions carried out by Florence Sakade and her editorial team, work which has been of assistance to generations of students (including the present editors).

Grateful acknowledgement is also due to Flavia Hodges, Tan Mike Tze, Nancy Goh, Nathan Burrows, Neil Chandler, Bruce Penno, Paul Eagle, Shozo Tsuji, Yasuko Tsuji, and Kazuko Seeley.

The 1,006
ESSENTIAL CHARACTERS

一	一			**ICHI, ITSU,** *hito-, hito(tsu),* one 一月　*ichigatsu,* January 一番　*ichiban,* first, best 一冊　*issatsu,* one (book, magazine)
1 1 stroke				
二	一	二		**NI,** *futa(tsu),* two 二月　*nigatsu,* February 二か月　*nikagetsu,* two months 二回　*nikai,* twice
2 2 strokes				
三	一	二	三	**SAN,** *mi-, mit(tsu),* three 三月　*sangatsu,* March 三人　*sannin,* three people 三日　*mikka,* three days, the third day
3 3 strokes				
四	丨	冂	冂	**SHI,** *yon, yo-, yot(tsu), yo(tsu),* four 四月　*shigatsu,* April 四日　*yokka,* four days, the fourth day 四十　*shijū, yonjū,* forty
	冂	四		
4 5 strokes				

五	一	丁	五	GO, *itsu(tsu)*, five
	五			五月 *gogatsu*, May
				五人 *gonin*, five people
				五十 *gojū*, fifty
5 4 strokes				

六	、	二	六	ROKU, *mut(tsu)*, *mu(tsu)*, six
	六			六月 *rokugatsu*, June
				六か月 *rokkagetsu*, six months
				六十 *rokujū*, sixty
6 4 strokes				

七	一	七		SHICHI, *nana(tsu)*, *nana*, seven
				七月 *shichigatsu*, July
				七か月 *nanakagetsu*, seven months
				七十 *shichijū*, *nanajū*, seventy
7 2 strokes				

八	ノ	八		HACHI, *yat(tsu)* *ya(tsu)*, eight
				八月 *hachigatsu*, August
				八か月 *hachikagetsu*, eight months
				八十 *hachijū*, eighty
8 2 strokes				

九	ノ	九		KYŪ, KU, *kokono(tsu)*, nine
				九月 *kugatsu*, September
				九十 *kujū*, *kyūjū*, ninety
				九時 *kuji*, nine o'clock
9 2 strokes				

十	一	十		**JŪ**, *tō*, ten
				十月　*jūgatsu*, October 十日　*tōka*, ten days, the tenth day 十回　*jikkai*, ten times
10 2 strokes				

百	一	丆	丆	**HYAKU**, hundred
	百	百	百	二百　*nihyaku*, two hundred 三百　*sanbyaku*, three hundred 百貨店　*hyakkaten*, department store
11 6 strokes				

千	ノ	二	千	**SEN**, *chi*, thousand
				千円　*sen'en*, a thousand yen 三千　*sanzen*, three thousand 五千　*gosen*, five thousand
12 3 strokes				

日	丨	冂	日	**NICHI, JITSU**; *hi*, day, sun; *~ka*, suffix for counting days
	日			日曜日　*nichiyōbi*, Sunday 昨日　*sakujitsu*, yesterday 朝日　*asahi*, morning sun
13 4 strokes				

月	ノ	冂	月	**GETSU, GATSU**; *tsuki*, month, moon
	月			月曜日　*getsuyōbi*, Monday 来月　*raigetsu*, next month 三日月　*mikazuki*, new moon
14 4 strokes				

3

火	丶	丷	少	**KA;** *hi*, fire
	火			火曜日 *kayōbi*, Tuesday 火ばち *hibachi*, charcoal brazier 火事 *kaji*, fire, conflagration
15 **4 strokes**				

水	亅	刁	水	**SUI;** *mizu*, water
	水			大水 *ō-mizu*, flood, inundation 水力 *suiryoku*, water power 水兵 *suihei*, sailor
16 **4 strokes**				

木	一	十	才	**BOKU, MOKU;** *ki*, tree, wood
	木			木曜日 *mokuyōbi*, Thursday 材木 *zaimoku*, lumber 木製 *mokusei*, made of wood
17 **4 strokes**				

金	丿	人	厶	**KIN,** gold; **KON** gold; *kane*, money
	今	仐	余	金曜日 *kin'yōbi*, Friday お金 *o-kane*, money 金魚 *kingyo*, goldfish
	余	金		
18 **8 strokes**				

土	一	十	土	**DO, TO;** *tsuchi*, earth, soil
				土曜日 *doyōbi*, Saturday 土地 *tochi*, ground, plot of land 土人 *dojin*, native
19 **3 strokes**				

年	ノ	⺊	⺨	NEN; *toshi*, year
	⺲	缶	年	六年生 *rokunensei*, sixth-grade pupil 年寄り *toshiyori*, old person 青年 *seinen*, youth
20 6 strokes				
左	一	ナ	𠂇	SA; *hidari*, left
	左	左		左派 *saha*, leftist (political), left wing 左側 *sasoku, hidarigawa*, left side 左手 *hidarite*, left hand
21 5 strokes				
右	ノ	ナ	𠂇	U, YŪ; *migi*, right
	右	右		左右 *sayū*, left and right 右派 *uha*, right wing (political) 右側 *usoku, migigawa*, right side
22 5 strokes				
上	⼁	⺊	上	JŌ; *ue*, top, above, on; *kami*, upper; *nobo(ru)*, to go up, to go toward Tōkyō; *a(geru)*, to raise; *a(garu)*, to rise
				上流 *jōryū*, upstream, upper class 海上 *kaijō*, on the sea, maritime 川上 *kawakami*, upstream
23 3 strokes				
下	一	丁	下	KA, GE; *shita*, bottom, under, beneath; *moto*, base; *shimo*, lower; *kuda(ru)*, to go down, to go away from Tōkyō; *sa(geru)*, to hang (v.t.), to lower; *sa(garu)*, to hang down; *kuda(saru)*, to bestow
				川下 *kawashimo*, downstream 下品 *gehin*, vulgar, coarse 地下鉄 *chikatetsu*, subway
24 3 strokes				

大	一	ナ	大	DAI, TAI; ō(kii), big, large, great
				大学　　daigaku, university, college 大変　　taihen, tremendous, serious 大広間　ō-hiroma, grand hall
25 3 strokes				

中	丨	冂	口	CHŪ; naka, middle, within, inside
	中			中学校　chūgakkō, middle school 中心　　chūshin, center, heart (of a city, etc.) 集中　　shūchū, concentration
26 4 strokes				

小	亅	小	小	SHŌ; ko, o-, chii(sai), small, minor
				小学校　shōgakkō, primary school 小屋　　koya, hut 小説　　shōsetsu, novel (fiction)
27 3 strokes				

入	ノ	入		NYŪ; iri, entering, attendance; i(reru), to put in; hai(ru), to enter
				入学　nyūgaku, entering school 輸入　yunyū, importation 入口　iriguchi, entrance
28 2 strokes				

出	乚	屮	屮	SHUTSU, SUI; de(ru), to come out, to go out; da(su), to put out, to take out, to bring out, to draw out
	出	出		出発　shuppatsu, setting out, departure, starting 出版　shuppan, publishing 出口　deguchi, exit
29 5 strokes				

6

目	丨	冂	月		MOKU, BOKU; *me*, eye; also used as an ordinal suffix
	月	目			横目　*yokome*, side glance 目的　*mokuteki*, purpose 目標　*mokuhyō*, mark, target
30 5 strokes					

見	丨	冂	月		KEN; *mi(ru)*, to see, to look; *mi(eru)*, to be visible, to be able to see; *mi(seru)*, to show, to display
	月	目	見		見事　*migoto*, splendid 見物　*kenbutsu*, sightseeing 見本　*mihon*, sample
31 7 strokes	見				

耳	一	丆	下		JI; *mimi*, ear
	午	王	耳		早耳　*hayamimi*, keen of hearing 耳鳴り　*miminari*, ringing in the ears 耳が遠い　*mimi ga tōi*, deaf
32 6 strokes					

音	丶	亠	立		ON, IN; *ne*, *oto*, sound
	立	立	产		音楽　*ongaku*, music 発音　*hatsuon*, pronunciation 母音　*boin*, vowel
33 9 strokes	音	音	音		

口	丨	冂	口		KŌ, KU; *kuchi*, mouth
					口ひげ　*kuchihige*, mostache 入口　*iriguchi*, entrance 口論　*kōron*, dispute
34 3 strokes					

手	ノ	ニ	三	SHU; *te*, hand
	手			握手　*akushu*, handshake 手袋　*tebukuro*, gloves 手紙　*tegami*, letter
35 4 strokes				

足	丶	ロ	口	SOKU; *ashi*, foot, leg; *ta(riru)*, to be sufficient; *ta(su)*, to add, to supplement
	尸	足	尺	足跡　*ashi-ato*, footprint 満足　*manzoku*, satisfaction 不足　*fusoku*, insufficiency
36 7 strokes	足			

立	丶	亠	亠	RITSU, RYŪ; *ta(tsu)*, (v.i.), to stand; *ta(teru)* (v.t.), to erect, to set up
	立	立		独立　*dokuritsu*, independence 役立つ　*yakudatsu*, useful 立場　*tachiba*, standpoint
37 5 strokes				

力	フ	力		RYOKU, RIKI; *chikara*, strength, power
				力持　*chikaramochi*, strong person 協力　*kyōryoku*, co-operation 努力　*doryoku*, endeavor
38 5 strokes				

人	ノ	人		JIN, NIN; *hito*, person
				人類　*jinrui*, human race 人間　*ningen*, human being 人口　*jinkō*, population
39 2 strokes				

子	⁷	了	子	SHI, SU; *ko*, child
				子ども *kodomo*, child, children 原子 *genshi*, atom 様子 *yōsu*, the state of things, appearance
40 3 strokes				

女	く	女	女	JO, NYO; *me*, female; *onna*, woman, girl
				女中 *jochū*, maid 少女 *shōjo*, maiden 女王 *joō*, queen
41 3 strokes				

男	⎸	冂	冂	DAN, NAN; *otoko*, man, male
	田	田	毘	男性 *dansei*, male sex, male 男子 *danshi*, male, boy 長男 *chōnan*, eldest son
42 7 strokes	男			

先	ノ	⼃	什	SEN; *saki*, previous, ahead
	生	步	先	先生 *sensei*, teacher 先日 *senjitsu*, the other day 行き先 *yukisaki*, destination
43 6 strokes				

生	ノ	⼃	什	SEI, SHŌ birth, life; *u(mareru)*, to be born; *u(mu)*, to give birth; *i(kiru)*, to live; *ki*, pure, genuine; *nama*, raw; *ha(eru)*, to grow, to spring up
	牛	生		一生 *isshō*, one's (whole) life 生活 *seikatsu*, livelihood 大学生 *daigakusei*, college student
44 5 strokes				

学	丶	ヽ丶	ヽ丶ソ	GAKU, learning, science; *mana(bu)*, to learn
				学校　*gakkō*, school
	ソソ	ソソ	学	医学　*igaku*, medicine
45 **8 strokes**	学	学		科学　*kagaku*, science

校	一	十	木	KŌ school; to correct, to investigate, to compare, to think
	术	杧	栌	校正　*kōsei*, proofreading
				校舎　*kōsha*, school building
46 **10 strokes**	栌	校	校	校友　*kōyū*, alumnus

王	一	丁	王	Ō, king
	王			王様　*ōsama*, king
				王子　*ōji*, prince
47 **4 strokes**				王国　*ōkoku*, kingdom, monarchy

玉	一	丁	王	GYOKU; *tama*, jewel, round object
	王	玉		水玉　*mizutama*, drop of water
				目玉　*medama*, eyeball
48 **5 strokes**				

貝	丨	冂	冃	*kai*, sea shell
	月	目	貝	貝殻　*kaigara*, shell
				貝拾い　*kaihiroi*, shell gathering
49 **7 strokes**	貝			真珠貝　*shinjugai*, pearl oyster

円	丶	冂	円
	円		
50 4 strokes			

EN, circle, yen (Japanese monetary unit); *maru(i)*, round

円満　　*enman*, perfection, satisfaction
千円札　*sen'ensatsu*, thousand-yen bill
円盤　　*enban*, disc

赤	一	十	土
	𠆢	歩	赤
51 7 strokes	赤		

SEKI, SHAKU; *aka*, *aka(i)*, red; *aka(rameru)* (v.t.), to colour up, to add blush; *aka(ramu)*, to turn red, to blush

赤ちゃん　*akachan*, baby, infant
赤十字　　*sekijūji*, Red Cross
赤銅　　　*shakudō*, alloy of copper and gold

青	一	二	主
	圭	青	青
52 8 strokes	青	青	

SEI, SHŌ; *ao*, *ao(i)*, blue, green, inexperienced

青年　　*seinen*, youth
青白い　*aojiroi*, pale
青空　　*aozora*, blue sky

白	丿	亻	白
	白	白	
53 5 strokes			

HAKU, BYAKU; *shiro*, *shiro(i)*, white

白人　*hakujin*, Caucasian
白状　*hakujō*, confession
白鳥　*hakuchō*, swan

| 夕 | 丿 | 夕 | 夕 |
| 54 3 strokes | | | |

SEKI; *yū*, evening

夕方　*yūgata*, evening
夕飯　*yūhan*, supper
夕風　*yūkaze*, evening breeze

名	ノ	ク	タ	MEI, MYŌ name, fame; *na*, name 名まえ　*namae*, name 有名　*yūmei*, famous, well-known 名人　*meijin*, an expert
55 6 strokes	タ	名	名	

早	l	冂	日	SŌ; *haya, haya(i)* early, fast 早口　*haya-guchi*, quick speaking 早春　*sōshun*, early spring 手早い　*tebayai*, quick, nimble
56 6 strokes	日	旦	早	

草	一	十	艹	SŌ; *kusa*, grass, vegetation 草原　*kusahara (kusawara)*, grassy plain 草案　*sōan*, draft (of a manuscript) 草取り　*kusatori*, weeding
	艹	芦	苩	
57 9 strokes	苩	莒	草	

山	l	山	山	SAN; *yama*, mountain 山道　*sandō, yamamichi*, mountain path 山脈　*sanmyaku*, mountain range 登山　*tozan*, mountain climbing
58 3 strokes				

川	ノ	川	川	SEN; *kawa*, river 谷川　*tanigawa*, mountain stream 川ばた　*kawabata*, riverside 川口　*kawaguchi*, mouth of a river
59 3 strokes				

田	丨	冂	冊	DEN; *ta*, rice field
	甲	田		田園　*den'en*, fields and gardens, rural districts
60 5 strokes				稲田　*inada*, rice field
				田植　*taue*, rice planting

町	丨	冂	冂	CHŌ; *machi*, town
	甲	田	田一	町外れ　*machihazure*, outskirts of a town
61 7 strokes	町			町内　*chōnai*, the neighborhood
				町長　*chōchō*, mayor of a town

村	一	十	才	SON; *mura*, village
	木	杧	村	村民　*sonmin*, villager
62 7 strokes	村			村長　*sonchō*, village mayor
				農村　*nōson*, a farm village

車	一	厂	冖	SHA; *kuruma*, wheel, vehicle
	戸	旦	車	自動車　*jidōsha*, automobile
63 7 strokes	車			自転車　*jitensha*, bicycle
				発車　*hassha*, departure of a vehicle

林	一	十	才	RIN; *hayashi*, woods
	木	朾	村	植林　*shokurin*, reforestation
64 8 strokes	材	林		密林　*mitsurin*, thick forest
				農林　*nōrin*, agriculture and forestry

13

森	一	十	オ	SHIN; *mori*, forest, grove
				森林　*shinrin*, forest
	木	木	杢	森閑　*shinkan*, silent
				森厳　*shingen*, solemn, awe-inspiring
65 12 strokes	森	森	森	

空	、	八	宀	KŪ, *sora*, sky; *a(ku)*, to become empty; *a(keru)*, to vacate; *kara*, emptiness
	宀	穴	空	青空　*aozora*, blue sky 空気　*kūki*, air 空港　*kūkō*, airport
66 8 strokes	空	空		

天	一	二	チ	TEN, *ame*, sky, heaven
	天			天気　*tenki*, weather 天井　*tenjō*, ceiling 天才　*tensai*, genius
67 4 strokes				

気	ノ	⸜	⸜	KI, spirit, energy, mind; KE
	气	気	気	天気　*tenki*, weather 元気　*genki*, good spirits, health 病気　*byōki*, sickness
68 6 strokes				

雨	一	一	冂	U; *ame*, rain
	币	雨	雨	大雨　*ō-ame*, heavy rain 雨戸　*amado*, rain door, shutter 梅雨　*baiu*, rainy season of early 　　　　summer
69 8 strokes	雨	雨		

花	一	艹	艹	KA; *hana*, flower
	艹	花	花	花屋　　*hanaya*, flower shop, florist 花びん　*kabin*, vase 花火　　*hanabi*, fireworks
70 7 strokes	花			

竹	ノ	ヒ	ケ	CHIKU; *take*, bamboo
	仁	竹	竹	竹やぶ　*takeyabu*, bamboo grove 竹細工　*takezaiku*, bamboo ware 竹かご　*takekago*, bamboo basket
71 6 strokes				

石	一	丆	石	SEKI, KOKU, SHAKU; *ishi*, stone
	石	石		小石　　*ko-ishi*, pebble 石炭　　*sekitan*, coal 磁石　　*jishaku*, magnet
72 5 strokes				

犬	一	ナ	大	KEN; *inu*, dog
	犬			小犬　　*ko-inu*, puppy 番犬　　*banken*, watchdog 狂犬病　*kyōkenbyō*, rabies
73 4 strokes				

虫	丶	口	口	CHŪ; *mushi*, insect, bug, worm
	中	虫	虫	害虫　　*gaichū*, harmful insect 虫歯　　*mushiba*, decayed tooth 昆虫　　*konchū*, insect, bug
74 6 strokes				

糸	ㄥ	ㄠ	幺	SHI; *ito*, thread
				毛糸　　*keito*, woolen yarn
	糸	糸	糸	糸口　　*itoguchi*, clue
				糸巻　　*itomaki*, spool for thread
75 6 strokes				

本	一	十	才	HON, book, suffix for counting long, slender objects; *moto*, basis, essence, (tree) root.
	木	本		一本　　*ippon*, one (bottle, rod, etc.)
				本箱　　*honbako*, bookcase
76 5 strokes				日本　　*Nihon, Nippon*, Japan

文	、	二	テ	BUN, writings, a sentence; MON, old unit of money; *fumi*, letter, book
	文			文化　　　　*bunka*, culture
				文学　　　　*bungaku*, literature
77 4 strokes				文部大臣　*Monbudaijin*, Minister of Education

字	、	∵	宀	JI, letter, mark; *aza*, section (of a village)
	宀	宁	字	字引　*jibiki*, dictionary
				文字　*moji, monji*, letter, character, ideograph
78 6 strokes				数字　*sūji*, number, numeral

正	一	丁	下	SEI, SHŌ; *tada(shii)*, correct, right; *tada(su)*, to correct, to rectify; *masa(ni)*, surely, truly
	正	正		正直　　　*shōjiki*, honesty
				正方形　*seihōkei*, square (geometrical figure)
79 5 strokes				正月　　　*shōgatsu*, New Year's

16

休	ノ	イ	仁
	什	休	休

KYŪ; *yasu(mi)*, rest, vacation; *yasu(mu)*, to rest

休憩　　*kyūkei*, rest, intermission
休日　　*kyūjitsu*, holiday
休養　　*kyūyō*, relaxation, recreation

80
6 strokes

引	⁊	ㄱ	弓
	引		

IN; *hiki*, pulling; *hi(ku)*, to pull, to draw

福引き　　*fukubiki*, lottery
引用　　*in'yō*, quotation, citation
引き立て　　*hikitate*, favor, patronage

81
4 strokes

羽	ヿ	㇆	㇆
	羽	羽	羽

U; *hane*, *ha*, feather, plumage; *-wa*, counter for birds

羽毛　　*umō*, feathers, plumage
一羽　　*ichiwa*, one (bird)
羽織　　*haori*, haori coat

82
6 strokes

雲	一	𠂆	千
	帀	帀	帀
	雲	雲	雲

UN; *kumo*, cloud

雲状　　*unjō*, cloudlike, nebulous
入道雲　　*nyūdōgumo*, gigantic clouds
星雲　　*seiun*, nebula

83
12 strokes

園	丨	冂	用
	周	周	周
	園	園	

EN; *sono*, garden

公園　　*kōen*, public park
花園　　*hanazono*, flower garden
動物園　　*dōbutsu-en*, zoo

84
13 strokes

遠	土	吉	声	EN, ON; *tō(i)*, far, distant
	声	声	袁	遠足　　*ensoku*, excursion, long walk 遠方　　*enpō*, long distance 永遠　　*eien*, eternity
85 13 strokes	袁	读	遠	

何	ノ	イ	仁	KA; *nani*, what, how many (interrogative prefix)
	仁	佢	佢	何人　　*nannin*, how many people? 何時間　*nanjikan*, how much time? 何時　　*nanji*, what time?
86 7 strokes	何			

科	一	二	千	KA, course, branch
	禾	禾	禾	学科　　*gakka*, a school subject 教科書　*kyōkasho*, textbook 科学　　*kagaku*, science
87 9 strokes	禾	科	科	

夏	一	一	丆	KA; *natsu*, summer
	丙	百	百	夏休み　*natsuyasumi*, summer vacation 初夏　　*shoka*, early summer 真夏　　*manatsu*, midsummer
88 10 strokes	頁	夏	夏	

家	丶	八	宀	KA, KE; *ie*, *ya*, house
	宀	宁	宁	家主　　*yanushi*, owner of a house, landlord 家族　　*kazoku*, family 農家　　*nōka*, farmhouse
89 10 strokes	家	家	家	

歌	一	百	可	KA; *uta*, song; *uta(u)*, to sing
				国歌 *kokka*, national anthem
	叵	哥	哥	歌劇 *kageki*, opera
				歌手 *kashu*, singer
90 14 strokes	歌	歌	歌	

画	一	丆	亓	GA a picture; KAKU, stroke of a Japanese character
	帀	兩	面	図画 *zuga*, a drawing
				映画 *eiga*, moving picture
				計画 *keikaku*, plan
91 8 strokes	画	画		

回	l	冂	冂	KAI, a turn; *mawa(su)*, to turn (v.t.); *mawa(ru)*, to turn (v.i.)
	冋	回	回	何回 *nankai*, how many times?
				回転 *kaiten*, revolution, rotation
				回数 *kaisū*, number of times, frequency
92 6 strokes				

会	丿	人	人	KAI, meeting; *a(u)*, to meet; E
	仐	会	会	会場 *kaijō*, place of meeting, site
				会長 *kaichō*, president (of a society), chairman (of a committee)
				会話 *kaiwa*, conversation
93 6 strokes				

海	丶	冫	氵	KAI; *umi*, sea, ocean
	汀	汀	汀	海岸 *kaigan*, seacoast, seaside
				海水浴 *kaisuiyoku*, sea bathing
				海外 *kaigai*, overseas, abroad
94 9 strokes	海	海	海	

19

絵	⟍	幺	糸	KAI; E, picture
	糸	糸	絵	浮世絵 *ukiyoe,* Japanese print 絵葉書 *ehagaki,* picture postcard 挿し絵 *sashie,* illustration
95 12 strokes	給	絵	絵	

外	ノ	ク	タ	GAI, GE outside, foreign; *hoka,* other; *soto,* outside
	列	外		外国 *gaikoku,* foreign country 外国人 *gaikokujin,* foreigner 外科 *geka,* surgery
96 5 strokes				

角	ノ	ク	⺈	KAKU, angle; *tsuno,* horn of an animal; *kado,* corner
	角	角	角	三角 *sankaku,* triangle 四角 *shikaku,* square 角度 *kakudo,* angle
97 7 strokes	角			

楽	ノ	⺀	白	GAKU, music; RAKU, comfort, ease; *tano(shii),* pleasant
	白	白	泊	楽しみ *tanoshimi,* pleasure 音楽会 *ongakukai,* concert, musicale 気楽 *kiraku,* ease, comfort
98 13 strokes	泊	泊	楽	

活	丶	冫	氵	KATSU energy
	氵	氵	汗	生活 *seikatsu,* life 活動 *katsudō,* activity 活字 *katsuji,* printer's type
99 9 strokes	汗	活	活	

間	ノ	ア	ヲ	KAN, KEN; *aida*, interval, space; *ma*, interval, room, time
	ヲ	ヲ゚	門	時間　　*jikan*, time 二時間　*nijikan*, two hours 昼間　　*hiruma*, daytime
100 12 strokes	門	門	間	

丸	ノ	九	丸	GAN; *maru(i)*, round (adj.); -*maru*, suffix in ship names; *maru(meru)*, to make (something) round
				丸薬　　*gan'yaku*, pill 日の丸　*hinomaru*, Rising Sun flag 丸太　　*maruta*, log (of timber)
101 3 strokes				

岩	ヽ	山	山	GAN; *iwa*, rock, crag
	屮	屵	岸	花こう岩　*kakōgan*, granite 岩石　　　*ganseki*, rock 岩屋　　　*iwaya*, cavern
102 8 strokes	岩	岩		

顔	立	产	产	GAN; *kao*, face
	彦	彦	彦	顔面　*ganmen*, face 顔色　*kao-iro*, complexion 顔付　*kaotsuki*, face, look, countenance
103 18 strokes	彦	顔	顔	

汽	ヽ	シ	シ	KI steam, vapor
	シ	氵	汽	汽車　*kisha*, steam-driven train 汽笛　*kiteki*, steam whistle 汽船　*kisen*, steamship, steamboat
104 7 strokes	汽			

21

記	丶	亠	言	KI chronicle; *shiru(su)*, to write down
	言	言	訂	日記　*nikki*, diary
				記念　*kinen*, remembrance, souvenir
				記者　*kisha*, journalist
105 10 strokes	記	記		

帰	丿	刂	汀	KI; *kae(ru)*, to return, to leave
	汀	汀	汀	帰り道　*kaerimichi*, (on) one's way back
				帰化人　*kikajin*, naturalized person
				帰国　*kikoku*, return to one's native country
106 10 strokes	归	帰	帰	

弓	了	弓	弓	KYŪ; *yumi*, bow, archery
				弓道　*kyūdō*, archery
				弓弦　*yumizuru*, bowstring
				弓状　*kyūjō*, arch, bow shape
107 3 strokes				

牛	丿	仁	二	GYŪ; *ushi*, cow, bull
	牛			小牛　*ko-ushi*, calf
				牛乳　*gyūnyū*, milk
				牛肉　*gyūniku*, beef
108 4 strokes				

魚	丿	ク	々	GYO; *uo*, fish; *sakana*, fish
	名	角	角	金魚　*kingyo*, goldfish
				魚市場　*uo-ichiba*, fish market
				魚つり　*uotsuri*, fishing
109 11 strokes	魚	魚	魚	

京

110
8 strokes

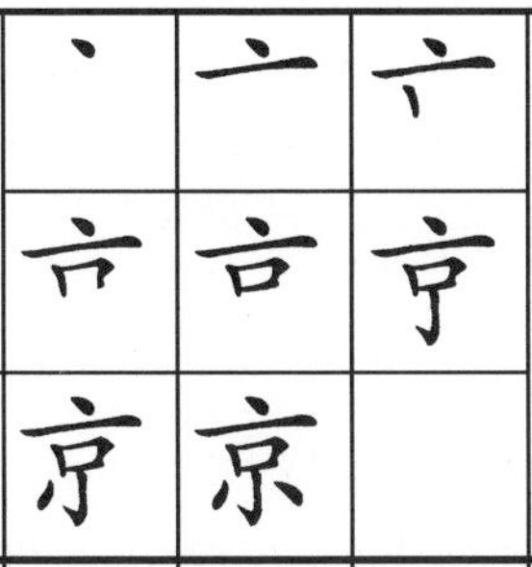

KYŌ, capital, KEI

東京 *Tōkyō,* capital of Japan
京都 *Kyōto,* ancient capital of Japan
上京 *jōkyō,* going to Tōkyō

強

111
11 strokes

KYŌ, GŌ; *tsuyo(i),* strong; *tsuyo(meru)* (v.t.), to reinforce, to emphasize; *shi(ite),* by force

勉強 *benkyō,* study
強弱 *kyōjaku,* strength and weakness
強情 *gōjō,* obstinacy

教

112
11 strokes

KYŌ; *oshi(eru),* to teach

教室 *kyōshitsu,* classroom
教育 *kyōiku,* education
教会 *kyōkai,* church

近

113
7 strokes

KIN; *chika(i),* near

近道 *chikamichi,* shortcut
近所 *kinjo,* neighborhood
最近 *saikin,* recently

兄

114
5 strokes

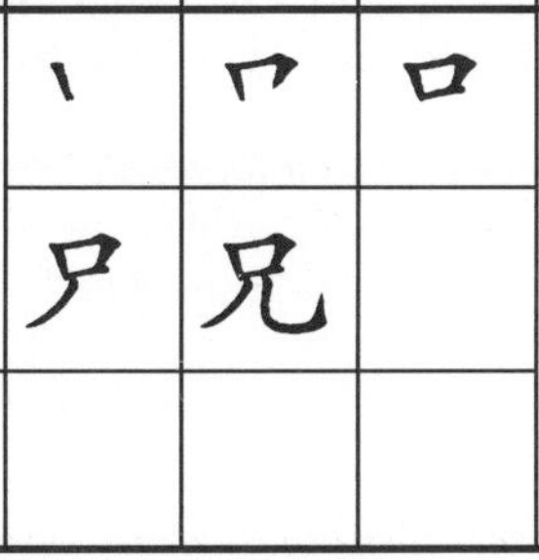

KEI, KYŌ; *ani,* older brother

兄弟 *kyōdai,* brothers (and sisters)
父兄 *fukei,* guardians (of pupils)

Character	Stroke order	Meaning and compounds
形 115 7 strokes		KEI, GYŌ; *katachi, ~gata,* shape, form 人形 *ningyō,* doll 長方形 *chōhōkei,* rectangle 半円形 *han'enkei,* semicircle
計 116 9 strokes	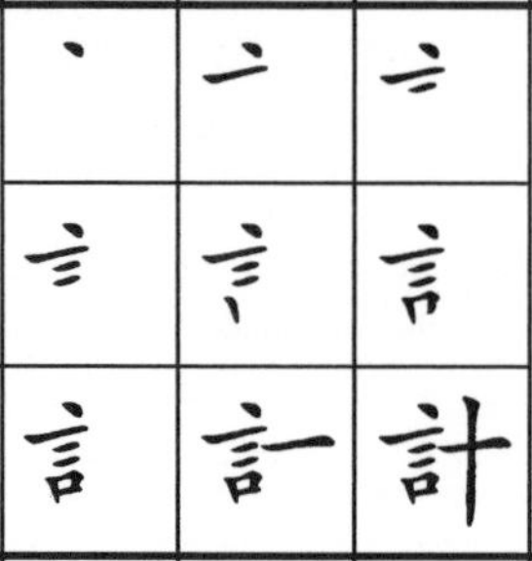	KEI; *haka(ru),* to measure; *haka(rau),* to arrange, to discuss 合計 *gōkei,* sum, total 寒暖計 *kandankei,* weather thermometer 体温計 *taionkei,* clinical thermometer
元 117 4 strokes		GEN, GAN; *moto,* beginning, foundation 根元 *kongen,* root, origin, source 元来 *ganrai,* originally, primarily 元日 *ganjitsu,* New Year's
言 118 7 strokes	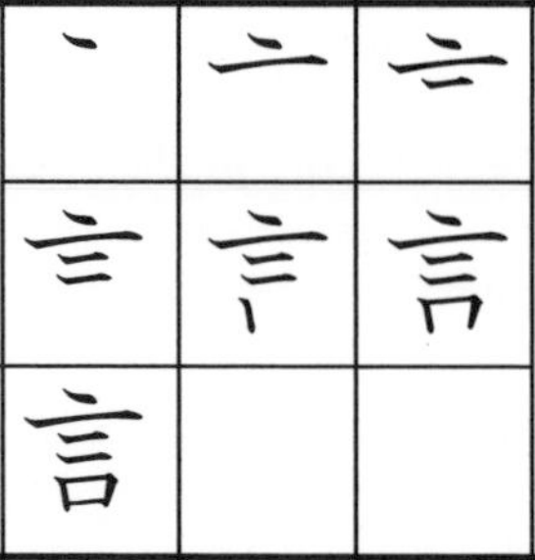	GEN, GON, speech, statement; *koto,* word, speech, expression; *i(u),* to say 方言 *hōgen,* dialect 無言 *mugon,* silence, muteness 言葉 *kotoba,* word, language
原 119 10 strokes		GEN original; *hara,* field, meadow 原因 *gen'in,* cause 高原 *kōgen,* plateau 草原 *kusawara,* grassy plain

戸	一	ラ	ヲ	**KO;** *to*, door
	戸			戸外 *kogai*, outdoors 木戸 *kido*, gate, door 江戸 *Edo*, old name for Tōkyō
120 4 strokes				

古	一	十	十	**KO;** *furu(i)*, old, ancient
	古	古		古代 *kodai*, ancient times 古今 *kokon*, past and present 考古学 *kōkogaku*, archeology
121 5 strokes				

午	ノ	レ	ニ	**GO** noon
	午			午前 *gozen*, morning, A.M. 午後 *gogo*, afternoon, P.M. 正午 *shōgo*, noon
122 4 strokes				

後	ノ	ク	彳	**GO, KŌ;** *ushi(ro)*, behind; *nochi*, after; *ato*, the rear, after, the remainder
	彳	彳	彳	食後 *shokugo*, after a meal 最後 *saigo*, last 前後 *zengo*, before and after, context
123 9 strokes	移	後	後	

語	、	ニ	言	**GO,** word, speech; *katari*, narration; *kata(ru)*, to tell, to speak
	言	言	訂	外国語 *gaikokugo*, foreign language 英語 *eigo*, English language 物語 *monogatari*, tale
124 14 strokes	訝	語	語	

工	一	丁	工	KŌ, KU worker, construction
				工夫　　*kōfu*, workman, laborer 工事中　*kōjichū*, under construction 工学　　*kōgaku*, engineering
125 3 strokes				

公	ノ	八	公	KŌ; *ōyake*, public
	公			主人公　*shujinkō*, hero, heroine 公園　　*kōen*, public park 公転　　*kōten*, revolution, turning
126 4 strokes				

広	、	亠	广	KŌ; *hiro(i)*, wide; *hiro(geru)* to spread (v.t.); *hiro(garu)*, to spread (v.i.); *hiro(maru)*, to be spread
	広	広		広場　*hiroba*, open space, plaza 広告　*kōkoku*, advertisement 広大　*kōdai*, vast
127 5 strokes				

交	、	亠	六	KŌ; *ma(jiru)*, to be mixed; *maji(waru)*, to associate with; *ka(wasu)*, to exchange
	六	亣	交	交際　*kōsai*, intercourse, association 交番　*kōban*, police box 交通　*kōtsū*, traffic
128 6 strokes				

光	丨	⺑	⺌	KŌ; *hikari*, light, ray; *hika(ru)*, to shine
	业	半	光	光年　*kōnen*, light-year 光波　*kōha*, light wave 観光　*kankō*, sightseeing
129 6 strokes				

考	一	十	土	KŌ; *kanga(e)*, thought, idea, opinion; *kanga(eru)*, to think 参考　*sankō*, reference 考案　*kōan*, idea, plan, scheme 考査　*kōsa*, examination
130 6 strokes	耂	耂	考	

行	ノ	ク	イ	KŌ, GYŌ, AN; *i(ku)*, *yu(ku)*, to go; *oko(nau)*, to hold, to conduct 行列　*gyōretsu*, procession, queue 急行　*kyūkō*, express 銀行　*ginkō*, bank
131 6 strokes	彳	行	行	

高	、	二	六	KŌ; *taka(i)*, high, costly; *taka(maru)*, to rise, to be elevated; *taka(meru)*, to lift, to boost 高等学校　*kōtōgakkō*, high school 最高　*saikō*, highest 高台　*takadai*, elevated land
132 10 strokes	宀	高	高	

黄	一	廿	丗	KŌ, Ō; *ki*, yellow 黄色　*ki-iro*, yellow 黄金　*ōgon*, gold 黄熱病　*ōnetsubyō*, yellow fever
133 11 strokes	芇	苗	带	
	黄	黄	黄	

合	ノ	人	合	GŌ; *a(u)*, to be together, to fit; *a(waseru)*, to join, to combine 合図　*aizu*, signal, sign 都合　*tsugō*, circumstances, convenience 組合　*kumiai*, union
134 6 strokes	今	合	合	

谷	ノ	ハ	⺍	KOKU; *tani*, valley
	父	父	谷	谷間　*tanima*, valley 谷底　*tanizoko*, bottom of a ravine
135 7 strokes	谷			

国	丨	冂	冂	KOKU; *kuni*, country
	円	甲	国	国語　*kokugo*, national language 　　　(Japanese) 国会　*kokkai*, the National Diet 全国　*zenkoku*, national
136 8 strokes	国	国		

黒	丶	冂	日	KOKU; *kuro, kuro(i)*, black
	甲	里	里	黒人　*kokujin*, negro 黒板　*kokuban*, blackboard 暗黒　*ankoku*, darkness, blackness
137 11 strokes	黒	黒	黒	

今	ノ	人	今	KON, KIN; *ima*, now, the present
	今			今月　*kongetsu*, this month 今度　*kondo*, next time 今夜　*kon'ya*, tonight
138 4 strokes				

才	一	寸	才	SAI, talent, suffix for counting age
				十六才　*jūroku-sai*, sixteen years old 天才　*tensai, genius* 才能　*sainō*, talent
139 3 strokes				

細	く	乡	幺	SAI; *hoso(i)*, slender, narrow; *koma(kai)*, minute, fine, detailed
	糸	糽	糾	細道　　*hosomichi*, narrow road 細工　　*saiku*, work, craftsmanship 細菌　　*saikin*, bacillus, germ
140 11 strokes	細	細	細	

作	ノ	イ	イ	SAKU, SA; *tsuku(ru)*, to make
	仁	作	作	作文　　*sakubun*, (literary) composition 名作　　*meisaku*, masterpiece 作曲　　*sakkyoku*, musical composition
141 7 strokes	作			

算	ノ	⼂	⼃	SAN reckoning
	竹	竹	筲	算数　　*sansū*, arithmetic, calculation 計算　　*keisan*, computation, figuring 予算　　*yosan*, budget
142 14 strokes	筲	算	算	

止	丨	卜	止	SHI; *to(maru)*, to stop (v.i.); *to(meru)*, to bring to a stop; *tome*, stop
	止			中止　　*chūshi*, discontinuation 禁止　　*kinshi*, prohibition 通行止　*tsūkōdome*, suspension of traffic
143 4 strokes				

市	、	亠	宀	SHI, city; *ichi*, market
	亣	市		市役所　*shiyakusho*, city office 市場　　*ichiba, shijō*, market 都市　　*toshi*, cities
144 5 strokes				

矢	ノ	㇅	二	SHI; *ya*, arrow
	失	矢		矢印　*yajirushi*, arrow(-sign)
145				弓矢　*yumiya*, bow and arrow
5 strokes				一矢　*isshi*, retort, shot in return

姉	く	乄	女	SHI; *ane*, elder sister
	女	女	妌	姉妹　*shimai, ane-imōto*, sisters
	妌	姉		姉娘　*anemusume*, elder daughter
146				姉婿　*anemuko*, elder sister's husband
8 strokes				

思	丶	冂	四	SHI; *omo(u)*, to think, to recall
	田	田	田	思想　*shisō*, thought, idea
	思	思	思	不思議　*fushigi*, strange
147				思い出　*omoide*, remembrance,
9 strokes				recollection

紙	幺	幺	糸	SHI; *kami*, paper
	糸	糸	糽	ボール紙　*bōrugami*, cardboard
	紅	紙	紙	表紙　*hyōshi*, cover, binding
148				紙くず　*kamikuzu*, wastepaper
10 strokes				

寺	一	十	土	JI; *tera*, temple
	圭	寺	寺	寺院　*ji-in*, Buddhist temple
149				山寺　*yamadera*, mountain temple
6 strokes				

Character	Stroke order	Readings and compounds
自 150 6 strokes	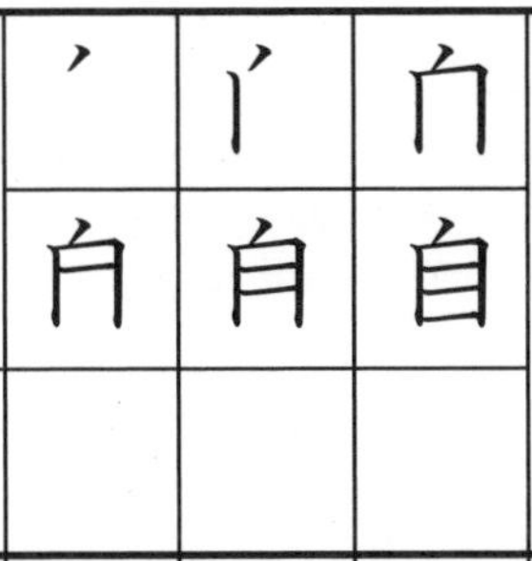	JI, SHI; *mizuka(ra),* self, in person 自分　*jibun,* self 自信　*jishin,* confidence 自由　*jiyū,* freedom
時 151 10 strokes		JI; *toki,* time 時々　*tokidoki,* sometimes 時計　*tokei,* watch, clock 時代　*jidai,* period, epoch
室 152 9 strokes	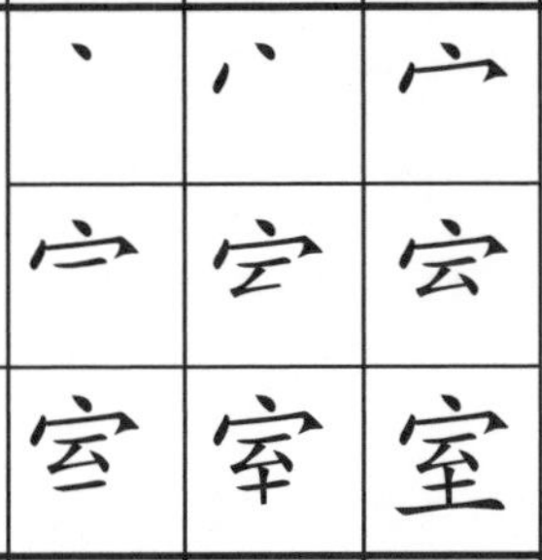	SHITSU, room; *muro,* storeroom, cave 教室　*kyōshitsu,* classroom 室内　*shitsunai,* indoors 温室　*onshitsu,* hothouse, greenhouse
社 153 7 strokes		SHA, a company; *yashiro,* Shintō shrine 社会　*shakai,* society, the world, the community 会社　*kaisha,* (business) company 神社　*jinja,* shrine
弱 154 10 strokes		JAKU; *yowa(i),* weak; *yowa(ru),* to grow weak, to be perplexed; *yowa(meru)* (v.t.), to weaken 弱虫　*yowamushi,* weakling 弱音　*yowane,* complaints 貧弱　*hinjaku,* scantiness, meagerness

首	、	゛	丷	SHU; *kubi*, neck
	丷	产	首	首輪　*kubiwa*, collar (dog) 手首　*tekubi*, wrist 首府　*shufu*, capital
155 9 strokes	首	首	首	

秋	ノ	二	千	SHŪ; *aki*, fall, autumn
	禾	禾	禾	初秋　*shoshū*, early autumn 秋風　*akikaze*, autumn breeze 秋分　*shūbun*, autumnal equinox
156 9 strokes	秋	秋	秋	

週	ノ	刀	月	SHŪ, week
	冃	用	周	週刊誌　*shūkanshi*, weekly magazine 来週　*raishū*, next week 今週　*konshū*, this week
157 11 strokes	周	调	週	

春	一	二	三	SHUN; *haru*, spring
	丰	夫	表	春風　*harukaze*, spring breeze 青春　*seishun*, springtime of life 晩春　*banshun*, late spring
158 9 strokes	春	春	春	

書	一	二	ヨ	SHO; *ka(ku)*, to write
	彐	彐	聿	辞書　*jisho*, dictionary 書物　*shomotsu*, book, volume 教科書　*kyōkasho*, textbook
159 10 strokes	書	書	書	

少 160 4 strokes	ノ 少	小	小	SHŌ; *suko(shi)*, *suku(nai)*, few, little, scarce 少年　*shōnen*, boy, lad 多少　*tashō*, more or less, somewhat 少佐　*shōsa*, major (army), lieutenant commander (navy)
場 161 12 strokes	一 圢 塌	十 圫 場	土 圽 場	JŌ; *ba*, place 工場　*kōjō*, *kōba*, factory 場所　*basho*, place 仕事場　*shigotoba*, place of work
色 162 6 strokes	ノ 久	ク 多	夕 色	SHOKU, SHIKI; *iro*, color 顔色　*kao-iro*, complexion 天然色　*tennenshoku*, natural color, technicolor 色彩　*shikisai*, color, hue
食 163 9 strokes	ノ 今 食	入 今 食	介 食 食	SHOKU, food; *ta(beru)*, to eat; *ku(u)*, to eat 食物　*shokumotsu*, food, edibles 食堂　*shokudō*, dining hall 食事　*shokuji*, a meal
心 164 4 strokes	丶 心	心	心	SHIN; *kokoro*, spirit, heart, mind 心持ち　*kokoromochi*, mood, feeling, sensation 真心　*magokoro*, sincerity, devotion 一心　*isshin*, whole-heartedness

33

新	、	二	立	SHIN; *atara(shii)*, new; *ara(tani)*, newly, afresh; *nii-*, first, new
	辛	亲	亲	新聞　　*shinbun*, newspaper 新年　　*shinnen*, the New Year 新学期　*shingakki*, new school term
165 13 strokes	新	新	新	

親	立	亲	奈	SHIN; *oya*, parent; *shita(shimu)*, to make friends with, to take kindly to; *shita(shii)*, intimate, familiar
	亲	親	親	両親　　*ryōshin*, parents 親切　　*shinsetsu*, kindness 親類　　*shinrui*, relative, relation
166 16 strokes	親	親	親	

図	丨	冂	冃	ZU, drawing, plan; TO; *haka(ru)*, to devise
	冈	冈	冈	図画　　*zuga*, drawing, a picture 地図　　*chizu*, map 図書館　*toshokan*, library
167 7 strokes	図			

数	丷	米	米	SŪ; *kazu*, number; *kazo(eru)*, to count
	娄	娄	娄	数字　　*sūji*, figure, numeral 数学　　*sūgaku*, mathematics 人数　　*ninzū*, the number of people
168 13 strokes	数	数	数	

西	一	厂	冂	SEI, SAI; *nishi*, west
	丙	西	西	西洋　　*seiyō*, the West, the Occident 大西洋　*Taiseiyō*, Atlantic Ocean 東西　　*tōzai*, east and west, Orient and Occident
169 6 strokes				

声	一	十	士	SEI, SHŌ; *koe,* voice
	吉	吉	吉	泣き声　*nakigoe,* crying voice 音声学　*onseigaku,* phonetics 声帯　*seitai,* the vocal cords
170 7 strokes	声			

星	丶	冂	曰	SEI, JŌ; *hoshi,* star
	曰	尸	臣	星座　*seiza,* constellation 火星　*kasei,* Mars 明星　*myōjō,* Venus
171 9 strokes	星	星	星	

晴	丨	冂	月	SEI; *ha(re),* fine weather; *ha(reru),* to clear (weather), to be dispelled; *ha(rasu),* to clear away, to dispel (doubts)
	日	日一	日十	
172 12 strokes	日キ	日キ	晴	秋晴れ　*akibare,* clear autumn weather 晴れ着　*haregi,* one's best clothes 晴天　*seiten,* fine weather

切	一	七	切	SETSU, SAI; *ki(ru),* to cut; *ki(reru),* to be sharp, to snap, to break, to run out, to expire
	切			
173 4 strokes				一切れ　*hitokire,* one slice 親切　*shinsetsu,* kindness 一切　*issai,* all, everything

雪	一	厂	宀	SETSU; *yuki,* snow
	乑	乑	乑	雪だるま　*yukidaruma,* snowman 雪解け　*yukidoke,* thaw 積雪　*sekisetsu,* snowdrift
174 11 strokes	雪	雪	雪	

船	ノ	刀	刀	SEN; *fune, funa,* boat, ship
	角	舟	舟	渡し船 *watashi-bune,* ferry 船員 *sen'in,* sailor 汽船 *kisen,* steamboat, steamship
175 11 strokes	船	船	船	

線	く	幺	糸	SEN, line, track, wire, string
	糺	絎	絎	地平線 *chiheisen,* horizon (on land) 光線 *kōsen,* light, beam, ray 直線 *chokusen,* straight line
176 15 strokes	線	線	線	

前	丶	丷	丷	ZEN; *mae,* before, in front of, previous
	广	疒	疒	午前 *gozen,* morning, A.M. 前後 *zengo,* before and after, context 以前 *izen,* ago, since, before
177 9 strokes	前	前	前	

組	ム	幺	幺	SO; *kumi,* class, group, set; *ku(mu),* to join, to unite
	糸	糾	糾	組み立て *kumitate,* construction, structure 一組 *hitokumi,* one set, one class 番組 *bangumi,* program
178 11 strokes	組	組	組	

走	一	十	土	SŌ; *hashi(ru),* to run
	キ	キ	走	競走 *kyōsō,* race, running match 走り書き *hashirigaki,* hasty writing 走り去る *hashirisaru,* to run away
179 7 strokes	走			

多	ノ	ク	タ	TA; ō(i), many, much, abundant
	多	多	多	多数 *tasū*, large number 多分 *tabun*, perhaps 多量 *taryō*, great quantity
180 6 strokes				

太	一	ナ	大	TAI, TA; *futo(i)*, big, deep (voice), bold (lines), shameless; *futo(ru)*, to grow fat
	太			太陽 *taiyō*, sun 丸太 *maruta*, log 太平洋 *Taiheiyō*, Pacific Ocean
181 4 strokes				

体	ノ	イ	仁	TAI, TEI body; *karada*, the body, health
	什	付	休	体育 *tai-iku*, physical education 団体 *dantai*, a group 車体 *shatai*, body of a vehicle
182 7 strokes	体			

台	ム	ム	仁	DAI, TAI; a stand
	台	台		台風 *taifū*, typhoon 舞台 *butai*, stage 燈台 *tōdai*, lighthouse
183 5 strokes				

地	一	十	土	CHI, JI, earth, ground
	扫	地	地	地上 *chijō*, on the ground 地下 *chika*, underground 地面 *jimen*, surface of the earth
184 6 strokes				

池	丶	冫	氵	CHI; *ike*, pond, lake
	汕	汕	池	電池　　*denchi*, electric cell, battery 池畔　　*chihan*, side of a pond, around a pond 用水池　*yōsuichi*, reservoir
185 6 strokes				

知	ノ	㇄	上	CHI; *shi(ru)*, to know; *shi(raseru)*, to inform
	矢	矢	矢	知識　　*chishiki*, knowledge 知人　　*chijin*, an acquaintance 承知　　*shōchi*, assent, agreement
186 8 strokes	知	知		

茶	一	十	艹	CHA, tea, tea plant, SA
	艹	艾	苂	茶色　　*cha-iro*, light brown 茶の湯　*cha-no-yu*, tea ceremony 茶わん　*chawan*, teacup, rice bowl
187 9 strokes	苯	茶	茶	

昼	㇆	コ	尸	CHŪ; *hiru*, noon, daytime
	尺	尺	屄	昼間　　*hiruma*, daytime 昼夜　　*chūya*, day and night 昼食　　*chūshoku*, noon meal, lunch
188 9 strokes	昼	昼	昼	

長	l	厂	F	CHŌ; head of an institution or organization; *naga(i)*, long
	F	巨	长	細長い　*hosonagai*, long and narrow 長ぐつ　*nagagutsu*, boots 校長　　*kōchō*, principal of a school
189 8 strokes	長	長		

鳥	ノ	イ	戸
	戸	白	白
190 11 strokes	鳥	鳥	鳥

CHŌ; *tori*, bird

鳥類   *chōrui*, birds (as a species)
小鳥   *kotori*, small bird
渡り鳥   *wataridori*, migratory bird

朝	一	十	十
	古	吉	吉
191 12 strokes	直	卓	朝

CHŌ; *asa*, morning

朝刊   *chōkan*, morning paper
朝食   *chōshoku*, breakfast
毎朝   *mai-asa*, every morning

直	一	十	亡
	古	古	直
192 8 strokes	直	直	

CHOKU, upright, honest, cheap; JIKI, direct; *tada(chini)*, immediately; *nao(su)*, to repair, to put right, to convert; *nao(ru)*, to be repaired, to change for the better

直角   *chokkaku*, right angle
正直   *shōjiki*, honesty
素直   *sunao*, gentle, obedient

通	⁷	⁷	了
	丂	肖	甬
193 10 strokes	诵	通	通

TSŪ; *tō(ru)*, to go along, to pass; *tō(su)*, to let pass, to continue; *kayo(u)*, to go back and forth, to commute

大通り   *ō-dōri*, main street
通信   *tsūshin*, correspondence, communication
通訳   *tsūyaku*, interpreter

弟	`	⸺	乂
	兰	兰	弟
194 7 strokes	弟		

TEI, DAI; *otōto*, younger brother

兄弟   *kyōdai*, brothers
弟妹   *teimai*, younger brothers and sisters

店	、	亠	广	**TEN**; *mise*, store
	庁	庁	庄	店番　*miseban*, tending a store 商店　*shōten*, store (shop) 売店　*baiten*, stand, stall
195 8 strokes	店	店		

点	丨	ト	ト	**TEN**, point, marks, dot
	占	占	占	点数　*tensū*, merit marks 点字　*tenji*, braille points 決勝点　*kesshōten*, goal
196 9 strokes	点	点	点	

電	一	一	一	**DEN** lightning, electricity
	雨	雨	雨	電気　*denki*, electricity 電話　*denwa*, telephone 電報　*denpō*, telegram
197 13 strokes	雷	雷	電	

刀	フ	刀		**TŌ**; *katana*, sword
				小刀　*kogatana*, pocketknife 大刀　*daitō*, long sword 軍刀　*guntō*, sabre
198 2 strokes				

冬	ノ	ク	夂	**TŌ**; *fuyu*, winter
	冬	冬		冬休み　*fuyuyasumi*, winter vacation 冬眠　*tōmin*, hibernation 冬期　*tōki*, winter season
199 5 strokes				

当	丨	丷	丷	TŌ; *a(taru)*, to hit, to be equal to, to win (v.i.); *a(teru)*, to hit, to apply, to guess (v.t.)
	彐	当	当	見当 *kentō*, guess 手当 *teate*, treatment, allowance 当然 *tōzen*, justly, naturally
200 6 strokes				

東	一	厂	冖	TŌ; *higashi*, east
	戸	由	申	東側 *higashigawa*, east side 東洋 *tōyō*, the East, the Orient 北東 *hokutō*, northeast
201 8 strokes	東	東		

答	ノ	ト	ケ	TŌ; *kota(e)*, answer; *kota(eru)*, to answer
	丿ヒ	竹	竺	答案 *tōan*, examination paper 問答 *mondō*, questions and answers 解答 *kaitō*, answer, solution
202 12 strokes	竺	答	答	

頭	一	豆	戸	TŌ, ZU; *atama*, head, top, brain; *kashira*, head, top, leader
	豆	豆	豆	先頭 *sentō*, leader, head 教頭 *kyōtō*, head teacher 頭痛 *zutsū*, headache
203 16 strokes	豆	頭	頭	

同	丨	冂	冂	DŌ; *ona(ji)*, same
	同	同	同	同時 *dōji*, the same time 同情 *dōjō*, sympathy 一同 *ichidō*, all (of us, them), all the persons concerned
204 6 strokes				

道	、	゛	宀	DŌ; *michi*, road, path
				水道　*suidō*, waterworks
	ソ	产	首	道具　*dōgu*, tool
				鉄道　*tetsudō*, railroad
205 12 strokes	首	道	道	

読	、	亠	言	DOKU, TOKU; *yo(mu)*, to read
				読者　　　*dokusha*, reader (person)
	言	詰	詰	読書　　　*dokusho*, reading
				読み返す　*yomikaesu*, to reread
206 14 strokes	誌	読	読	

内	丨	冂	内	NAI, DAI; *uchi*, inside, home, within, during, among, between
	内			案内　*annai*, guidance, invitation
				内海　*uchiumi, naikai*, inland sea
207 4 strokes				内容　*naiyō*, contents

南	一	十	十	NAN; *minami*, south
	内	南	南	南部　*nanbu*, southern part
				南極　*Nankyoku*, South Pole
208 9 strokes	南	南	南	西南　*seinan*, southwest

肉	丨	冂	内	NIKU, meat, flesh
	内	肉	肉	牛肉　*gyūniku*, beef
				筋肉　*kinniku*, muscles
209 6 strokes				肉屋　*nikuya*, butcher, butcher shop

馬	丨	厂	厅	BA; *uma*, horse
	斤	厍	馬	馬車　　*basha*, carriage 競馬場　*keibajō*, race track
210 10 strokes	馬	馬	馬	

売	一	十	士	BAI; *u(ri)*, sale; *u(ru)*, to sell
	士	声	声	売り出し　*uridashi*, opening sale, 　　　　　　bargain sale 商売　　　*shōbai*, business 発売　　　*hatsubai*, sale
211 7 strokes	売			

買	丶	冖	四	BAI; *ka(u)*, to buy, to purchase
	四	四	罒	売買　　*baibai*, purchase and sale, 　　　　　buying and selling 買い物　*kaimono*, shopping 買い手　*kaite*, buyer
212 12 strokes	買	買		

麦	一	十	丰	BAKU; *mugi*, barley, wheat
	主	韦	麦	麦わら　*mugiwara*, (barley) straw 麦刈り　*mugikari*, mowing barley 小麦　　*komugi*, wheat
213 7 strokes	麦			

半	丶	丷	丷	HAN; *naka(ba)*, half
	兰	半		半分　　　*hanbun*, half 一時半　*ichiji-han*, one-thirty, half-past 　　　　　　one 半島　　　*hantō*, peninsula
214 5 strokes				

番	一	⌒	⌒	**BAN**, number, guard, order, (one's) turn
				番組　　*bangumi*, program
	丷	平	采	交番　　*kōban*, police-box
				順番　　*junban*, order, one's turn
215 **12 strokes**	采	番	番	

父	⼃	八	父	**FU**; *chichi*, father
				父兄会　*fukeikai*, parents' association
	父			祖父　　*sofu*, grandfather
				父母　　*fubo*, parents
216 **4 strokes**				

風	ノ	几	凡	**FŪ**; *kaze*, wind
				風景　　*fūkei*, scenery
	凡	同	同	台風　　*taifū*, typhoon
				南風　　*minamikaze*, south wind
217 **9 strokes**	風	風	風	

分	ノ	八	今	**BUN, BU**, part, share; **FUN**, a minute; *wa(keru)* (v.t.), to divide; *wa(kareru)*, to be separated, to branch off; *wa(karu)*, to know, to understand
	分			
				自分　　*jibun*, self
218 **4 strokes**				二分　　*nifun*, two minutes
				十分　　*jippun*, ten minutes

聞	｜	ｌﾞ	尸	**BUN**; *ki(ku)*, to hear, to listen to, to ask, to obey; *ki(koeru)*, to be heard
	尸	尸ﾞ	門	新聞　　*shinbun*, newspaper
				新聞社　*shinbunsha*, newspaper office
				見聞　　*kenbun*, information, experience
219 **14 strokes**	門	門	聞	

米	丶	丷	业	BEI America, rice; MAI rice; *kome*, rice
	半	米	米	米国　*Beikoku*, America, the United States 米作　*beisaku*, rice-growing (crop) 白米　*hakumai*, polished rice
220 6 strokes				

歩	丶	丨⊦	𣥂	HO, BU; *ayu(mu)*, *aru(ku)*, to walk, to step
	止	屮	歨	第一歩　*dai-ippo*, the first step 進歩　*shinpo*, progress 散歩　*sanpo*, a walk, a stroll
221 8 strokes	歨	歩		

母	㇄	几	母	BO; *haha*, mother
	母	母		母の日　*Haha-no-hi*, Mother's Day 母国　*bokoku*, mother country 母親　*haha-oya*, mother
222 5 strokes				

方	丶	亠	方	HŌ, direction, side; *kata [gata]*, side, way of ~ing, person
	方			両方　*ryōhō*, both sides 作り方　*tsukurikata*, way of making 夕方　*yūgata*, evening
223 4 strokes				

北	丨	士	土	HOKU; *kita*, north
	北	北		北極　*Hokkyoku*, North Pole 南北　*nanboku*, north and south 北風　*kitakaze*, north wind
224 5 strokes				

每	ノ	ト	仁	MAI every (prefix)
	与	与	每	每日　　*mainichi*, every day 每朝　　*mai-asa*, every morning 每週　　*maishū*, every week
225 6 strokes				

妹	く	ㄑ	女	MAI; *imōto*, younger sister
	女	女'	妌	弟妹　　*teimai*, younger brothers and sisters 姉妹　　*shimai*, sisters
226 8 strokes	妌	妹		

万	一	丁	万	MAN, ten thousand; BAN
				万年筆　　*mannenhitsu*, fountain pen 万一　　　*man'ichi*, if by any chance 万国　　　*bankoku*, all countries
227 3 strokes				

明	l	冂	日	MEI, MYŌ bright; *aka(rui)*, light, bright; *aki(raka)*, bright; *a(keru)*, to dawn, to break (day); *a(kasu)*, to disclose (a secret), to pass the night
	日	日﹣	明	夜明け　　*yoake*, dawn
228 8 strokes	明	明		説明　　　*setsumei*, explanation 発明　　　*hatsumei*, invention

鳴	ロ	ロ'	叮	MEI; *na(ku)*, to sing (birds), to cry (animals), to howl (animals), to chirp (insects); *na(ru)* (v.i.), to ring, to sound; *na(rasu)* (v.t.), to ring (a bell), to sound (a drum), to complain, to be famous
	叭	叭	鸣	
229 14 strokes	鸣	鳴	鳴	鳴き声　　*nakigoe*, cry (of animals) 悲鳴　　　*himei*, scream, cry of distress 鳴動　　　*meidō*, rumbling

毛	´	⁼	三	MŌ; *ke*, hair
	毛			毛糸　　*keito*, woolen thread, yarn 毛虫　　*kemushi*, caterpillar 毛布　　*mōfu*, blanket
230 4 strokes				

門	｜	ｒ	ｒ	MON, gate; *kado*, gate
	ｒ	ｒ	門	校門　　*kōmon*, school gate 専門　　*senmon*, specialty 門口　　*kadoguchi*, door, entrance
231 8 strokes	門	門		

夜	、	亠	广	YA; *yo, yoru*, evening, night
	疒	疒	疒	夜中　　　*yonaka*, midnight 十五夜　*jūgoya*, night of the full moon 今夜　　　*kon'ya*, tonight
232 8 strokes	夜	夜		

野	丶	口	日	YA; *no*, field, plain
	甲	里	里	野原　　*nohara*, field 野球　　*yakyū*, baseball 野外　　*yagai*, outdoors
233 11 strokes	野	野	野	

友	一	ナ	方	YŪ; *tomo*, friend
	友			友だち　*tomodachi*, friend 友人　　*yūjin*, friend 友情　　*yūjō*, friendship
234 4 strokes				

用	ノ	刀	月	YŌ, business; *mochi(iru)*, to use
	月	用		用意　*yōi*, preparation
				用心　*yōjin*, heed, care, caution
235				用事　*yōji*, business
5 strokes				

曜	I	Π	Ħ	YŌ term used for days of the week
	日	日'	日'	木曜日　*mokuyōbi*, Thursday
				土曜日　*doyōbi*, Saturday
236	日'	日彐	曜	水曜日　*suiyōbi*, Wednesday
18 strokes				

来	一	一	一	RAI; *ku(ru)*, to come; *kita(ru)*, to arrive, next; *kita(su)*, to cause, to induce
	三	半	来	来年　*rainen*, next year
				以来　*irai*, since, from that time
237	来			将来　*shōrai*, the future
7 strokes				

里	丶	冂	冂	RI, Japanese linear unit (2.44 miles); *sato* village, country, one's native home (usually as viewed by a woman married into another family)
	日	甲	甲	郷里　*kyōri*, one's native place, home
238	里			村里　*murazato*, village
7 strokes				一里　*ichiri*, one ri

理	一	丁	于	RI, reason, logic
	王	玑	珇	理解　*rikai*, understanding
				整理　*seiri*, arrangement, adjustment
239	玾	理	理	料理　*ryōri*, cooking
11 strokes				

話	、	二	三	WA; *hanashi*, story; *hana(su)*, to speak
	言	言	言	世話 *sewa*, aid 電話 *denwa*, telephone 会話 *kaiwa*, conversation
240 13 strokes	言	計	話	

悪	一	一	二	AKU, badness, evil; *waru(i)*, bad, evil
	亞	亜	亜	悪口 *warukuchi*, evil talk, gossip 悪人 *akunin*, bad man, villain 悪路 *akuro*, bad road
241 11 strokes	亜	悪		

安	、	八	宀	AN; *yasu(i)*, cheap, inexpensive
	宀	安	安	安心 *anshin*, peace of mind 安全 *anzen*, safe 不安 *fuan*, uneasiness
242 6 strokes				

暗	l	刀	月	AN; *kura(i)*, dark
	日	日'	日宀	真っ暗 *makkura*, pitch dark 暗号 *angō*, code, cryptograph 暗記 *anki*, memorization
243 13 strokes	日宀	暗	暗	

医	一	丁	匸	I to heal, to cure
	三	歹	矢	医者 *isha*, physician, doctor 医学 *igaku*, medical science 医院 *i-in*, medical practitioner's office
244 7 strokes	医			

委 245 8 strokes	´	二	千
	千	禾	禾
	委	委	

I to entrust with

委員　　*i-in*, committee, delegate
委員長　*i-inchō*, chairman of a committee
委任　　*i-nin*, charge, trust, commission

意 246 13 strokes	`	亠	立
	立	产	音
	音	音	意

I, mind, heart, attention, care

注意　*chūi*, care, attention
意見　*iken*, opinion, admonition
意味　*imi*, meaning

育 247 8 strokes	`	亠	云
	云	产	育
	育	育	

IKU; *soda(teru)*, to bring up, to educate, to raise; *soda(tsu)*, to grow up

教育　*kyōiku*, education
体育　*tai-iku*, physical education
育児　*ikuji*, upbringing of a child

員 248 10 strokes	`	冖	口
	尸	呂	冒
	冒	員	員

IN member, official, personnel

満員　*man'in*, no vacancy, full house
一員　*ichi-in*, (one) member
職員　*shokuin*, staff, personnel

院 249 10 strokes	⁊	𝟹	阝
	阝	阝`	陀
	陀	陀	院

IN temple, academy, board, suffix for "institution"

病院　　*byōin*, hospital
美容院　*biyōin*, beauty shop
下院　　*ka-in*, House of Representatives, Lower House

50

飲	ノ	今	今	IN; *no(mu)*, to drink
	食	食	食	飲料水 *inryōsui* drinking water 飲み水 *nomimizu*, drinking water 飲み物 *nomimono*, drinks
250 12 strokes	飲	飲	飲	

運	丶	冖	冖	UN, luck; *hako(bu)*, to carry, to transport
	冒	冝	軍	運よく *un'yoku*, luckily 運動 *undō*, exercise, motion 運命 *unmei*, fate
251 12 strokes	軍	運	運	

泳	丶	丶	氵	EI; *oyo(gu)*, to swim
	氵	汀	沪	水泳 *suiei*, swimming 平泳ぎ *hira-oyogi*, breast stroke 水泳大会 *suiei taikai*, swimming meet
252 8 strokes	沪	泳		

駅	丨	厂	厂	EKI, station
	馬	馬	馬	駅前 *ekimae*, in front of the station 駅長 *ekichō*, station master 駅員 *eki-in*, station employee
253 14 strokes	馬	駅	駅	

央	丶	冂	央	Ō center, middle
	央	央		中央 *chūō*, center 中央線 *Chūō-sen*, the Chūō Line (electric railway in Tōkyō) 震央 *shin'ō*, the epicenter, the center of an earthquake
254 5 strokes				

横	木	杧	栌	Ō ; *yoko*, the side, the width
	栌	栏	横	横書き　*yokogaki*, writing from left to right
255 15 strokes	横	横	横	横断　*ōdan*, crossing, intersection 横顔　*yokogao*, side view of a person's face, profile

屋	⁻	⁻	尸	OKU; *ya*, shop
	尸	尺	层	屋根　*yane*, roof 時計屋　*tokeiya*, watch shop
256 9 strokes	屋	屋	屋	屋上　*okujō*, housetop, roof

温	⟍	⟍	氵	ON; warm; *atata(kai)*, warm (to the touch); *atata(maru)*, to warm oneself; *atata(meru)*, to heat
	汩	汩	汩	温度　*ondo*, temperature 温泉　*onsen*, hot spring
257 12 strokes	温	温	温	体温　*taion*, body temperature

化	ノ	イ	イ	KA, KE; *ba(keru)*, to take the form of; *ba(kasu)*, to bewitch
	化			変化　*henka*, change, variation, alteration
258 4 strokes				化学　*kagaku*, chemistry 化粧　*keshō*, make-up

荷	一	艹	艹	KA; *ni*, a load, burden
	艻	芢	荮	荷物　*nimotsu*, baggage 荷船　*nibune*, freighter
259 10 strokes	荷	荷	荷	荷作り　*nizukuri*, packing

界	丶	冂	四	KAI world
				世界　　　*sekai*, world
	甲	田	尹	世界一　　*sekai-ichi*, best in the world
				限界　　　*genkai*, boundary, limits
260 9 strokes	界	界	界	

開	丨	冂	尸	KAI; *hira(ku)*, to open (v.t. & i.); *a(keru)* (v.t.), to open; *hira(keru)*, to be civilized, to open; *a(ku)* (v.i.) to be open
	尸	門	門	開会　　*kaikai*, opening a meeting 満開　　*mankai*, full bloom
261 12 strokes	門	閈	開	開発　　*kaihatsu*, development, exploitation

階	⁊	3	阝	KAI, story of a building, floor, grade
				階段　　*kaidan*, stairs, stairway
	阝	阝	阝	階級　　*kaikyū*, class, caste
				三階　　*sangai*, 3rd floor
262 12 strokes	阰	階	階	

寒	宀	宀	宁	KAN, the coldest season of the year; *samu(i)*, cold
	宁	审	宝	極寒　　*gokkan*, bitter cold 寒中　　*kanchū*, cold season
263 12 strokes	寒	寒	寒	寒流　　*kanryū*, cold current

感	丿	厂	厂	KAN, feeling, thought
				感想　　*kansō*, thoughts, impressions
	后	咸	咸	感心　　*kanshin*, admiration
				感覚　　*kankaku*, sensation
264 13 strokes	咸	感		

漢	シ	氵	氵	KAN China; ~kan, suffix for "man"
	氵	漭	漭	漢字　　kanji, Chinese character 漢文　　kanbun, Chinese composition 悪漢　　akkan, villain, crook
265 13 strokes	漭	漢	漢	

館	ノ	ケ	ヶ	KAN building, hall
	今	今	食	図書館　　toshokan, library 映画館　　eigakan, movie theater 旅館　　　ryokan, inn, hotel
266 16 strokes	食	鈝	館	

岸	'	山	山	GAN; kishi, bank, shore
	屮	戸	岸	海岸　　kaigan, seashore 岸壁　　ganpeki, quay, wharf 川岸　　kawagishi, riverbank
267 8 strokes	岸	岸		

起	土	キ	キ	KI; o(kiru), to rise, to get up; o(kosu), to raise, to awaken (v.t.); o(koru), to occur, to develop
	走	走	起	早起き　　hayaoki, early rising 起原　　　kigen, origin 起重機　　kijūki, crane, derrick
268 10 strokes	起	起		

期	一	十	廿	KI, GO period, term
	甘	其	其	学期　　gakki, school term 期待　　kitai, expectation 時期　　jiki, the times, season
269 12 strokes	其	期	期	

客	、	ハ	宀	KYAKU, guest; KAKU
	宀	宀	安	お客さん　*o-kyaku-san*, guest 客車り　*kyakusha*, railroad passenger car 客船　*kyakusen*, passenger boat
270 9 strokes	安	客	客	

究	、	ハ	宀	KYŪ study; *kiwa(meru)*, to study thoroughly
	宀	穴	究	研究　*kenkyū*, research 研究会　*kenkyūkai*, research society 研究家　*kenkyūka*, researcher
271 7 strokes	究			

急	ノ	ク	ク	KYŪ; *iso(gu)*, to hurry
	刍	刍	刍	急病　*kyūbyō*, sudden illness 急行　*kyūkō*, express 大急ぎ　*ō-isogi*, great haste
272 9 strokes	急	急	急	

級	㇗	纟	幺	KYŪ, rank, grade
	糹	糹	糸	学級　*gakkyū*, school class 上級　*jōkyū*, high class 同級生　*dōkyūsei*, classmate
273 9 strokes	糺	級	級	

宮	、	ハ	宀	KYŪ, GŪ, KU; *miya*, shrine, prince (of the blood)
	宀	宀	宮	宮殿　*kyūden*, palace 神宮　*jingū*, Shintō shrine 宮様　*miya-sama*, royal prince
274 10 strokes				

球	丁	王	玗	**KYŪ**, sphere, globe; *tama*, ball
	玗	玗	球	野球 *yakyū*, baseball 地球 *chikyū*, the earth, the globe 電球 *denkyū*, electric light bulb
275 11 strokes	球	球	球	

去	一	十	土	**KYO, KO** past; *sa(ru)*, to leave, to depart
	去	去		去年 *kyonen*, last year 過去 *kako*, the past, past tense
276 5 strokes				

橋	木	朽	杼	**KYŌ**; *hashi*, bridge
	杼	杯	橋	桟橋 *sanbashi*, pier 土橋 *dobashi*, earthen bridge 鉄橋 *tekkyō*, iron bridge
277 16 strokes	橋	橋	橋	

業	丶	丷	业	**GYŌ**, occupation, business, industry, studies; **GŌ**, karma; *waza*, act, deed
	业	业	业	職業 *shokugyō*, occupation, profession 産業 *sangyō*, industry 工業 *kōgyō*, industry, manufacturing industry
278 13 strokes	丵	業	業	

曲	丨	冂	巾	**KYOKU**, melody; *ma(garu)*, to bend, to twist, to turn, (v.i.); *ma(geru)*, to bend, to twist, to turn (v.t.)
	曲	曲	曲	曲線 *kyokusen*, curved line 作曲 *sakkyoku*, musical composition 曲がり道 *magarimichi*, crooked road, winding lane
279 6 strokes				

局	ァ	ュ	尸	KYOKU, bureau, board, office, department
	尸	吊	局	放送局　*hōsōkyoku*, broadcasting station 編集局　*henshūkyoku*, editorial department
280 7 strokes	局			郵便局　*yūbinkyoku*, post office

銀	ノ	ハ	彡	GIN, silver
	牟	金	釒	銀行　*ginkō*, bank 銀色　*gin'iro*, silver color 銀貨　*ginka*, silver coin
281 14 strokes	釸	銀	銀	

区	一	フ	又	KU, ward, section
	区			区別　*kubetsu*, distinction, classification 地区　*chiku*, area 区画　*kukaku*, boundary, block, division
282 4 strokes				

苦	一	十	艹	KU, pain, anxiety; *kuru(shii)*, painful; *niga(i)*, bitter
	艹	苎	芢	苦労　*kurō*, troubles, toil 苦心　*kushin*, pains, hard work 苦戦　*kusen*, hard fighting
283 8 strokes	苦	苦		

具	丨	冂	冃	GU, tool, utensil; ingredients
	月	目	且	道具　*dōgu*, tool, utensil, instrument 具合　*guai*, condition, state 具体的　*gutaiteki*, concrete, definite
284 8 strokes	具	具		

57

君 285 7 strokes	フ ヨ ヨ 尹 尹 君 君	KUN Mister, Master; *kimi*, you (familiar form) 佐藤君 *Satō-kun*, Mr. Satō 貴君 *kikun*, you (lit., masc.) 諸君 *shokun*, gentlemen, ladies and gentlemen, you
係 286 9 strokes	ノ イ イ 仁 仔 係 係 係 係	KEI; *kakari*, charge, duty, in charge (of); *kaka(ru)*, to affect, to concern 係員 *kakari-in*, clerk in charge 関係 *kankei*, relation, connection, participation, implication 記録係 *kirokugakari*, person in charge of records, recorder
軽 287 12 strokes	一 戸 車 車 車 軽 軽 軽 軽	KEI; *karu*, *karu(i)*, light (in weight), slight, easy; *karo(yaka)*, airy, light 軽卒 *keisotsu*, rashness, hastiness 軽音楽 *kei-ongaku*, light music 気軽 *kigaru*, light-hearted
血 288 6 strokes	ノ イ 白 血 血 血	KETSU; *chi*, blood 血液 *ketsueki*, blood 出血 *shukketsu*, bleeding, hemorrhage 血管 *kekkan*, blood vessel
決 289 7 strokes	丶 冫 氵 沪 沪 決 決	KETSU; *ki(maru)*, to be decided; *ki(meru)*, to decide 決心 *kesshin*, making up one's mind 決定 *kettei*, decision 解決 *kaiketsu*, solution

研 290 9 strokes	一 石 石	ナ 石 研	オ 石 研	KEN study; *to(gu)*, to sharpen, to wash (rice) 研究　　*kenkyū*, study, research 研究室　*kenkyūshitsu*, laboratory 研究所　*kenkyūjo*, research institute
県 291 9 strokes	丨 月 県	冂 目 県	月 且 県	KEN, prefecture 県道　　*kendō*, prefectural road 県庁　　*kenchō*, prefectural office 県知事　*kenchiji*, prefectural governor
庫 292 10 strokes	丶 广 盾	亠 庁 盾	广 庐 庫	KO warehouse 書庫　　*shoko*, library 倉庫　　*sōko*, warehouse 冷蔵庫　*reizōko*, icebox, refrigerator
湖 293 12 strokes	丶 氵 洺	丷 沽 湖	氵 沽 湖	KO; *mizu-umi*, lake 湖水　*kosui*, lake 湖岸　*kogan*, shore of a lake 湖畔　*kohan*, border of a lake
向 294 6 strokes	ノ 向	イ 向	门 向	KŌ; *mu(ku)*, to turn toward, to be suited for; *mu(kau)*, to face, to head for; *mu(kō)*, the opposite side, beyond 向こう　　*mukō*, opposite 向こう側　*mukōgawa*, opposite side 方向　　　*hōkō*, direction, course

幸	一	十	土	KŌ; *saiwa(i)*, blessings, good luck, happiness, fortune; *sachi*, happiness, luck; *shiawa(se)*, happiness, good fortune
	圭	赱	圭	
295 8 strokes	幸	幸		不幸 *fukō*, unhappiness, misfortune 幸福 *kōfuku*, happiness 幸運 *kōun*, good fortune

港	氵	汁	汁	KŌ; *minato*, harbor
	洪	浐	洪	港町 *minatomachi*, port town 入港 *nyūkō*, entry into port 空港 *kūkō*, airport
296 12 strokes	港	港	港	

号	丶	口	口	GŌ, number, issue (of a magazine)
	므	号		番号 *bangō*, number 記号 *kigō*, symbol 信号 *shingō*, signal, code
297 5 strokes				

根	一	十	木	KON, root (math.), perseverance; *ne*, root
	朾	朾	朾	根気 *konki*, patience, perseverance 大根 *daikon*, giant white radish 根本 *konpon*, basis
298 10 strokes	根	根	根	

祭	丿	ク	夕	SAI; *matsu(ri)*, festival; *matsu(ru)*, to deify, to worship as a god, to offer prayers for the sake of
	夗	夘	夗	
299 11 strokes	怒	祭	祭	村祭り *muramatsuri*, village festival 祭日 *saijitsu*, national holiday 文化祭 *bunkasai*, cultural festival

皿	ヽ	口	皿	sara, plate, dish, bowl
	皿	皿		皿洗い　　　sara-arai, dishwashing 皿洗い機　sara-araiki, dishwasher 灰皿　　　　haizara, ashtray
300 5 strokes				

仕	ノ	イ	仁	SHI, JI work; tsuka(eru), to serve
	什	仕		仕事　　shigoto, work 給仕　　kyūji, office boy, waiter 仕方　　shikata, way of doing
301 5 strokes				

死	一	ァ	歹	SHI, death; shi(nu), to die
	歹	歼	死	死体　　　shitai, corpse 死傷者　　shishōsha, dead and injured, 　　　　　casualties 必死　　　hisshi, certain death, desperation
302 6 strokes				

使	ノ	イ	亻	SHI; tsuka(u), to use
	仁	佢	佢	使い　　tsukai, errand, messenger 使命　　shimei, mission, errand 使用　　shiyō, use
303 8 strokes	伊	使		

始	く	女	女	SHI; haji(maru), to begin (v.i.); haji(meru), to begin (v.t.)
	如	如	始	開始　　kaishi, commencement, start 始末　　shimatsu, circumstances, the 　　　　particulars; management
304 8 strokes	始	始		始業　　shigyō, beginning of work or class

61

指	一	寸	扌	SHI; *yubi*, finger; *sa(su)*, to point at, to indicate
	扌	护	护	親指　　*oyayubi*, thumb 指輪　　*yubiwa*, ring 指揮者　*shikisha*, conductor, commander
305 9 strokes	指	指	指	

歯	丨	卜	止	SHI; *ha*, tooth
	止	艹	歨	虫歯　　*mushiba*, decayed tooth 歯医者　*ha-isha*, dentist 歯車　　*haguruma*, gear, cogwheel
306 12 strokes	柴	歯	歯	

詩	、	二	三	SHI, poetry, poem
	言	言	言	詩人　　*shijin*, poet 詩集　　*shishū*, anthology of poetry 叙事詩　*jojishi*, epic poem
307 13 strokes	詰	詩	詩	

次	、	冫	冫	JI, SHI; *tsugi*, next; *tsu(gu)*, to rank next to
	沙	次	次	次第　　*shidai*, order, reason, as soon as 次官　　*jikan*, vice-minister 目次　　*mokuji*, table of contents
308 6 strokes				

事	一	一	戸	JI; *koto*, thing, action, affair, fact
	戸	丐	写	仕事　　*shigoto*, work 用事　　*yōji*, business 大事　　*daiji*, great matter, serious affair, importance
309 8 strokes	写	事		

持	一	十	才	JI; *mo(chi)*, durability; *mo(tsu)*, to have, to hold
	才	扩	扩	気持　*kimochi*, feeling 持参　*jisan*, bringing 支持　*shiji*, support
310 9 strokes	扩	持	持	

式	一	二	亍	SHIKI, ceremony, form, model; ~*shiki*, ~-style (suffix for "style", "type")
	式	式	式	式場　*shikijō*, ceremonial hall 卒業式　*sotsugyō-shiki*, graduation 　　　　ceremony, commencement
311 6 strokes				旧式　*kyūshiki*, old-style

実	丶	八	宀	JITSU, reality; *mi*, nut, fruit; *mino(ru)*, to bear fruit
	宀	宀	宝	実際　*jissai*, actual state, reality 真実　*shinjitsu*, truth 果実　*kajitsu*, fruit
312 8 strokes	実	実		

写	'	冖	写	SHA; *utsu(su)*, to copy, to imitate, to take (a photograph)
	写	写		写真　*shashin*, photograph 写生　*shasei*, sketch, drawing from 　　　　nature
313 5 strokes				映写　*eisha*, projection

者	一	十	土	SHA; *mono*, person
	少	尹	者	若者　*wakamono*, young man 医者　*isha*, doctor 学者　*gakusha*, scholar
314 8 strokes	者	者		

主	、	二	宀
	宁	主	
315 5 strokes			

SHU, SU; *nushi*, master, owner; *omo*, main, foremost

主人 — *shujin*, master
民主主義 — *minshushugi*, democracy
持主 — *mochinushi*, owner

守	、	八	宀
	宀	守	守
316 6 strokes			

SHU, SU; *mamo(ru)*, to protect, to guard, to defend, to obey (the law), to keep (a promise); *mori*, nursemaid, baby-sitter

お守り — *o-mamori*, amulet, charm
留守 — *rusu*, absence
保守 — *hoshu*, conservatism

取	一	厂	厂
	耳	耳	耳
	取	取	
317 8 strokes			

SHU; *to(ru)*, to take

取り出す — *toridasu*, to take out
取材 — *shuzai*, choice of subject
取扱い — *toriatsukai*, treatment, handling

酒	、	氵	氵
	沂	汅	洒
	酒	酒	
318 10 strokes			

SHU; *sake*, rice wine, liquor

ぶどう酒 — *budōshu*, wine
酒飲み — *sakenomi*, drinker
酒屋 — *sakaya*, liquor shop

受	丶	丷	丷
	丷	丷	爫
	受	受	
319 8 strokes			

JU; *u(keru)*, to receive; *u(karu)*, to pass (an exam)

受持 — *ukemochi*, charge, matter in hand
受付 — *uketsuke*, receptionist, information desk
受話機 — *juwaki*, telephone receiver

州 320 6 strokes	＼ 州	リ 州	少 州	SHŪ, province, state (U.S.A.); *su*, shallows, a sandbank 本州　　*Honshū* (main island of Japan) 九州　　*Kyūshū* (Japan's third largest island) ユタ州　*Yuta-shū*, State of Utah
拾 321 9 strokes	一 扌 拾	十 扒 拾	才 扲 拾	SHŪ; JŪ, ten (used in legal documents); *hiro(u)*, to pick up 拾い物　*hiroimono*, something picked up, windfall, bargain 命拾い　*inochibiroi*, narrow escape (from death) 拾弐円　*jūni-en*, 12 yen
終 322 11 strokes	ㄥ 糸 終	幺 糸 終	幺 紒 終	SHŪ; *o(wari)*, end; *o(waru)*, to come to an end; *o(eru)*, to finish 終戦　*shūsen*, end of a war 終業　*shūgyō*, end of work 最終　*saishū*, the last
習 323 11 strokes	コ 羽 習	ヨ 羽 習	习 羽 習	SHŪ; *nara(u)*, to learn, to study 練習　*renshū*, practice 習字　*shūji*, penmanship 習慣　*shūkan*, habit, custom
集 324 12 strokes	ノ 广 隹	イ 什 隹	イ 佳 集	SHŪ; *atsu(meru)*, to collect (v.t.); *atsu(maru)*, to gather together (v.i.); *tsudo(u)*, to meet, to gather 編集　*henshū*, editing 詩集　*shishū*, anthology of poems 文集　*bunshū*, literary anthology

住	ノ	イ	イ	JŪ dwelling; *su(mu)*, to dwell, to live; *su(mai)*, dwelling
	仁	仟	住	住所　　*jūsho*, address 衣食住　*i-shoku-jū*, necessities of life 　　　　　(clothing, food, shelter)
325 7 strokes	住			住宅　　*jūtaku*, dwelling, living quarters

重	一	二	千	JŪ, CHŌ; *omo(i)*, heavy; *kasa(neru)*, to pile (things) up; *kasa(naru)*, to be piled up; ~*e*, ~fold
	点	盲	盲	体重　　*taijū*, weight (of the body) 厳重　　*genjū*, strictness
326 9 strokes	重	重	重	二重　　*futae, nijū*, duplicate, double, twofold

宿	丶	丷	宀	SHUKU; *yado*, inn; *yado(ru)*, to lodge at; *yado(su)*, to provide shelter
	宀	宀	宀	宿屋　　*yadoya*, inn 宿題　　*shukudai*, homework
327 11 strokes	宿	宿	宿	下宿　　*geshuku*, boardinghouse

所	一	コ	ヨ	SHO; *tokoro*, place
	戸	戸	所	台所　　*daidokoro*, kitchen 場所　　*basho*, place
328 8 strokes	所	所		近所　　*kinjo*, neighborhood

暑	丶	口	日	SHO; *atsu(i)*, hot
	日	旦	昇	残暑　　*zansho*, lingering summer heat 避暑　　*hisho*, summering, going to a 　　　　　summer resort
329 12 strokes	暑	暑	暑	暑中　　*shochū*, midsummer

助	丨	冂	月	JO; *tasu(karu)*, to be aided, to be rescued; *tasu(keru)*, to aid, to rescue; *~suke*, suffix for masculine names
	月	且	町	助手　*joshu*, assistant 補助　*hojo*, assistance 助力　*joryoku*, help, aid
330 7 strokes	助			

昭	丨	冂	月	SHŌ bright
	日	昭	昭	昭和　*Shōwa*, Emperor Hirohito or his reign (1926–1989)
331 9 strokes	昭	昭	昭	

消	⺡	⺡	⺡	SHŌ; *ki(eru)*, to vanish, to go out, to melt away; *ke(su)*, to extinguish, to switch off, to put out (a light)
	沪	沪	消	消しゴム　*keshigomu*, eraser 消防　*shōbō*, fire fighting 消毒　*shōdoku*, disinfection
332 10 strokes	消	消		

商	丶	亠	亠	SHŌ; *akina(u)*, to sell, to deal in
	产	产	产	商人　*shōnin*, merchant 商売　*shōbai*, business, trade, transaction 商業　*shōgyō*, commerce, trade
333 11 strokes	产	商	商	

章	亠	立	产	SHŌ, chapter
	音	音	音	文章　*bunshō*, sentence 記章　*kishō*, medal, badge 勲章　*kunshō*, decoration, order (for honors)
334 11 strokes	章	章		

勝	月	月	朦	SHŌ; *ka(tsu)*, to win; *masa(ru)*, to excel
	朦	朦	朦	勝負　*shōbu*, victory or defeat, match 勝敗　*shōhai*, the outcome (of a battle) 勝手　*katte*, selfish, willful
335 12 strokes	朦	勝	勝	

乗	一	二	三	JŌ; *no(ru)*, to ride; *no(seru)*, to give a ride to, to place upon
	千	禾	丘	乗り物　*norimono*, vehicle 乗客　*jōkyaku*, passenger 遠乗り　*tōnori*, a long ride
336 9 strokes	乖	乗	乗	

植	一	十	木	SHOKU; *u(eru)*, to plant, to set up (type)
	木	杧	杧	植物　*shokubutsu*, plant, vetegation 植民地　*shokuminchi*, colony 田植え　*taue*, rice planting
337 12 strokes	枯	植	植	

申	丶	冂	日	SHIN; *mō(su)*, to say
	日	申		申し込み　*mōshikomi*, application, proposal 申告　*shinkoku*, report, filing a return 申し合わせ　*mōshiawase*, arrangement
338 5 strokes				

身	丿	亻	冃	SHIN; *mi*, body
	自	身	身	身体　*shintai*, body 身長　*shinchō*, height (of the body) 身分　*mibun*, social position
339 7 strokes	身			

神 340 9 strokes	丶	ラ	ネ
	ネ	ネ	初
	初	初	神

SHIN, JIN; *kami*, god

神経質　*shinkeishitsu*, nervous temperament
精神　　*seishin*, soul, spirit
神様　　*kamisama*, god

真 341 10 strokes	一	十	广
	市	市	首
	直	真	真

SHIN; *ma*, truth, reality

写真機　*shashinki*, camera
真夏　　*manatsu*, midsummer

深 342 11 strokes	丶	冫	氵
	氵	汀	沪
	泙	浬	深

SHIN; *fuka(i)*, deep, profound, thick (fog), close (connection); *fuka(sa)*, depth, profundity; *fuka(meru)* (v.t.), to make deeper, to intensify

深夜　　*shin'ya*, midnight
深呼吸　*shinkokyū*, deep breath
深刻　　*shinkoku*, serious, significant

進 343 11 strokes	ノ	イ	仁
	什	隹	隹
	隹	淮	進

SHIN; *susu(mu)*, to advance, to proceed; *susu(meru)* (v.t.), to move forward, to stimulate

進行　　*shinkō*, progress, advance
進級　　*shinkyū*, promotion
行進　　*kōshin*, march, parade

世 344 5 strokes	一	十	廿
	廿	世	

SEI, SE; *yo*, world, age, reign

世界　　*sekai*, the world
世紀　　*seiki*, century
世間　　*seken*, the world, society, life

整	一	己	束	SEI; *totono(eru)*, to put in order, to get ready; *totono(u)*, to be ready
	束	束	刺	整理 *seiri*, adjustment, arrangement, reorganization
345 16 strokes	敕	敕	整	整備 *seibi*, adjustment, complete equipment, consolidation

昔	一	十	廿	SEKI, SHAKU; *mukashi*, in the past, olden times
	丗	芾	芕	昔話 *mukashibanashi*, old tale, folklore 今昔 *konjaku*, past and present 大昔 *ōmukashi*, high antiquity, in the
346 8 strokes	昔	昔		remote past

全	ノ	入	入	ZEN whole; *matta(ku)*, entirely
	今	全	全	全体 *zentai*, the whole 全部 *zenbu*, all, the whole 完全 *kanzen*, perfect
347 6 strokes				

相	一	十	才	SŌ, appearance, aspect, phase; SHŌ minister of state; *ai-*, each other, mutual
	木	机	机	相談 *sōdan*, consultation, talk 相手 *aite*, companion, the other party 首相 *shushō*, prime minister
348 9 strokes	机	相	相	

送	、	`'`	兰	SŌ; *oku(ru)*, to send
	兰	关	关	放送 *hōsō*, broadcast 輸送 *yusō*, transportation 送金 *sōkin*, sending money
349 9 strokes	送	送	送	

想	一	十	才	SŌ, idea, thought
	木	杧	相	想像　*sōzō*, imagination 理想　*risō*, ideal 予想　*yosō*, expectation
350 13 strokes	相	想	想	

息	′	⸢	白	SOKU, son; *iki*, breath
	自	自	自	ため息　*tameiki*, sigh 休息　*kyūsoku*, rest 消息　*shōsoku*, news, letter, 　　　circumstances
351 10 strokes	息	息	息	

速	一	⸢	戸	SOKU; *haya(i)*, speedy, quick; *haya(meru)* (v.t.), to hasten, to accelerate; *sumi(yaka)*, speedy, prompt
	束	束	束	速度　*sokudo*, speed 速記　*sokki*, stenography, shorthand 速達　*sokutatsu*, express mail, special 　　　delivery
352 10 strokes	凍	速	速	

族	゛	方	方	ZOKU, family, tribe, clan
	扩	扩	扩	家族　*kazoku*, family, household 民族　*minzoku*, race, people, nation 水族館　*suizokukan*, aquarium
353 11 strokes	扩	族	族	

他	ノ	イ	イ	TA, other
	仲	他		他国　*takoku*, other countries 他人　*tanin*, other people, stranger その他　*sonota*, the others, the rest; and 　　　so forth
354 5 strokes				

| 打 355 5 strokes | 一 | 十 | 才 |
| | 打 | 打 | |

DA; *u(tsu)*, to strike, to beat

舌打ち   *shita-uchi*, smacking one's lips, click of the tongue
打者   *dasha*, batter, hitter
三塁打   *sanrui-da*, three-base hit

対 356 7 strokes	、	ソ	フ
	文	文	対
	対		

TAI, opposite, against; TSUI, pair, set

反対   *hantai*, opposition, opposite, objection, reverse
対面   *taimen*, interview, confrontation
二対一   *ni-tai-ichi*, (score of) 2 to 1

待 357 9 strokes	ノ	ク	イ
	彳	彳	彳
	往	待	待

TAI; *ma(tsu)*, to wait for

待合室   *machiaishitsu*, waiting room
接待   *settai*, reception
招待   *shōtai*, invitation

| 代 358 5 strokes | ノ | イ | 仁 |
| | 代 | 代 | |

DAI, generation, price; *ka(eru)*, to substitute, to use instead; *ka(waru)*, to take the place of, to relieve; *yo*, generation, era, reign

時代   *jidai*, period, era, age
現代   *gendai*, the present age
代表   *daihyō*, representative

第 359 11 strokes	ノ	ト	ケ
	竹	竺	竺
	笃	第	第

DAI grade, prefix for ordinal numbers

第一回   *dai-ikkai*, the first time
及第   *kyūdai*, passing an examination
落第   *rakudai*, failure (in an examination), rejection

題	日	旦	早	DAI, subject, topic, theme, title (of book, story, etc.)
	早	是	是	問題 *mondai,* question, problem 話題 *wadai,* topic of conversation 宿題 *shukudai,* homework
360 18 strokes	是	是	題	

炭	'	屮	山	TAN; *sumi,* charcoal
	屮	产	岸	炭坑 *tankō,* coal mine 石炭 *sekitan,* coal 木炭 *mokutan,* charcoal
361 9 strokes	炭	岽	炭	

短	ノ	ヒ	上	TAN shortness, defect; *mijika(i),* short, brief
	乍	矢	矢	短気 *tanki,* quick temper 最短 *saitan,* shortest 長短 *chōtan,* long and short, merits and demerits
362 12 strokes	知	短	短	

談	、	二	言	DAN, talk
	言	言	言	相談 *sōdan,* consultation 談話 *danwa,* conversation, talk 歓談 *kandan,* pleasant chat
363 15 strokes	訬	談	談	

着	、	ヽヽ	丷	CHAKU; *ki(ru),* to wear; *tsu(ku),* to reach, to arrive; *ki(seru),* to dress, to plate
	ヂ	半	羊	着物 *kimono,* Japanese robe 一着 *itchaku,* first arrival, a suit (of clothes)
364 12 strokes	羊	着	着	上着 *uwagi,* coat

注 365 8 strokes	丶 氵 沪 汪 注	冫 氵 汙 注	氵 汀

CHŪ; *soso(gu)*, to pour, to concentrate on

注意 *chūi*, attention, care, warning, advice
注目 *chūmoku*, attention, observation
注文 *chūmon*, order, request, demand

柱 366 9 strokes	一 木 杧 柱	十 术 杧 柱	才 杧 柱

CHŪ; *hashira*, post, pillar

帆柱 *hobashira*, mast
柱時計 *hashiradokei*, wall clock
電柱 *denchū*, telegraph (electric) pole

丁 367 2 strokes	一	丁	

CHŌ Japanese linear unit (120 yds.), division of a ward or town, leaf of a book; TEI "D" grade

横丁 *yokochō*, side street, alleyway
丁度 *chōdo*, exactly, just
丁寧 *teinei*, politeness

帳 368 11 strokes	丿 巾 帖	冂 帐 帳	巾 帐 帳

CHŌ curtain, register

帳面 *chōmen*, notebook, account book
手帳 *techō*, memo book, notebook
日記帳 *nikkichō*, diary

調 369 15 strokes	言 訂 調	言 訊 調	訂 訊

CHŌ; *shira(be)*, melody, inspection; *shira(beru)*, to investigate, to examine, to inspect

調子 *chōshi*, tune, key, rhythm, tone, way, condition
調査 *chōsa*, investigation, examination
調節 *chōsetsu*, adjustment

追	´	イ	亽	TSUI; *o(u)*, to run after, to drive away
	戶	自	自	追いかける *oikakeru*, to chase 追求 *tsuikyū*, pursuit 追放 *tsuihō*, banishment, exile, purge
370 **9 strokes**	𠂤	追	追	

定	丶	丷	宀	TEI, JŌ; *sada(meru)*, to fix, to decide, to establish; *sada(ka)*, certain
	宀	宁	宇	定員 *tei-in*, regular staff, full number of personnel 定期 *teiki*, fixed period or term, regularity; prefix for "regular" 予定 *yotei*, previous arrangement, program, schedule
371 **8 strokes**	定	定		

庭	丶	亠	广	TEI; *niwa*, garden
	广	庀	庍	庭園 *teien*, garden 校庭 *kōtei*, school playground 家庭 *katei*, home
372 **10 strokes**	庄	庭	庭	

笛	ノ	⺊	⺮	TEKI; *fue*, flute, whistle
	⺮	竹	笃	警笛 *keiteki*, alarm whistle, warning horn 汽笛 *kiteki*, steam whistle, siren 口笛 *kuchibue*, whistling
373 **11 strokes**	笛	笛	笛	

鉄	ノ	⺈	牟	TETSU, iron, steel
	金	金	釒	鉄道 *tetsudō*, railroad 地下鉄 *chikatetsu*, subway 鉄橋 *tekkyō*, iron bridge, railway bridge
374 **13 strokes**	釒	鉄	鉄	

転 375 11 strokes	一 車 転	冐 軒 転	亘 軒	TEN to turn round, to change, to fall, to tumble; *koro(geru)*, to roll over; *koro(bu)*, to tumble, to fall down 転校　*tenkō*, change of schools 転任　*tennin*, change of post 運転　*unten*, driving, working, operation
都 376 11 strokes	土 者 者ㇷ	耂 者 者ろ	耂 者 都	TO, TSU; *miyako*, capital, metropolis 都会　*tokai*, city 首都　*shuto*, capital 都合　*tsugō*, circumstances, conditions
度 377 9 strokes	丶 庐 庐	亠 庐 庐	广 庐 度	DO, TO, TAKU degree, time, times; *tabi*, occasion, counter for number of times 一度　*ichido*, once 速度　*sokudo*, speed 程度　*teido*, degree, level, extent
投 378 7 strokes	一 扌 投	扌 扩	扌 投	TŌ; *na(geru)*, to throw, to give up 投票　*tōhyō*, voting 投資　*tōshi*, investment 投書　*tōsho*, contribution (to a magazine, newspaper, etc)
豆 379 7 strokes	一 豆 豆	丆 戸	戸 豆	TŌ, ZU; *mame*, peas, beans; *mame-*, baby/miniature 豆腐　*tōfu*, bean-curd 大豆　*daizu*, soy beans 豆本　*mamehon*, miniature book

76

島	亻	亻	戶	**TŌ**; *shima*, island
	自	自	鳥	半島　　*hantō*, peninsula 群島　　*guntō*, group of islands 島国　　*shimaguni*, island country
380 10 strokes	鳥	島	島	

湯	丶	丷	氵	**TŌ**; *yu*, hot water
	沪	沪	沪	湯気　　*yuge*, steam 湯船　　*yubune*, bathtub 熱湯　　*nettō*, boiling water
381 12 strokes	湡	湯	湯	

登	ノ	ノ	ヌ	**TŌ, TO**; *nobo(ri)*, climbing (n.); *nobo(ru)*, to climb
	癶	癶	癶	登山　　*tozan*, mountain climbing 登校　　*tōkō*, attending school 木登り　*ki-nobori*, tree climbing
382 12 strokes	咎	登	登	

等	ノ	𠂉	𠂉	**TŌ**, class, quality; *hito(shii)*, like, equal
	竹	竺	竺	上等　　　　*jōtō*, high-class, very good, 　　　　　　superior 一等　　　　*ittō*, first class, most, best 高等学校　　*kōtōgakkō*, senior high 　　　　　　school
383 12 strokes	笁	等	等	

動	二	盲	重	**DŌ**; *ugo(ku)*, to move
	重	重	動	動物　　*dōbutsu*, animal 自動車　*jidōsha*, automobile 運動　　*undō*, motion, physical exercise, 　　　　athletic sports
384 11 strokes	動			

童	、	亠	产	DŌ child
	立	立	音	児童 *jidō*, child, boys and girls 童話 *dōwa*, nursery tale 童謡 *dōyō*, nursery song
385 12 strokes	音	童	童	

農	冖	曲	曲	NŌ, *farming*
	曲	严	農	農場 *nōjō*, farm 農業 *nōgyō*, agriculture 農家 *nōka*, farmhouse
386 13 strokes	農	農	農	

波	、	〰	氵	HA; *nami*, wave
	氵	沪	沪	大波 *ō-nami*, big wave 防波堤 *bōhatei*, breakwater 電波 *denpa*, electric wave
387 8 strokes	波	波		

配	一	冂	西	HAI; *kuba(ru)*, to distribute, to deliver
	西	酉	酉	配給 *haikyū*, ration, distribution (of food or goods) 配達 *haitatsu*, delivery 心配 *shinpai*, worry
388 10 strokes	酉	配	配	

倍	丿	亻	亻	BAI, two times, double; suffix denoting "times"
	伫	仵	倍	数倍 *sūbai*, several times 何倍 *nanbai*, how many times? 倍率 *bairitsu*, magnifying power
389 10 strokes	倍	倍	倍	

箱	ノ	⺊	⺮	*hako*, box, case 下駄箱　*getabako*, shoe cabinet 郵便箱　*yūbinbako*, mailbox, postbox 箱庭　*hakoniwa*, miniature garden
	⺮	竹	竿	
390 15 strokes	箔	箱	箱	
畑	丶	⺍	⺍	*hata*, *hatake*, field, farm, cultivated field 田畑　*tahata*, fields 麦畑　*mugibatake*, wheat (barley) field 花畑　*hanabatake*, flower garden
	火	火	灯	
391 9 strokes	畑	畑	畑	
発	ノ	⺈	⺈	HATSU to expose, to open, to shoot, to happen 発音　*hatsuon*, pronounciation 発表　*happyō*, announcement 出発　*shuppatsu*, departure
	癶	癶	癶	
392 9 strokes	癶	発	発	
反	一	厂	厂	HAN, antithesis, anti-; TAN, unit of measure (for land and cloth); *so(ru)* (v.i.), to curve; *so(rasu)* (v.t.), to bend (something) 反対　*hantai*, opposition, contrast 反省　*hansei*, self-examination 反射　*hansha*, reflection
	反			
393 4 strokes				
坂	一	十	土	HAN; *saka*, slope, hill 坂道　*sakamichi*, sloping road 上り坂　*noborizaka*, ascent, uphill road 急坂　*kyūhan*, steep slope
	土	圢	坊	
394 7 strokes	坂			

板	一	十	才	HAN; *ita*, board (of wood)
	木	朳	朽	板の間 *ita-no-ma*, wooden floor 掲示板 *keijiban*, notice-board 看板 *kanban*, poster, signboard, shingle
395 8 strokes	朽	板		

皮	ノ	厂	广	HI; *kawa*, skin, leather
	皮	皮		毛皮 *kegawa*, fur 皮肉 *hiniku*, irony 皮膚 *hifu*, skin
396 5 strokes				

悲	ノ	ナ	彐	HI; *kana(shii)*, sad
	彐	非	非	悲劇 *higeki*, tragedy, tragic event 悲壮 *hisō*, pathetic 慈悲 *jihi*, mercy
397 12 strokes	非	非	悲	

美	ヽ	ヅ	゛	BI, beauty; *utsuku(shii)*, beautiful
	羊	羊	羊	美術 *bijutsu*, fine arts 美人 *bijin*, a beauty, pretty girl, beautiful woman 美術館 *bijutsukan*, art museum
398 9 strokes	羊	美	美	

鼻	⼁	冂	自	BI; *hana*, nose
	自	畠	畠	鼻先 *hanasaki*, tip of one's nose, under one's very nose 鼻紙 *hanagami*, paper handkerchief 鼻血 *hanaji*, nosebleed
399 14 strokes	畠	鼻	鼻	

筆

400
12 strokes

HITSU; *fude,* writing brush

万年筆	*mannenhitsu,* fountain pen
鉛筆	*enpitsu,* pencil
筆者	*hissha,* writer

氷

401
5 strokes

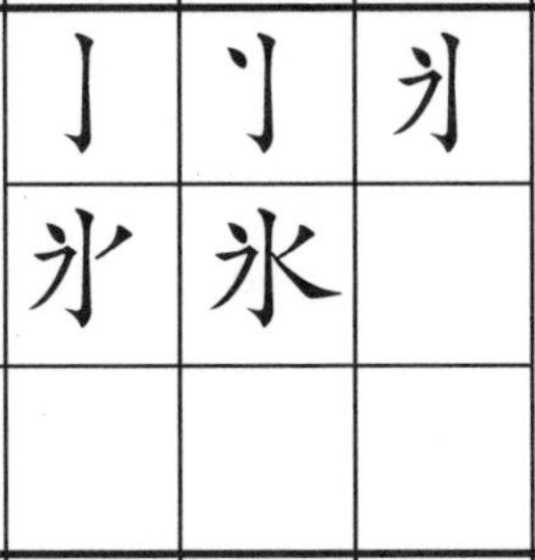

HYŌ; *kōri,* ice

氷すべり	*kōrisuberi,* ice skating
氷山	*hyōzan,* iceberg
砕氷船	*saihyōsen,* icebreaker

表

402
8 strokes

HYŌ, list, table, schedule; *omote,* the outside, surface; *ara(wasu),* to show, to indicate, to expose, to express, to represent

表紙	*hyōshi,* cover of a book
表面	*hyōmen,* surface
時間表	*jikanhyō,* schedule, timetable

秒

403
9 strokes

BYŌ, second (unit of time)

秒針	*byōshin,* second hand
一秒	*ichibyō,* one second
数秒	*sūbyō,* several seconds

病

404
10 strokes

BYŌ; *yamai,* illness; *ya(mu),* to fall ill

病気	*byōki,* illness, sickness
病院	*byōin,* hospital
病人	*byōnin,* sick person

品	丶	丬	口	HIN, elegance, dignity; *shina*, goods 品物　　*shinamono*, article, goods 手品　　*tejina*, jugglery, sleight of hand 作品　　*sakuhin*, work, works
	口	吕	吕	
405 9 strokes	品	品	品	

負	ノ	ク	ケ	FU; *o(u)*, to bear, to owe; *ma(keru)*, to be defeated, to reduce a price; *ma(kasu)*, to defeat 勝負　　*shōbu*, victory or defeat, game 負傷　　*fushō*, wound 背負う　*se-ou*, to carry on one's back
	负	角	角	
406 9 strokes	負	負	負	

部	丶	二	立	BU, department, copy, part 全部　　*zenbu*, all, whole 東部　　*tōbu*, eastern part 部分　　*bubun*, part
	立	立	音	
407 11 strokes	音㇏	部㇏	部	

服	ノ	刀	月	FUKU, dress, European clothes 洋服　　*yōfuku*, European clothes 礼服　　*reifuku*, full dress 制服　　*seifuku*, uniform
	月	月㇏	肝	
408 8 strokes	服	服		

福	丶	ラ	ネ	FUKU, good fortune 幸福　　　*kōfuku*, happiness 福の神　　*fuku-no-kami*, God of Wealth 祝福　　　*shukufuku*, blessing
	ネ	衤	祀	
409 13 strokes	福	福	福	

物	ノ	⺊	牛	BUTSU, MOTSU; *mono*, thing, article, object
	牛	牜	牞	食べ物　*tabemono*, food
				名物　*meibutsu*, noted product, special product
410　8 strokes	牣	物		貨物　*kamotsu*, freight

平	一	⺕	二	HEI, BYŌ; *tai(ra)*, evenness, flatness; *hira(tai)*, even, level, simple
	平	平		平和　*heiwa*, peace
				平気　*heiki*, calmness, indifference
411　5 strokes				平等　*byōdō*, equality

返	一	厂	反	HEN; *kae(su)*, to return, to give back
	反	返	返	返事　　　*henji*, answer
				繰り返す　*kurikaesu*, to repeat
				恩返し　　*ongaeshi*, repayment of a favor, returning a favor
412　7 strokes	返			

勉	ノ	⺈	ク	BEN to exert oneself, to make efforts
	厶	缶	缶	勉強　　*benkyō*, study
				勤勉　　*kinben*, diligence
				勉強家　*benkyōka*, studious person
413　10 strokes	免	免	勉	

放	、	二	亠	HŌ; *hana(su)*, to let go, to release; *hana(tsu)*, to set free, to send forth, to shoot
	方	方	扩	放送　　*hōsō*, broadcasting
				放課後　*hōkago*, after school
414　8 strokes	扷	放		開放　　*kaihō*, freedom, opening

83

味 415 8 strokes	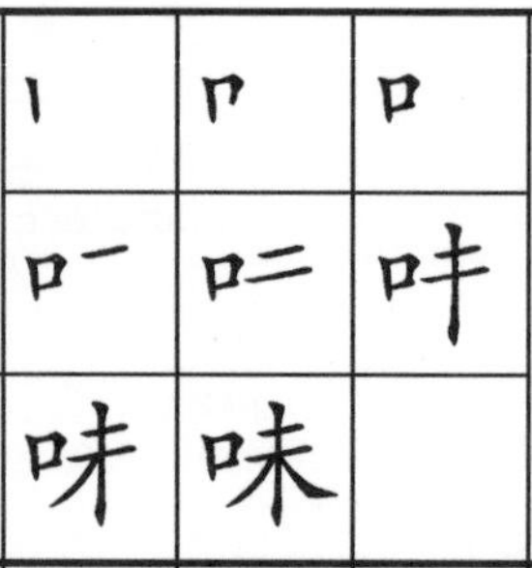	MI; *aji,* taste, relish, experience; *aji(wau),* to savor, to appreciate 無味 *mumi,* tastelessness 味方 *mikata,* friend, ally 興味 *kyōmi,* interest, ejoyment
命 416 8 strokes		MEI, order, command; MYŌ; *inochi,* life 命令 *meirei,* order, command 使命 *shimei,* mission 生命 *seimei,* life, soul
面 417 9 strokes		MEN, side, phase, mask; *omote,* face, outside, front, surface; *omo* (lit.), face, surface; *tsura,* face 表面 *hyōmen,* surface 正面 *shōmen,* the front 場面 *bamen,* scene
問 418 11 strokes	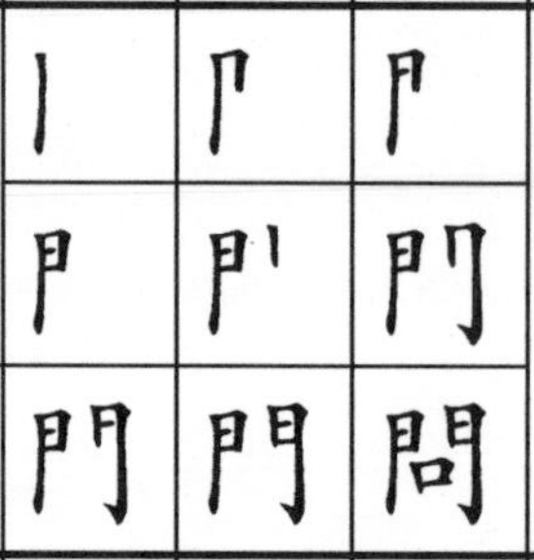	MON; *to(u),* to ask, to question, to care, to accuse 問題 *mondai,* problem, issue, trouble 学問 *gakumon,* learning 疑問 *gimon,* doubt, question
役 419 7 strokes		YAKU, office, duty, role, use, service; EKI (lit.), war 役所 *yakusho,* public office 役人 *yakunin,* government official 役者 *yakusha,* actor, actress

薬	一	十	艹	YAKU; *kusuri*, medicine, chemicals
	苩	苩	萡	薬学　*yakugaku*, pharmacy (study) 火薬　*kayaku*, gunpowder 薬局　*yakkyoku*, pharmacy, pharmacist's office
420 16 strokes	萍	萍	薬	

由	丶	冂	巾	YU, YŪ; *yoshi*, a reason, significance
	由	由		自由　*jiyū*, liberty, freedom 不自由　*fujiyū*, inconvenience, discomfort 理由　*riyū*, reason
421 5 strokes				

油	丶	丶丶	氵	YU; *abura*, oil
	氵	沪	汕	油絵　*abura-e*, oil painting 石油　*sekiyu*, petroleum 油田　*yuden*, oil field
422 8 strokes	油	油		

有	一	ナ	冇	YŪ, U; *a(ru)*, to exist, to have, to measure, to have experience, to happen, to consist of
	冇	有	有	有名　*yūmei*, fame, well-known 有益　*yūeki*, benefit, profit 有志　*yūshi*, volunteer
423 6 strokes				

遊	丶	二	亏	YŪ; *aso(bu)*, to play, to be idle
	方	㣺	㣺	遊星　*yūsei*, planet 遊戯　*yūgi*, game, sports, children's play 遊覧　*yūran*, excursion, sightseeing
424 12 strokes	斿	游	遊	

予	フ	マ	3
	予		
425 4 strokes			

YO previous

予防　*yobō*, prevention
予定　*yotei*, previous arrangement, schedule
予想　*yosō*, anticipation

羊	丶	丷	丷
	半	半	羊
426 6 strokes			

YŌ; *hitsuji*, sheep, ram, ewe

羊毛　*yōmō*, wool
羊皮　*yōhi*, sheepskin
子羊　*kohitsuji*, a lamb

洋	丶	冫	氵
	氵	汀	汀
427 9 strokes	泮	浂	洋

YŌ, ocean

西洋　*seiyō*, the West, the Occident
洋間　*yōma*, Western-style room
洋服　*yōfuku*, Western-style clothes

葉	一	十	艹
	苎	芏	茊
	莊	笹	葉
428 12 strokes			

YŌ; *ha*, leaves, foliage

葉緑素　*yōryokuso*, chlorophyll
落ち葉　*ochiba*, fallen leaves
葉巻　*hamaki*, cigar

陽	⁊	了	阝
	阝	阳	陧
	陽	陽	陽
429 12 strokes			

YŌ positive, male principle in nature

太陽　*taiyō*, sun
太陽系　*taiyōkei*, solar system
陽気　*yōki*, season, weather, cheerfulness

様 430 14 strokes	木 栌 栏 栏 样 様	栌 栏 样 梯 様 様	栏 栏 栏 梯 様 様	**YŌ**, way, style, manner; *sama*, Mr., Mrs., Miss, etc. (polite suffix for personal names); state, way, form, condition 神様　*kamisama*, god 様子　*yōsu*, appearance, manner, state
落 431 12 strokes	一 艹 莎 莎	十 艹 茨 落	艹 艹 莎 落	**RAKU**; *o(chiru)*, to fall (v.i.), to be omitted, to be inferior to; *o(tosu)*, to omit, to make worse, to let drop, to lose 落第　*rakudai*, failure (in an examination), rejection 落成　*rakusei*, completion (building, etc.)
流 432 10 strokes	丶 氵 泸 泸	氵 泸 済 流	氵 泸 流 流	**RYŪ, RU**; *naga(re)*, stream, current, flow; *naga(reru)*, to flow (v.i.); *naga(su)*, to set afloat, to wash away, to pour (v.t.) 流れ星　*nagareboshi*, shooting star 流行　*ryūkō*, fashion, vogue 電流　*denryū*, electric current
旅 433 10 strokes	亠 方 方 旅	方 方 旅 旅	方 方 旅 旅	**RYO**; *tabi*, travel, journey 旅人　*tabibito*, traveler 旅行　*ryokō*, trip, travel 旅館　*ryokan*, inn, hotel
両 434 6 strokes	一 冊	一 両	冂 両	**RYŌ**, old Japanese monetary unit; two, both 両手　*ryōte*, both hands 両方　*ryōhō*, both, both sides 両親　*ryōshin*, parents, father and mother

緑	糸	糹	糹	RYOKU, ROKU; *midori*, green
	糹	紵	紵	新緑　*shinryoku*, fresh verdure
435 14 strokes	紵	緑	緑	緑地　*ryokuchi*, green tract of land 緑色　*midori-iro*, green (color)

礼	丶	ラ	ネ	REI, salutation, courtesy, bow, thanks
	ネ	礼		礼儀　*reigi*, courtesy, manners, etiquette 無礼　*burei*, impoliteness, discourtesy
436 5 strokes				失礼　*shitsurei*, discourtesy, rudeness

列	一	フ	歹	RETSU, row, line
	歹	列	列	行列　*gyōretsu*, row, procession 列車　*ressha*, train
437 6 strokes				整列　*seiretsu*, standing in a row

練	糸	糹	糹	REN; *ne(ru)*, to polish (one's style), to discipline (one's mind), to parade, to knead (a dough)
	紵	紳	綀	
				練習　*renshū*, practice
438 14 strokes	紳	練	練	熟練　*jukuren*, skill, dexterity 訓練　*kunren*, drill, training

路	口	早	早	RO road, route, path; *~ji*, suffix denoting "way"
	足	𧾷	𧾷	
				道路　*dōro*, road
439 13 strokes	𧾷	路	路	線路　*senro*, railway track 航路　*kōro*, sea route

和

440
8 strokes

WA, harmony, peace, Japan; *yawa(ragu),* to soften, to calm down (v.i.); *nago(yaka),* calm, harmonious

平和 *heiwa,* peace
和服 *wafuku,* Japanese clothes, kimono
調和 *chōwa,* harmony

愛

441
13 strokes

AI, love; *ai(suru),* to love

愛情 *aijō,* love, affection
愛国心 *aikokushin,* patriotism
愛児 *aiji,* one's beloved child

案

442
10 strokes

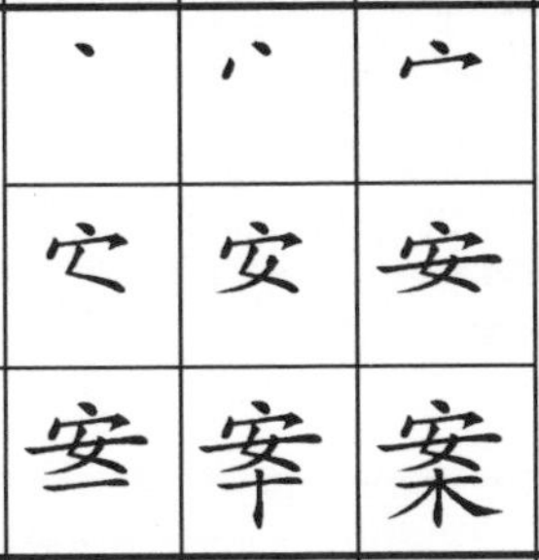

AN, plan, idea; *an(jiru),* to be anxious about, to be concerned about

案外 *angai,* unexpectedly
案内 *annai,* guide, guidance
名案 *meian,* good idea, good plan

以

443
5 strokes

I with, through, on account of

以上 *ijō,* above, more than
以外 *igai,* besides, outside of
以前 *izen,* before, formerly

衣

444
6 strokes

I; *koromo,* clothes, garment, priest's robe

衣類 *irui,* clothing
衣食住 *i-shoku-jū,* clothing, food and shelter
衣替え *koromogae,* change of dress

位	ノ	イ	イ	I; *kurai*, rank, position, grade; about (approximately)
	伫	付	付	地位　*chi-i*, rank, social standing 位置　*ichi*, location, situation 学位　*gaku-i*, academic degree
445 7 strokes	位			

囲	丨	冂	冂	I; *kako(mu)*, to surround, to enclose, to besiege
	月	用	囲	胸囲　*kyōi*, girth of the chest, chest measurement 周囲　*shūi*, circumference, surroundings 範囲　*han'i*, extent, sphere, limits
446 7 strokes	囲			

胃	丶	冂	冂	I, stomach
	冊	田	甲	胃袋　*ibukuro*, stomach 胃病　*ibyō*, stomach trouble 胃腸　*i-chō*, stomach and intestines
447 9 strokes	胃	胃	胃	

印	ノ	丫	乍	IN, seal, stamp; *shirushi*, sign, symbol, trace
	乍	臼	印	印刷　*insatsu*, printing 矢印　*yajirushi*, arrow sign 目印　*mejirushi*, mark
448 6 strokes				

英	一	十	艹	EI England, excellent
	艹	苎	苩	英語　*eigo*, English language 英雄　*eiyū*, hero 日英　*Nichi-Ei*, Japan and England
449 8 strokes	英	英		

栄	丶	丷	丷	EI, honor; *saka(e)*, prosperity; *saka(eru)*, to prosper; *ha(eru)*, to excel, to shine
	丷	兴	学	光栄　*kōei*, honor 繁栄　*han'ei*, prosperity 栄養　*eiyō*, nutrition
450 9 strokes	学	栄	栄	

塩	土	圡	圹	EN; *shio*, salt
	垆	垆	圴	塩水　*shiomizu*, salt water 塩田　*enden*, salt bed 食塩　*shokuen*, table salt
451 13 strokes	塩	塩	塩	

億	ノ	イ	仁	OKU, one hundred million
	俨	倍	倍	二十億年　*nijūoku-nen*, two billion years 数億円　*sūoku-en*, several hundred million yen
452 15 strokes	億	億	億	

加	フ	カ	加	KA; *kuwa(eru)*, to add, to join, to increase (v.t.); *kuwa(waru)*, to join, to enter (v.i.)
	加	加		参加　*sanka*, participation 加入　*kanyū*, entrance, joining 増加　*zōka*, increase
453 5 strokes				

果	丶	冂	日	KA fruit, result; *hate*, end, result; *hata(su)*, to carry out, to realize, to fulfill; *ha(teru)*, to end, to die
	日	旦	早	結果　*kekka*, result, effect 効果　*kōka*, effect 果実　*kajitsu*, fruit
454 8 strokes	早	果		

貨	ノ	イ	イ	KA treasure, goods
	化	竹	俏	百貨店 *hyakkaten*, department store 銀貨 *ginka*, silver coin 雑貨 *zakka*, miscellaneous goods, sundries
455 11 strokes	俏	貨	貨	

課	`	ニ	言	KA, section, lesson
	言	訂	評	課外 *kagai*, extra-curricular 課題 *kadai*, theme, homework 学課 *gakka*, lesson
456 15 strokes	評	評	課	

芽	一	十	艹	GA; *me*, bud, sprout, shoot
	艹	芦	芒	木の芽 *ki-no-me*, leaf bud 新芽 *shinme*, sprout, bud, shoot 芽ばえ *mebae*, bud, sprout
457 8 strokes	芽	芽		

改	`	フ	己	KAI; *arata(meru)*, to change, to reform, to revise; *arata(maru)*, to be reformed
	己	己	改	改良 *kairyō*, improvement 改心 *kaishin*, conversion, reform 改札口 *kaisatsuguchi*, ticket gate
458 7 strokes	改			

械	十	才	杆	KAI shackles
	杆	栌	枡	機械 *kikai*, machine 器械 *kikai*, instrument, apparatus
459 11 strokes	枎	械	械	

害	丶	丷	宀	GAI, harm calamity
	宀	中	宇	害虫　　gaichū, harmful insect 損害　　songai, loss, damage 障害　　shōgai, obstacle, hindrance
460 10 strokes	宝	害		

街	ノ	ク	彳	GAI, KAI; machi, street, town, quarters
	彳	彳	彳	商店街　shōtengai, shopping centre 市街　　shigai, the streets; city, town 街道　　kaidō, highway, route
461 12 strokes	往	街	街	

各	ノ	ク	夂	KAKU; ono-ono, each, every
	久	各	各	各地　　kakuchi, every place 各人　　kakujin, each person 各駅　　kaku-eki, each station
462 6 strokes				

覚	丶	丷	丷	KAKU; obo(eru), to remember, to understand; sa(masu), to awake (v.t.); sa(meru), to wake up (v.i.)
	灬	灬	甞	覚え書　oboegaki, memorandum note 感覚　　kankaku, sensation, sense, 　　　　feeling
463 12 strokes	甞	覚	覚	自覚　　jikaku, consciousness, self- 　　　　consciousness

完	丶	八	宀	KAN end, completion
	宀	宀	宇	完全　　kanzen, perfection 完成　　kansei, completion 完結　　kanketsu, completion, finish, 　　　　termination
464 7 strokes	完			

官	`	八	宀	KAN, government, government position
	宀	宁	宇	官庁　　*kanchō,* government office 裁判官　*saibankan,* judge 警官　　*keikan,* policeman, police officer
465 8 strokes	官	官		

管	ノ	⺊	⺈	KAN to control, to administer; *kuda,* tube, pipe
	⺮	⺮	竺	鉄管　*tekkan,* iron pipe (tube) 血管　*kekkan,* blood vessel 管理　*kanri,* administration, control, charge
466 14 strokes	竿	管	管	

関	｜	門	門	KAN; *seki,* barrier; *kan(suru),* to relate to
	門	門	閂	関心　　*kanshin,* concern, interest 玄関　　*genkan,* entrance hall, entrance 機関車　*kikansha,* engine, locomotive
467 14 strokes	閂	関	関	

観	ノ	⼆	乍	KAN to look at carefully, to show
	牛	牟	牟	観光　*kankō,* sightseeing 観察　*kansatsu,* observation 観測　*kansoku,* observation, survey
468 18 strokes	奔	雚	観	

願	一	厂	厂	GAN; *nega(i),* wish, petition, request; *nega(u),* to ask, to request, to wish, to beg
	盾	原	原	願書　*gansho,* written application 志願　*shigan,* volunteering, desire, application
469 19 strokes	原	原	願	

希	ノ	メ	宇	KI rare; desire
	产	产	齐	希望　　kibō, hope, desire 希望者　kibōsha, aspirant, applicant 希薄　　kihaku, thin, weak, sparse
470 7 strokes	希			

季	一	二	千	KI, season
	千	禾	丢	季節　kisetsu, season 四季　shiki, the four seasons 雨季　uki, rainy season
471 8 strokes	季	季		

紀	し	幺	幺	KI history, chronicle
	糸	糸	糸	世紀　　　seiki, century, period 二十世紀　nijisseiki, twentieth century 紀元　　　kigen, era, epoch
472 9 strokes	紀	紀	紀	

喜	一	十	士	KI; yoroko(bi), joy, happy event, congratulation; yoroko(bu), to rejoice, to be glad
	吉	吉	吉	大喜び　ō-yorokobi, great joy, great delight
473 12 strokes	壴	喜		喜劇　kigeki, comedy 歓喜　kanki, joy, ecstasy

旗	广	扩	斻	KI; hata, flag
	斻	斻	斻	国旗　kokki, national flag 校旗　kōki, school flag 星条旗　seijōki, the Stars and Stripes
474 14 strokes	旗	旗	旗	

器	口	吅	吅	KI; *utsuwa*, vessel, utensil, capacity, caliber
	𣦓	哭	哭	食器　*shokki*, tableware 陶器　*tōki*, pottery, ceramics 洗面器　*senmenki*, wash basin
475 15 strokes	器			
機	木	松	松	KI; *hata*, loom
	櫟	榉	椛	機械　*kikai*, machine, mechanism 機会　*kikai*, opportunity, chance 危機　*kiki*, crisis, emergency
476 16 strokes	機	機	機	
議	言	言	詳	GI discussion
	詳	詳	議	会議　*kaigi*, conference 議論　*giron*, argument, discussion 議会　*gikai*, Diet
477 20 strokes	議			
求	一	寸	寸	KYŪ; *moto(me)*, request, demand; *moto(meru)*, to request, to search for, to buy, to wish for
	寸	求	求	求人　*kyūjin*, offer of a job 請求　*seikyū*, demand 求職　*kyūshoku*, seeking employment
478 7 strokes	求			
泣	丶	丶丶	氵	KYŪ; *na(ku)*, to cry, weep, sob
	氵	泣	泣	泣き声　*nakigoe*, crying, sobbing 泣き虫　*nakimushi*, crybaby 感泣　*kankyū*, weeping with emotion
479 8 strokes	泣	泣		

救	一	十	寸	KYŪ; *suku(i)*, rescue, help; *suku(u)*, to rescue, to help
	求	求	求	救済　　*kyūsai*, relief 救助　　*kyūjo*, rescue 救急車　*kyūkyūsha*, ambulance
480 11 strokes	求	救	救	

給	㇐	㇀	幺	KYŪ to supply
	糸	糸	糸	給料　　*kyūryō*, pay, salary 供給　　*kyōkyū*, supply 月給　　*gekkyū*, monthly salary
481 12 strokes	紷	給	給	

挙	`	``	```	KYO to conduct, to perform; *a(geru)*, to raise, to hold (a function)
	丷	丷	兴	選挙　　*senkyo*, election 挙行　　*kyokō*, performance 挙手　　*kyoshu*, raising one's hand, a show of hands
482 10 strokes	兴	誉	挙	

漁	㇒	氵	氵	GYO; RYŌ, fishing
	沱	沱	渔	漁船　　*gyosen*, fishing boat 漁業　　*gyogyō*, fishing industry 漁師　　*ryōshi*, fisherman
483 14 strokes	漁	漁	漁	

共	一	十	廾	KYŌ; *tomo*, both, as well as, together
	丗	共	共	共通　　*kyōtsū*, commonness 共和国　*kyōwakoku*, republic 共産党　*kyōsantō*, Communist Party
484 6 strokes				

協

485
8 strokes

KYŌ to be in harmony

協力 *kyōryoku,* cooperation
協会 *kyōkai,* society, association
協議 *kyōgi,* conference, consultation

鏡

486
19 strokes

KYŌ; *kagami,* mirror

鏡台 *kyōdai,* dressing table, mirror stand
双眼鏡 *sōgankyō,* binoculars
顕微鏡 *kenbikyō,* microscope

競

487
20 strokes

KYŌ, KEI; *kiso(u),* to rival, to compete; *se(ru),* to bid, to compete for

競争 *kyōsō,* competition
競技 *kyōgi,* match, tournament, sporting events
競馬 *keiba,* horse race

極

488
12 strokes

KYOKU, terrestrial poles, magnetic poles, zenith; GOKU very, extremely; *kiwa(maru)* (v.i.), to reach an end, an extreme; *kiwa(mi),* apex

極端 *kyokutan,* extremity
北極 *hokkyoku,* North Pole
至極 *shigoku,* very, quite

訓

489
10 strokes

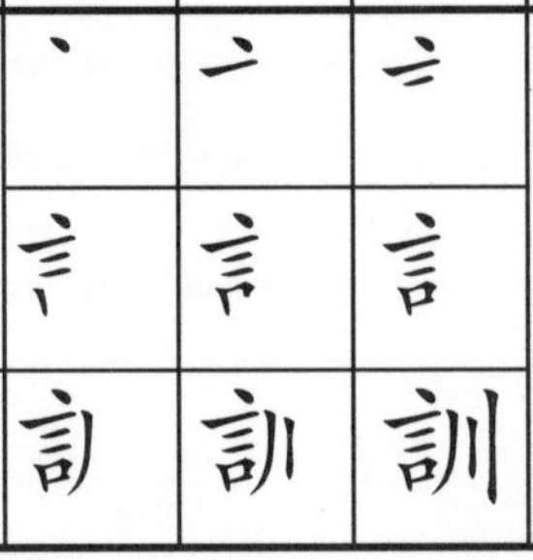

KUN, precept, Japanese rendering of a Chinese character (i.e., "kun" reading)

教訓 *kyōkun,* teachings, lesson
訓練 *kunren,* training, drill
訓辞 *kunji,* address of instructions

軍	⟍	⟍	⟍	GUN, army, military authorities
				軍備　*gunbi*, armaments
				軍隊　*guntai*, troops, army
				軍艦　*gunkan*, warship
490 9 strokes				

郡				GUN, county, district
				郡部　*gunbu*, rural district, counties
				郡長　*gunchō*, head of a county
491 10 strokes				

径				KEI; path, course, direct
				径路　　　　*keiro*, course, path
				直径　　　　*chokkei*, diameter
				直情径行　*chokujōkeikō*, impulsiveness
492 8 strokes				

型				KEI; *kata*, type, model, mold, conventionality
				模型　*mokei*, model
				小型　*kogata*, small size
				大型　*ō-gata*, large size
493 9 strokes				

景				KEI, KE view, scene
				風景　　*fūkei*, scenery, view
				不景気　*fukeiki*, bad times, depression
				光景　　*kōkei*, spectacle, scene
494 12 strokes				

芸	一	十	艹	GEI, arts, accomplishments
	艹	芢	芸	芸術 *geijutsu,* art 民芸 *mingei,* folk art 芸者 *geisha,* Japanese singing and
495 7 strokes	芸			dancing girl

欠	ノ	⺈	ケ	KETSU lack, absence; *ka(keru),* to be broken off, to lack (v.i.); *ka(ku),* to lack, to want (v.t.)
	欠			欠点 *ketten,* fault 欠席 *kesseki,* absence
496 4 strokes				欠乏 *ketsubō,* shortage

結	ㇱ	ㇱ	幺	KETSU; *musu(bi),* end, knot; *musu(bu),* to tie, to bind, to conclude, to link; *yu(u),* to dress (the hair); *yu(waeru),* to fasten, to bind
	糸	糸	紆	結果 *kekka,* result
497 12 strokes	紆	紆	結	結婚 *kekkon,* marriage 連結 *renketsu,* coupling, connection, linking

建	㇕	㇕	㇕	KEN, KON; *ta(teru),* to build, to establish; *ta(tsu),* to be built; ~*date,* ~-storied building
	㇕	㇕	聿	建物 *tatemono,* a building 建築 *kenchiku,* construction, architecture, building
498 9 strokes	津	建	建	二階建 *nikaidate,* two-storied building

健	イ	イ	イⱻ	KEN; *suko(yaka),* healthy, sound
	イⱻ	イ	イⱻ	強健 *kyōken,* robust 保健 *hoken,* (preservation of) health
499 11 strokes	律	健	健	健全 *kenzen,* healthy, sound

験				KEN effect; to examine
	一	厂	厂	実験 *jikken,* experiment 経験 *keiken,* experience 試験 *shiken,* examination, experiment
	馬	馬	駅	
500 18 strokes	駖	験	験	

固				KO; *kata(meru),* to harden, to make hard (v.t.); *kata(maru),* to become hard; *kata(i),* hard, firm
	丨	冂	冂	固有 *koyū,* peculiar, one's own 固体 *kotai,* a solid (body) 強固 *kyōko,* firmness, solidity, stability
	円	円	固	
501 8 strokes	周	固		

功				KŌ, merits, effect, service; KU
	一	丁	工	成功 *seikō,* success 功績 *kōseki,* meritorious deed 功労 *kōrō,* service
	巧	功		
502 5 strokes				

好				KŌ; *kono(mu),* to like, love; *su(ki),* fond of, like
	く	女	女	好意 *kōi,* goodwill, kindness 好き嫌い *sukikirai,* likes and dislikes 好き好む *sukikonomu,* like, prefer
	女	好	好	
503 6 strokes				

候				KŌ, season, sign; to inquire after
	ノ	イ	亻	気候 *kikō,* climate, weather 天候 *tenkō,* weather 候補 *kōho,* candidacy, candidate
	亻	仁	仔	
504 10 strokes	仔	候	候	

101

航	丿	ノ	月	KŌ to sail on the water
	月	舟	舟	航海　　*kōkai*, voyage, navigation 航路　　*kōro*, sea route, air route 航空　　*kōkū*, aviation, air voyage
505 10 strokes	舟	舮	航	
康	、	亠	广	KŌ to enjoy
	广	庐	户	健康　　　*kenkō*, health, good health 不健康　*fukenkō*, bad health
506 11 strokes	序	庚	康	
告	丿	广	丄	KOKU; *tsu(geru)*, to tell, to inform
	生	生	告	報告　　*hōkoku*, report 広告　　*kōkoku*, advertisement 忠告　　*chūkoku*, advice
507 7 strokes	告			
差	、	⸌	⸜	SA, difference, remainder (math.); *sa(su)*, to thrust, to insert
	羊	羊	羊	差別　　　*sabetsu*, distinction, discrimination 大差　　　*taisa*, great difference 差出人　*sashidashinin*, sender, addresser
508 10 strokes	羊	羑	差	
菜	一	十	艹	SAI; *na*, greens, rape (vegetable)
	艹	艹	芯	野菜　　　*yasai*, vegetables 菜の花　*na-no-hana*, rape blossoms 菜園　　　*saien*, vegetable garden
509 11 strokes	莁	茟	菜	

最	ヽ	冂	曰
	旦	㝵	冐	SAI prefix for forming superlatives; *motto(mo)*, most
510 12 strokes	冐	冐	最	最初　saisho, the first, beginning 最後　saigo, the last 最善　saizen, the best

SAI prefix for forming superlatives; *motto(mo)*, most

最初　*saisho*, the first, beginning
最後　*saigo*, the last
最善　*saizen*, the best

材	一	十	才
	才	材	村
511 7 strokes	材		

ZAI, material (for work), timber, ability, talent

木材　*mokuzai*, lumber, wood
材料　*zairyō*, raw material, ingredients
人材　*jinzai*, capable man

昨	l	冂	日
	日	日'	昨
512 9 strokes	昨	昨	昨

SAKU yesterday, ancient times

昨日　*sakujitsu*, yesterday
昨年　*sakunen*, last year
昨夜　*sakuya*, last night

札	一	十	才
	木	札	
513 5 strokes			

SATSU, paper money; *fuda*, label, namecard, tag, placard; bid

札入れ　*satsu-ire*, wallet
名札　*nafuda*, nameplate, name-tag
入札　*nyūsatsu*, bid, bidding

刷	ˋ	ˊ	尸
	尸	吊	吊
514 8 strokes	刷	刷	

SATSU; *su(ru)*, to print; *~zuri*, suffix for "printing"

印刷　　　　*insatsu*, printing
校正刷り　　*kōseizuri*, proofs (printing)
謄写版刷り　*tōshaban-zuri*, mimeographed copy

殺	ノ	ㄨ	㸐
	𠂉	杀	杀
515 **10 strokes**	杀	殺	殺

SATSU, SAI, SETSU; *koro(su)*, to kill

殺人　　*satsujin*, homicide, murder
殺風景　*sappūkei*, tasteless, dreary
自殺　　*jisatsu*, suicide

察	丶	ハ	宀
	宀	灾	灾
516 **14 strokes**	夵	窣	察

SATSU; *sas(suru)*, to guess, to perceive, to sympathize with

観察　*kansatsu*, observation
視察　*shisatsu*, inspection
警察　*keisatsu*, police

参	ㄥ	ㄙ	ㅿ
	乒	矢	矣
517 **8 strokes**	参	参	

SAN, three (used in legal papers);
mai(ru), to go, to come, to surrender, to
be nonplussed, to visit for worship

参加　　*sanka*, participation
参観　　*sankan*, visit
参考書　*sankōsho*, reference book

産	丶	亠	亠
	产	立	产
518 **11 strokes**	产	产	産

SAN, childbearing, product, fortune;
u(mu), to give birth to, to produce;
u(mareru), to be born

産物　*sanbutsu*, products
産地　*sanchi*, place of production
産業　*sangyō*, industry

散	一	十	卄
	卅	苷	苷
519 **12 strokes**	散	散	散

SAN; *chi(ru)*, to fall (leaves), to be
scattered (v.i.); *chi(rasu)*, to scatter, to
disperse (v.t.); *chi(rakaru)*, to be in order;
chi(rakasu), to scatter

散歩　*sanpo*, walk, stroll
解散　*kaisan*, breakup, dissolution
胃散　*isan*, medical powder for the
　　　stomach

残 520 10 strokes	一	丁	万	ZAN; *noko(ri)*, remainder; *noko(ru)*, to be left over, to remain; *noko(su)*, to leave, to save
	歹	歼	歼	残念　　*zannen*, regret, disappointment 残金　　*zankin*, balance, money left over
	残	残	残	残り物　*nokorimono*, remains, left-overs

士 521 3 strokes	一	十	士		SHI man, figure 武士　*bushi*, samurai 紳士　*shinshi*, gentleman 勇士　*yūshi*, brave man, hero

氏 522 4 strokes	⼁	匚	氏		SHI Mister (used as suffix); *uji*, family name, lineage 氏名　　　*shimei*, full name 氏族制度　*shizoku-seido*, the clan or the family system 諸氏　　　*shoshi*, Messrs., gentlemen
	氏				

史 523 5 strokes	丶	⼍	口		SHI annals, history, chronicles 歴史　*rekishi*, history 女史　*joshi*, Madame, Mrs., Miss 史上　*shijō*, in history, in the annals
	史	史			

司 524 5 strokes	丁	刁	司	SHI to rule, to manage 司会者　*shikaisha*, master of ceremonies, moderator, chairman
	司	司		司令　　*shirei*, order, command 司令部　*shireibu*, headquarters

試	言	訁	訁	SHI; *kokoro(mi)*, trial, test; *kokoro(miru)*, to try; *tame(su)*, to try, to test
	訁	訁	試	試験　　　*shiken*, examination 試運転　　*shi-unten*, test driving, trial run 試合　　　*shiai*, match, contest
525 13 strokes	試			
児	丨	丨丨	丨冂	JI, NI infant, child
	旧	旧	尸	児童　　　*jidō*, child, boys and girls, 　　　　　juvenile 孤児　　　*koji*, orphan 小児まひ　*shōni-mahi*, infantile 　　　　　paralysis
526 7 strokes	児			
治	丶	丷	氵	JI, CHI; *osa(meru)*, to rule over; *osa(maru)*, to be peaceful; *nao(ru)* (v.i.), to heal; *nao(su)* (v.t.), to cure
	沪	汋	汋	政治　　*seiji*, politics, administration 自治　　*jichi*, self-government 治療　　*chiryō*, medical treatment
527 8 strokes	治	治		
辞	丿	二	千	JI, word, speech; *ji(suru)*, to resign, to take one's leave, to decline; *ya(meru)*, to retire, to quit
	舌	舌	舌	辞書　　*jisho*, dictionary 辞職　　*jishoku*, resignation 祝辞　　*shukuji*, congratulatory address
528 13 strokes	舌	舌	辞	
失	丿	二	二	SHITSU; *ushina(u)*, to lose, to miss 失礼　　*shitsurei*, impoliteness 失敗　　*shippai*, failure 失望　　*shitsubō*, despair, disappointment
	牛	失		
529 5 strokes				

借 530 10 strokes	ノ 什 佴	イ 伊 借	仁 借 借	SHAKU; *ka(ri)*, borrowing, debt; *ka(riru)*, to borrow, to rent, to substitute temporarily, to obtain (help) 借金　　*shakkin*, debt, loan 借り物　*karimono*, borrowed thing 拝借　　*haishaku*, loan, borrowing
種 531 14 strokes	ᅳ 禾 稆	ニ 禾 種	千 秆 種	SHU kind, sort; *tane*, seed 種まき　*tanemaki*, sowing seed 種類　　*shurui*, sort, kind 人種　　*jinshu*, human race
周 532 8 strokes	ノ 内 周	几 冏 周	几 周	SHŪ circumference; to go round; *mawa(ri)*, border, periphery 周囲　*shūi*, circumference, surroundings 周辺　*shūhen*, outskirts 一周　*isshū*, one round
祝 533 9 strokes	丶 ネ 礽	ラ ネ 祀	ネ 礽 祝	SHUKU; *iwa(i)*, celebration; *iwa(u)*, to celebrate 祝賀　*shukuga*, celebration 祝福　*shukufuku*, blessing 祝日　*shukujitsu*, festival day
順 534 12 strokes	ノ 川 順	川 川 順	川 順 順	JUN, order, turn 順序　*junjo*, order, procedure, method 順番　*junban*, order, turn 順調　*junchō*, normal condition, smooth progress

107

初	⟍	ラ	ネ
	ネ	ネ	初
535 7 strokes	初		

SHO; *hatsu*, first; *haji(me)*, beginning; *-someru*, to begin-

初秋 *shoshū*, early autumn
初雪 *hatsuyuki*, first snow of the year
初期 *shoki*, first stage

松	一	十	才
	木	朴	朴
536 8 strokes	松	松	

SHŌ, *matsu*, pine

松葉 *matsuba*, pine needles
松林 *matsubayashi*, pine forest
松竹梅 *shōchikubai*, pine-bamboo-plum decorations

笑	ノ	⺈	⺮
	⺮	⺮	竺
537 10 strokes	竺	竿	笑

SHŌ; *wara(u)*, to laugh, smile; *e(mu)*, to smile, beam

大笑い *ōwarai*, loud laughter
苦笑 *kushō*, forced laugh
微笑 *bishō/hohoemi*, smile

唱	⎮	⼝	口
	口	叩	唱
538 11 strokes	唱	唱	唱

SHŌ; *tona(eru)*, to chant, to recite, to say

独唱 *dokushō*, vocal solo
合唱 *gasshō*, chorus
唱歌 *shōka*, song, singing

焼	火	火	灯
	炉	炉	炉
539 12 strokes	焼	焼	焼

SHŌ, *ya(ku)*, to burn, to bake, to grill, to toast (v.t.), to burn with jealousy; *ya(keru)*, to be burned, to be roasted, to be jealous of

夕焼け *yūyake*, evening glow, sunset colors
焼失 *shōshitsu*, destruction by fire

象 540 12 strokes	ノ ク ク 名 名 牟 务 象 象			**SHŌ** image; **ZŌ**, elephant 対象　*taishō*, object 印象　*inshō*, impression 象げ　*zōge*, ivory
照 541 13 strokes	l 冂 日 日 日﹃ 日刀 昭 照 照			**SHŌ**; *te(rasu)*, to shine on, to compare with, to shed light on; *te(ru)*, to shine; *te(reru)*, to be shy, to be embarrassed 日照り　*hideri*, drought 照明　*shōmei*, illumination 対照　*taishō*, contrast
賞 542 15 strokes	｀ ｀ヽ ﾘﾘﾉ ﾘﾘﾉ 屵 屵 賞 賞 賞			**SHŌ**, prize 賞品　*shōhin*, prize (thing) 賞金　*shōkin*, prize (money) 鑑賞　*kanshō*, appreciation
臣 543 7 strokes	l 厂 厂 臣 臣 臣 臣			**SHIN, JIN** retainer, subject 大臣　*daijin*, cabinet minister 忠臣　*chūshin*, loyal retainer
信 544 9 strokes	ノ イ イ 仁 仁 仁 信 信 信			**SHIN**, sincerity, trust, faith; *shin(jiru)*, to believe, to trust, to believe in 信用　*shin'yō*, trust, confidence, belief, credit 信号　*shingō*, signal 通信　*tsūshin*, communication

成	ノ	厂	万	SEI, JŌ; *na(ru)*, to become, to be completed, to consist of, to come to, to succeed; to come, to go (honorific); *na(su)*, to do, to perform
	成	成	成	
545 6 strokes				成長　*seichō*, growth 完成　*kansei*, completion 賛成　*sansei*, agreement, approval

省	ノ	⼩	小	SEI to look; *habu(ku)*, to omit, to cut down; *kaeri(miru)*, to reflect upon (oneself); SHŌ suffix for "government department"
	少	少	省	
546 9 strokes	省	省	省	省略　*shōryaku*, omission 外務省　*Gaimushō*, Ministry of Foreign Affairs (Japan) 反省　*hansei*, self-examination

清	シ	冫	汁	SEI; *kiyo(i)*, *kiyo(raka)*, pure, clear; *kiyo(meru)* (v.t.), to cleanse, purge, to exorcize
	汗	泩	清	
547 11 strokes	清	清	清	清潔　*seiketsu*, cleanliness 清書　*seisho*, fair copy 血清　*kessei*, (blood) serum

静	十	主	青	SEI, JŌ; *shizu(ka)*, quiet, silent, peaceful; *shizu(maru)*, to become quiet; *shizu(meru)*, to make calm, to soothe
	青	青	静	
548 14 strokes	静	静	静	静止　*seishi*, stillness, standstill 静物　*seibutsu*, still life 安静　*ansei*, complete rest

席	、	亠	广	SEKI, seat, place
	广	庐	庐	出席　*shusseki*, attendance, presence 欠席　*kesseki*, absence 座席　*zaseki*, seat
549 10 strokes	庐	席	席	

110

積

550
16 strokes

SEKI, product (math.); *tsumo(ri),* intention; *tsu(mu),* to pile up, to load, to accumulate (v.t.); *tsumo(ru),* to be piled up

面積	*menseki,* area
積極的	*sekkyokuteki,* positive, active, progressive
積荷	*tsumini,* cargo, a load

折

551
7 strokes

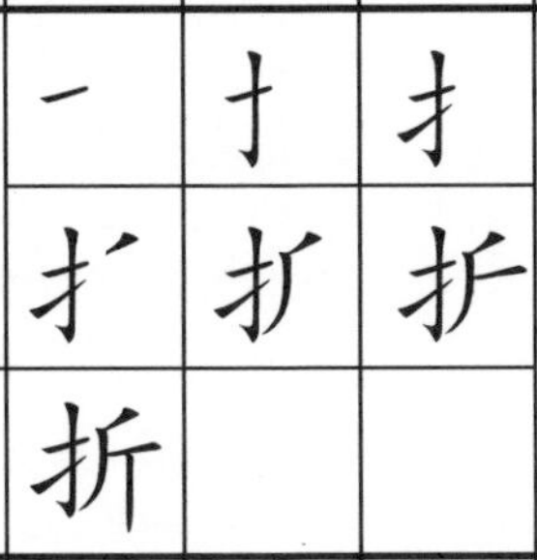

SETSU; *o(ru),* to break, to fold, to bend

曲折	*kyokusetsu,* winding, complications
折合	*oriai,* mutual relations, compromise
折り目	*orime,* crease

節

552
13 strokes

SETSU, paragraph, season, time; *fushi,* joint, knot, tune

節約	*setsuyaku,* economy, frugality
調節	*chōsetsu,* regulation, control
使節	*shisetsu,* delegate, envoy

説

553
14 strokes

SETSU, opinion, theory; ZEI; *to(ku),* to explain, to persuade, to preach

説明	*setsumei,* explanation
伝説	*densetsu,* legend
社説	*shasetsu,* editorial

浅

554
9 strokes

SEN; *asa(i),* shallow

浅見	*senken,* superficial view
浅薄	*senpaku,* superficial
遠浅	*tōasa,* shoaling beach, shallowness extending far from shore

戦	⍀	当	当	SEN; *tataka(i)*, fight, war, struggle; *takaka(u)*, to fight, to make war, to struggle, to compete in games
	単	単	戦	戦争　　*sensō*, war 終戦　　*shūsen*, end of a war 戦場　　*senjō*, battlefield
555 13 strokes	戦	戦		

選	⼐	⼐	⼰	SEN; *era(bu)*, to choose, to select
	己己	己己	巽	選挙　　*senkyo*, election 選手　　*senshu*, player, champion 当選　　*tōsen*, victory in an election
556 15 strokes	巽	選	選	

然	ノ	ク	タ	ZEN, NEN yes, but, however
	タ	夘	然	自然　　*shizen*, nature 当然　　*tōzen*, natural, just, as a matter of course 天然　　*tennen*, nature
557 12 strokes	然	然	然	

争	ノ	⼇	⼛	SŌ; *araso(i)*, quarrel, dispute, competition; *araso(u)*, to struggle, to dispute, to quarrel
	⼛	乎	争	競争　　　　*kyōsō*, competition 言い争う　　*ii-arasou*, to quarrel 争奪戦　　　*sōdatsusen*, scramble, contest, challenge
558 6 strokes				

倉	ノ	人	人	SŌ; *kura*, warehouse
	今	今	合	倉庫　　*sōko*, warehouse 船倉　　*sensō*, hold (of a ship) 米倉　　*komegura*, rice granary
559 10 strokes	倉	倉	倉	

巣	丶	⺍	⺍
	⺍	屵	当
560 11 strokes	単	単	巣

SŌ; *su*, nest, den, breeding place

巣箱　　*subako*, nesting box
巣立つ　*sudatsu*, to leave the nest, home
営巣　　*eisō*, nest building

束	一	一	一
	三	申	申
561 7 strokes	束		

SOKU; *taba*, bundle, bunch; bind

約束　*yakusoku*, appointment; promise
束縛　*sokubaku*, restriction, restraint
花束　*hanataba*, bouquet, bunch of
　　　flowers

側	ノ	イ	仈
	佴	佀	側
562 11 strokes	側	側	側

SOKU; *kawa*, side

内側　*uchigawa*, the inside
右側　*migigawa*, *usoku*, right side
側面　*sokumen*, the side

続	糸	糸	糸
	紵	続	続
563 13 strokes	続	続	

ZOKU; *tsuzu(ki)*, continuation, sequel, range; *tsuzu(ku)*, to continue, to follow, to last (v.i.); *tsuzu(keru)*, to continue, to resume (v.t.)

続出　*zokushutsu*, successive occurrence
手続　*tetsuzuki*, procedure
相続　*sōzoku*, inheritance

卒	丶	一	亠
	宀	立	衣
564 8 strokes	卒	卒	

SOTSU, a private, common soldier; to finish

卒業　　*sotsugyō*, graduation
卒業生　*sotsugyōsei*, graduate
兵卒　　*heisotsu*, private (soldier)

孫	㇇	了	孑	SON; *mago*, grandchild 子孫　　*shison*, descendants
孑	孖	孫
565 **10 strokes**	孫	孫	孫

帯	一	十	卄	TAI; *obi*, girdle; *o(biru)*, to wear 地帯　　*chitai*, zone 熱帯　　*nettai*, torrid zone, tropics 帯封　　*obifū*, half wrapper
卅	卌	世
566 **10 strokes**	芇	带	帯

隊	㇀	了	阝	TAI, a party, a corps, band, unit 兵隊　　*heitai*, soldier 楽隊　　*gakutai*, band (musical) 隊長　　*taichō*, captain, commander, 　　　　leader
阝	阝ソ	阼
567 **12 strokes**	防	隊	隊

達	土	士	圭	TATSU; *tas(suru)*, to arrive, to reach, to attain (one's object) 発達　　*hattatsu*, development 配達　　*haitatsu*, delivery 達人　　*tatsujin*, an expert
圭	幸	圭
568 **12 strokes**	幸	達	達

単	丶	丷	丷	TAN single 単純　　*tanjun*, simple 簡単　　*kantan*, simple, easy 単価　　*tanka*, unit price
丷	丷	単
569 **9 strokes**	単	単	単

置

570
13 strokes

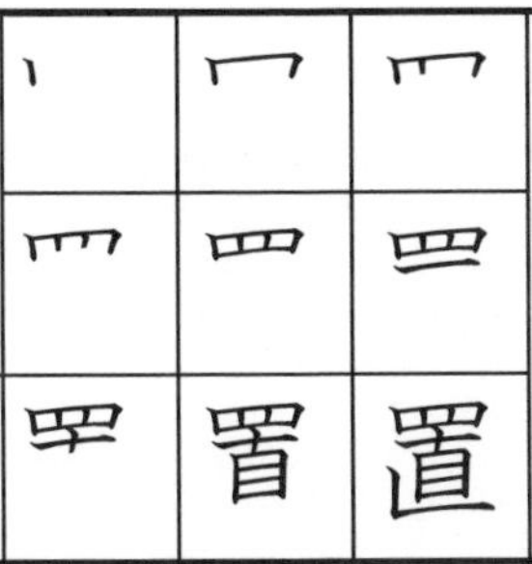

CHI; *o(ku),* to put, to place

位置 *ichi,* position
置物 *okimono,* ornament (for a *tokonoma*)
物置 *mono-oki,* storeroom

仲

571
6 strokes

CHŪ; *naka,* relationship

仲がいい *naka ga ii,* to be on good terms with
仲間 *nakama,* workmate, colleague, associate
仲裁 *chūsai,* mediation

貯

572
12 strokes

CHO to store, to save

貯水地 *chosuichi,* reservoir
貯蔵 *chozō,* storage
貯金 *chokin,* savings

兆

573
6 strokes

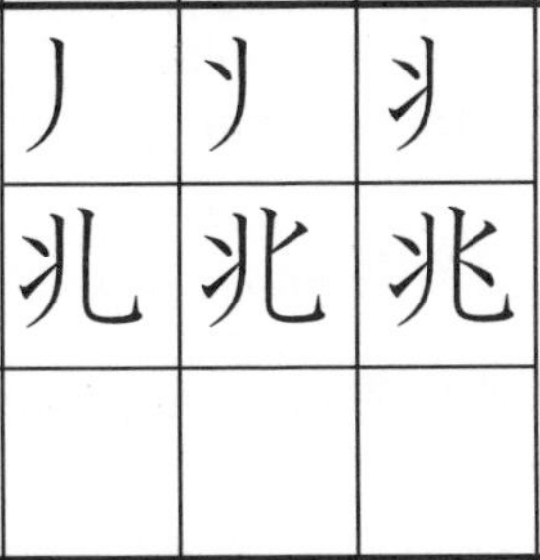

CHŌ, trillion (U.S.), sign; *kiza(shi),* sign, omen; *kiza(su),* to show signs

兆候 *chōkō,* sign, omen
二兆円 *nichōen,* two trillion yen
前兆 *zenchō,* omen, portent

腸

574
13 strokes

CHŌ, the intestines

盲腸 *mōchō,* (vermiform) appendix
大腸 *daichō,* large intestine
腸カタル *chōkataru,* intestinal catarrh

低	ノ	イ	亻
	亻	仁	低
575 7 strokes	低		

TEI; *hiku(i)*, low, short

低気圧　*tei-kiatsu*, low atmospheric pressure
低空　　*teikū*, low altitude
低地　　*teichi*, low ground

底	、	宀	广
	户	庀	庄
576 8 strokes	底	底	

TEI; *soko*, bottom, depth

谷底　　*tanizoko*, bottom of a ravine
海底　　*kaitei*, bottom of the sea
徹底的　*tetteiteki*, thoroughgoing, out-and-out

停	ノ	イ	亻
	亻	伫	伫
577 11 strokes	停	停	停

TEI to stop

停止　　*teishi*, stop, suspension
停電　　*teiden*, electricity stoppage
停留所　*teiryūjo*, stopping place, streetcar (bus) stop

的	ノ	イ	白
	白	白	白
578 8 strokes	的	的	

TEKI like, similar, suffix for forming adjectives from nouns; *mato*, mark, target

目的　　*mokuteki*, purpose
世界的　*sekaiteki*, international, world-wide
社会的　*shakaiteki*, social

典	丶	冂	巾
	曲	曲	曲
579 8 strokes	典	典	

TEN ceremony, celebration

辞典　　*jiten*, dictionary
古典　　*koten*, classics
祭典　　*saiten*, festival, rite

伝	ノ	イ	イ	DEN; *tsuta(eru)* to report, to impart, to transmit; *tsuta(waru)*, to be reported, imparted, transmitted, *tsuta(u)*, to follow along
	仁	伝	伝	
580 6 strokes				伝記　　　*denki*, biography 伝染病　*densenbyō*, epidemic 宣伝　　　*senden*, propaganda
徒	ノ	ク	イ	TO companion
	彳	彴	往	生徒　　　*seito*, pupil, student 徒歩　　　*toho*, going on foot 徒競走　*tokyōsō*, running match
581 10 strokes	徒	徒		
努	く	タ	女	DO; *tsuto(meru)*, to make efforts
	如	奴	努	努力　　　*doryoku*, effort 努力家　*doryokuka*, hard worker
582 7 strokes	努			
灯	ヽ	ヽ	少	TŌ light, lamp
	火	灯	灯	電灯　　　　　*dentō*, electric light 安全灯　　　*anzentō*, safety lamp 懐中電灯　*kaichūdentō*, flashlight, electric torch
583 6 strokes				
堂	ヽ	ヽ	ツ	DŌ, temple, hall
	ツ	半	峃	食堂　　　　　*shokudō*, dining room, eating house 公会堂　　　*kōkaidō*, town hall, public hall
584 11 strokes	堂	堂	堂	国会議事堂　*Kokkai-gijidō*, the Diet Building

働	ノ	イ	信	DŌ; *hatara(ki)*, work (n.); *hatara(ku)*, to work, to do (evil), to come into play
	俥	偅	偅	労働者 *rōdōsha*, laborer 働き手 *hatarakite*, bread winner, worker 働き者 *hatarakimono*, hard worker
585 13 strokes	働	働		

特	ノ	㇒	牛	TOKU special
	牛	牛	牡	特別 *tokubetsu*, special, particular 特長 *tokuchō*, strong point 特急 *tokkyū*, limited express
586 10 strokes	牛	特	特	

得	ノ	㇒	彳	TOKU, profit, benefit, advantage; *e(ru)*, to get, to obtain; *-u(ru)*, *-e(masu)*, to be able to
	袓	袓	得	得意 *tokui*, proud satisfaction; customer; one's forte 納得 *nattoku*, understanding, compliance
587 11 strokes	得			得点 *tokuten*, score (in a game)

毒	一	十	丰	DOKU, poison
	主	走	青	気の毒 *ki-no-doku*, sorry, pitiful 毒草 *dokusō*, poisonous herb 中毒 *chūdoku*, poisoning
588 8 strokes	毒	毒		

熱	土	耂	夫	NETSU, heat, fever, craze, zeal; *nes(suru)*, to heat, to become hot; *atsu(i)*, hot
	幸	封	執	熱病 *netsubyō*, fever 熱心 *nesshin*, zeal
589 15 strokes	執	熱	熱	熱帯 *nettai*, tropical zone

念	ノ	人	今	**NEN**, thought, feeling, desire
	今	今	念	記念 *kinen*, commemoration 残念 *zannen*, regret, disappointment 念願 *nengan*, one's heart's desire
590 8 strokes	念	念		

敗	l	⊓	目	**HAI**; *yabu(reru)*, to be defeated
	貝	貝	貝	敗戦 *haisen*, lost battle 腐敗 *fuhai*, putrefaction, corruption 失敗 *shippai*, failure
591 11 strokes	財	敗	敗	

梅	木	术	朾	**BAI**; *ume*, plum, plum tree
	杧	栂	梅	梅雨 *baiu/tsuyu*, rainy season 梅酒 *umeshu*, plum brandy 梅干し *umeboshi*, pickled plums
592 10 strokes	梅			

博	一	十	十	**HAKU** learned; to spread; abundant
	忄	博	博	博士 *hakushi*, doctor (degree) 博物館 *hakubutsukan*, museum 博覧会 *hakurankai*, exposition
593 12 strokes	博	博		

飯	ノ	𠆢	今	**HAN**; *meshi*, boiled rice, a meal
	食	食	食	朝飯 *asahan*, *asameshi*, breakfast 昼飯 *hirumeshi*, lunch 夕飯 *yūhan*, *yūmeshi*, supper
594 12 strokes	飲	飯	飯	

飛	て	て	飞	HI; *to(bu)*, to fly; *to(basu)*, to let fly, to launch
	飞	飞	飛	飛び込む　*tobikomu*, to jump in, to dive into, to rush in 飛行機　*hikōki*, airplane 飛行場　*hikōjō*, airport
595 9 strokes	飛	飛	飛	

費	一	二	弓	HI; *tsui(yasu)*, to spend, to consume, to squander
	弗	弗	曹	費用　*hiyō*, expense 旅費　*ryohi*, traveling expenses 出費　*shuppi*, expenditure
596 12 strokes	費			

必	、	ソ	必	HITSU; *kanara(zu)*, without fail, by all means, invariably, necessarily
	必	必		必要　*hitsuyō*, need 必死　*hisshi*, inevitable death, desperation 必勝　*hisshō*, sure victory
597 5 strokes				

票	一	一	一	HYŌ, vote
	西	西	西	投票　*tōhyō*, voting 伝票　*denpyō*, chit 五十票　*gojippyō*, fifty votes
598 11 strokes	票	票	票	

標	一	十	才	HYŌ mark, sign; to write down, to express
	木	杧	栖	標本　*hyōhon*, specimen 標語　*hyōgo*, motto 目標　*mokuhyō*, mark, object
599 15 strokes	栖	標	標	

不	一	フ	不	FU dis-, in-, un-, mal-, ill-
	不			不自由 *fujiyū,* inconvenience, want
				不平 *fuhei,* discontent, complaint
600				不幸 *fukō,* misfortune, unhappiness, death
4 strokes				

夫	一	二	丰	FU, FŪ; *otto,* husband
	夫			工夫 *kōfu,* laborer, coolie
				夫婦 *fūfu,* husband and wife
601				夫人 *fujin,* married lady, Mrs.
4 strokes				

付	ノ	イ	什	FU; *tsu(ku),* to adhere, to stick (v.i.); *tsu(keru),* to attach, to stick (v.t.)
	付	付		付近 *fukin,* neighborhood
				寄付 *kifu,* contribution
602				受付 *uketsuke,* acceptance, information office
5 strokes				

府	ヽ	亠	广	FU, urban prefecture, center
	广	庁	庁	政府 *seifu,* government
	府	府		首府 *shufu,* capital
603				府県 *fuken,* prefectures
8 strokes				

副	一	戸	戸	FUKU vice-, sub-, secondary
	畐	畐	畐	副詞 *fukushi,* adverb
	畐	副	副	副会長 *fukukaichō,* vice-president (of a society)
604				副業 *fukugyō,* side job
11 strokes				

粉	、	⺍	半	FUN; *kona, ko,* powder
				火の粉　*hi-no-ko,* spark
	米	米	米	小麦粉　*komugiko,* wheat flour
				製粉　*seifun,* milling (flour)
605 **10 strokes**	粉	粉	粉	

兵	⺅	⺁	⺁	HEI, soldier; HYŌ
				兵隊　*heitai,* soldier
	丘	丘	兵	兵器　*heiki,* arms
				兵士　*heishi,* soldier
606 **7 strokes**	兵			

別	⼁	口	口	BETSU, distinction, exception; different, particular; *waka(reru),* to part (from)
	号	另	別	特別　*tokubetsu,* special
				別問題　*betsumondai,* another question
				別れ　*wakare,* parting, separation
607 **7 strokes**	別			

辺	フ	刀	刀	HEN, side, neighborhood; *atari,* vicinity
	辺	辺	辺	底辺　*teihen,* the base (geom.)
				周辺　*shūhen,* outskirts
				近辺　*kinpen,* neighborhood
608 **5 strokes**				

変	、	二	亠	HEN, odd; disturbance, accident, change; *ka(waru),* to change, to be uncommon, to move (v.i.); *ka(eru),* to change, to reform
	亦	亦	亦	変化　*henka,* change, variety, conjugation
609 **9 strokes**	変	変	変	大変　*taihen,* serious, great, terrible

122

便 610 9 strokes	ノ 亻 仁 仁 便	イ 仃 佰 伊 便	仁 佰 佰 便	BEN, convenience, bodily waste; BIN, mail; *tayo(ri)*, tidings, communication, a letter 便利　　*benri*, convenience 便所　　*benjo*, toilet 航空便　*kōkūbin*, air mail
包 611 5 strokes	ノ 勺 包	ク 包	勺	HŌ; *tsutsu(mu)*, to wrap, to cover 小包　　　*kozutsumi*, postal package 包み紙　*tsutsumigami*, wrapping paper 包囲　　　*hōi*, encirclement
法 612 8 strokes	丶 氵 法	丶丶 汁 法	氵 汁	HŌ, law, doctrine, reason, method 方法　*hōhō*, way, method 法律　*hōritsu*, law 文法　*bunpō*, grammar
望 613 11 strokes	丶 亡 望	亠 朝 望	亡 胡 望	BŌ, MŌ; *nozo(mi)*, desire, wish; *nozo(mu)*, to desire, to expect, to see 失望　*shitsubō*, disappointment 希望　*kibō*, hope, wish 絶望　*zetsubō*, despair
牧 614 8 strokes	ノ 牛 牧	仁 牛 牧	牛 牛	BOKU; *maki*, pasture 牧場　*bokujō, makiba*, stock farm 牧草　*bokusō*, grass 放牧　*hōboku*, grazing

123

末	一	二	寸	MATSU; *sue*, end, future, youngest child, trifle
	才	末		末っ子 *suekko*, youngest child 月末 *getsumatsu*, end of the month 始末 *shimatsu*, management, circumstances
615 5 strokes				

満	氵	汀	汒	MAN fullness; *mi(chiru)*, to rise (tide), to wax (moon); *mi(tasu)*, to fill, to meet (a requirement)
	浐	浐	浩	満員 *man'in*, filled to capacity 満月 *mangetsu*, full moon
616 12 strokes	満	満	満	満七歳 *man-shichisai*, full seven years old

未	一	二	寸	MI yet, never, till now, un-
	才	未		未来 *mirai*, future 未開 *mikai*, uncivilized, uncultivated 未知 *michi*, unknown, strange
617 5 strokes				

脈	ノ	刀	月	MYAKU, pulse, hope, range
	肝	肝	肛	山脈 *sanmyaku*, mountain range 静脈 *jōmyaku*, (blood) vein 鉱脈 *kōmyaku*, vein of ore
618 10 strokes	脈	脈	脈	

民	⁻	⁼	₱	MIN; *tami*, people, subjects
	₣	民		市民 *shimin*, townsman 国民 *kokumin*, nation 民族 *minzoku*, race
619 5 strokes				

無	ノ	ト	ヒ
	仁	血	缸
620 12 strokes	無	無	無

MU, BU; *na(shi)* (lit.), *na(i)*, to be non-existent, not to have, to be missing, to lack, to be deceased

無理　*muri*, unreasonable, compulsory, impossible, excessive
無線　*musen*, wireless (radio)
無事　*buji*, safe, peaceful, well

約	㇄	乡	幺
	糸	糸	糸
621 9 strokes	約	約	約

YAKU, promise, abridgment; approximately, about (prefix)

約束　　　*yakusoku*, promise, appointment, regulations
予約　　　*yoyaku*, subscription, pre-engagement
約四十分　*yaku-yonjippun*, about forty minutes

勇	㇇	マ	マ
	丙	丙	甬
622 9 strokes	甬	勇	勇

YŪ; *isa(mashii)*, brave

勇気　*yūki*, courage
勇士　*yūshi*, brave man
勇敢　*yūkan*, bravery

要	一	一	丆
	西	西	西
623 9 strokes	要	要	要

YŌ, the main point, necessity; *yō(suru)*, to require, to need; *i(ru)*, to need, to be required

必要　*hitsuyō*, necessity, need
要求　*yōkyū*, request, demand
重要　*jūyō*, important

養	、	丷	丷
	艹	羊	羊
624 15 strokes	美	養	養

YŌ; *yashina(u)*, to bring up, to support, to recuperate, to cultivate

教養　*kyōyō*, culture
養成　*yōsei*, training
養殖　*yōshoku*, raising, culture

浴 625 10 strokes	`丶` `氵` `氵` `汱` `浴`	`氵` `氵` `氵` `浴` `浴`	`氵` `氵` `浴` `浴`	YOKU; *a(biru)*, to bathe oneself in (water, the sun); *a(biseru)*, to pour (liquid) on, to shower with (abuse) 水浴び　*mizu-abi*, bathing 入浴　*nyūyoku*, taking a bath 日光浴　*nikkō-yoku*, sun bath
利 626 7 strokes	`一` `禾` `利`	`二` `禾`	`千` `利`	RI, advantage, profit, interest (on money); *ki(ku)*, to function well 利用　*riyō*, utilization 利益　*rieki*, gains, benefit 権利　*kenri*, a right, a claim
陸 627 11 strokes	`フ` `阝` `陸`	`了` `阝` `陸`	`阝` `陸` `陸`	RIKU, land 大陸　*tairiku*, continent 上陸　*jōriku*, landing 着陸　*chakuriku*, landing (of an airplane)
良 628 7 strokes	`丶` `ヨ` `良`	`ウ` `自`	`ヨ` `良`	RYŌ; *yo(i)*, good, well, fine, right, satisfactory 改良　*kairyō*, improvement 良心　*ryōshin*, conscience 最良　*sairyō*, the best, the ideal
料 629 10 strokes	`丶` `半` `米`	`丷` `米` `料`	`丷` `米` `料`	RYŌ, charge, materials 原料　*genryō*, raw material 料理　*ryōri*, cooking 料金　*ryōkin*, charge

量	丶	冂	𠃌
	曰	旦	昌
630 12 strokes	量	量	量

RYŌ, quantity, measure; *haka(ru)*, to weigh, to measure

雨量　*uryō*, rainfall
重量　*jūryō*, weight
分量　*bunryō*, quantity

輪	車	車	軪
	軩	輪	軩
631 15 strokes	輪	輪	輪

RIN; *wa*, ring, circle, wheel

三輪車　*sanrinsha*, tricycle, three-wheeled vehicle
車輪　*sharin*, wheel
首輪　*kubiwa*, collar (for a dog)

類	丷	米	米
	米	米	米
632 18 strokes	類	類	類

RUI, a kind, a variety

種類　*shurui*, kind, sort
親類　*shinrui*, a relative
分類　*bunrui*, classification

令	丿	人	人
	今	令	
633 5 strokes			

REI proclamation, law, order

号令　*gōrei*, (word of) command
命令　*meirei*, command, order
指令　*shirei*, order, instructions

冷	丶	冫	冫
	冫	冷	冷
634 7 strokes	冷		

REI; *tsume(tai)*, cold; *hi(eru)*, to grow cold, feel chilly; *hi(yasu)*, to cool (v.t.); *sa(meru)* (v.i.), to cool off; *sa(masu)* (v.t.), to let cool

冷水　*reisui*, cold water
冷気　*reiki*, cold air
冷蔵　*reizō*, cold storage, refrigeration

例	ノ	イ	仁	REI, example; *tato(eru)*, to liken to; *tato(eba)*, for example
	伢	伢	伢	例外　*reigai*, exception 実例　*jitsurei*, (concrete) example 例年　*reinen*, ordinary year, every year
635 8 strokes	伢	例		

歴	一	厂	斤	REKI to pass, to travel about
	斤	麻	厤	歴史　*rekishi*, history 経歴　*keireki*, background (of a person), career 履歴書　*rirekisho*, personal history
636 14 strokes	厤	歷	歴	

連	一	厂	币	REN, a ream (of paper), a group; ~*ren*, suffix for "group"; *tsu(reru)*, to take along; *tsu(ranaru)*, to range; ~*zure*, suffix for "companion"
	旨	亘	車	連絡　*renraku*, connection, communication, contact 連盟　*renmei*, league
637 10 strokes	連	連	連	

老	一	十	土	RŌ, old age; *o(i)*, old age, the aged; *o(iru)*, to grow old; *fu(keru)*, to grow old
	耂	耂	老	老人　*rōjin*, old man 老木　*rōboku*, aged tree 養老院　*yōrōin*, asylum for the aged
638 6 strokes				

労	、	〝	〟	RŌ, labor, service, trouble
	〝	〟	学	苦労　*kurō*, toil, care 勤労　*kinrō*, labor 労働者　*rōdōsha*, laborer
639 7 strokes	労			

録	金	釒	釦	**ROKU** to copy, to write down
	釔	鉅	鈩	記録 *kiroku,* record 新記録 *shinkiroku,* new record 録音 *rokuon,* (sound) recording, transcription
640 16 strokes	鈩	録	録	

圧	一	厂	厂	**ATSU** pressure
	圧	圧		気圧 *kiatsu,* atmospheric pressure 圧力 *atsuryoku,* pressure 電圧 *den'atsu,* voltage
641 5 strokes				

移	ノ	二	千	**I**; *utsu(ru),* to move (to a place, into a house), to change (v.i.), to sink into, to be infectious; *utsu(su),* to remove (v.t.), to infect
	禾	禾	禾	移民 *imin,* immigration (emigration), immigrant
642 11 strokes	移	移	移	移り変わる *utsurikawaru,* to change, to shift

因	丨	冂	冂	**IN**, cause; *yo(ru),* to be due to, to be based on
	円	因	因	原因 *gen'in,* cause 因果 *inga,* cause and effect, fate 因襲 *inshū,* long-established custom
643 6 strokes				

永	丶	刁	刁	**EI** long, eternal, perpetual; *naga(i),* everlasting
	永	永		永遠 *eien,* eternity 永眠 *eimin,* death 永住 *eijū,* permanent residence
644 5 strokes				

129

営	丶	⺌	⺍	EI; *itona(mi)*, occupation; *itona(mu)*, to run (a hotel), to perform (a religious service)
	⺍	兴	労	経営　*keiei*, management, operation 営業　*eigyō*, business, trade, operation
645 12 strokes	労	営		

衛	彳	彳	衤	EI to protect, to defend
	衠	律	律	衛生　*eisei*, hygiene 防衛　*bōei*, defense 守衛　*shuei*, guard, watchman
646 16 strokes	律	律	衛	

易	丨	冂	日	EKI, divination; I easy
	日	月	昜	容易　*yōi*, easy 貿易　*bōeki*, trade 易者　*ekisha*, fortuneteller
647 8 strokes	昜	易		

益	丶	丷	丷	EKI, benefit, profit; *eki(suru)*, to benefit
	兰	兴	兴	利益　*rieki*, gain, benefit 有益　*yūeki*, instructive, profitable 益虫　*ekichū*, useful insect
648 10 strokes	益	益	益	

液	氵	氵	汐	EKI, liquid, fluid, juice
	汐	汸	浐	液体　*ekitai*, liquid 血液　*ketsueki*, blood 消毒液　*shōdoku-eki*, antiseptic solution
649 11 strokes	浐	浐	液	

演 650 14 strokes	氵 氵 氵	氵 沛 演	氵 演 演	EN; *en(jiru)*, to act, to perform a play, to create (a comic scene), to commit (a blunder) 演説　　*enzetsu*, speech 演技　　*engi*, acting 演奏　　*ensō*, (musical) performance
応 651 7 strokes	丶 广 応	二 応	广 応	Ō, *ō(jiru)*, to answer, to comply with, to apply for, to accept 応援　　　*ōen*, aid, cheering 応用　　　*ōyō*, practical application 応接間　　*ōsetsuma*, parlor
往 652 8 strokes	丿 彳 彳	彳 彳 往	彳 行	Ō to go; ancient times 往来　　　*ōrai*, (street) traffic, going and coming, street 往復　　　*ōfuku*, going and returning, round trip 立往生　　*tachi-ōjō*, standstill
桜 653 10 strokes	木 杧 桜	术 桜	术 桜	Ō; *sakura*, cherry tree, cherry blossom, pink 桜花　　　*ōka*, cherry blossoms (lit.) 桜肉　　　*sakuraniku*, horsemeat 山桜　　　*yamazakura*, wild cherry
恩 654 10 strokes	丨 円 因	冂 因 恩	冃 因 恩	ON, favor, kindness 恩人　　　*onjin*, benefactor 謝恩　　　*shaon*, expression of gratitude 恩返し　　*ongaeshi*, requital of another's favor

可	一	一	可	KA, good, approval
	口	可		可決　　*kaketsu,* approval 可能　　*kanō,* possibility 不可能　*fukanō,* impossibility
655 5 strokes				

仮	ノ	イ	仁	KA, KE; *kari,* temporary, false
	仜	仮	仮	仮定　*katei,* supposition 仮装　*kasō,* disguise 仮病　*kebyō,* pretended illness
656 6 strokes				

価	ノ	イ	仁	KA; *atai,* price, value
	仁	�	価	定価　*teika,* fixed price 価値　*kachi,* value 物価　*bukka,* prices of commodities
657 8 strokes	価	価		

河	丶	冫	氵	KA; *kawa,* river
	沪	沪	沪	河口　*kakō,* mouth of a river 銀河　*ginga,* Milky Way 運河　*unga,* canal
658 8 strokes	沪	河		

過	l	冂	冂	KA; *su(giru),* to elapse, to pass, to exceed; *su(gosu),* to pass (a day), to go to excess; *ayama(chi),* error, mishap
	冋	咼	咼	
659 12 strokes	咼	渦	過	通過　*tsūka,* passage 経過　*keika,* progress, lapse 過去　*kako,* past, past tense

賀	マ	カ	カロ	GA congratulations
				年賀 *nenga*, New Year's greetings 年賀状 *nengajō*, New Year's card 祝賀 *shukuga*, celebration, congratulation
	智	賀	賀	
660 12 strokes	智	賀	賀	

快	'	`	忄	KAI; *kokoroyo(i)*, pleasant, refreshing
				快晴 *kaisei*, fine weather 愉快 *yukai*, pleasant 快活 *kaikatsu*, cheerful
	忄	忙	快	
661 7 strokes	快			

解	⺈	角	角	KAI, explanation; *to(ku)*, to untie, to solve; *to(keru)* (v.i.), to relent, become loose; *hodo(ku)*, to untie
	解	解	解	理解 *rikai*, understanding 解散 *kaisan*, breaking up, dissolution 分解 *bunkai*, analysis, decomposition
662 13 strokes	解	解	解	

格	一	十	才	KAKU, status, case (in grammar)
				性格 *seikaku*, personality, character 人格 *jinkaku*, character 価格 *kakaku*, price
	木	杦	松	
663 10 strokes	格			

確	石	石	矿	KAKU; *tashi(ka)*, sure, accurate, reliable; *tashi(kameru)*, to ascertain, to confirm
	矿	矿	矿	正確 *seikaku*, correctness 確実 *kakujitsu*, certainty 確定 *kakutei*, decision
664 15 strokes	碎	碎	確	

額	ヽ	宀	宀	GAKU, framed picture, amount (of money); *hitai*, forehead
	宀	宀	客	金額 *kingaku*, amount of money 総額 *sōgaku*, sum total 多額 *tagaku*, large sum
665 18 strokes	額	額	額	

刊	一	二	干	KAN publication, edition
	刊	刊		刊行 *kankō*, publication 週刊 *shūkan*, weekly publication 新刊 *shinkan*, new publication
666 5 strokes				

幹	一	十	古	KAN; *miki*, trunk of a tree
	卓	卓	卓	幹部 *kanbu*, the executive, leading members 根幹 *konkan*, basis, root 幹線 *kansen*, trunk line
667 13 strokes	幹	幹	幹	

慣	ヽ	ハ	小	KAN; *na(reru)*, to get accustomed (to), to become inured (to)
	忄	忄	忄	習慣 *shūkan*, habit, custom 慣用 *kan'yō*, common use, practice
668 14 strokes	忄	慣	慣	見慣れる *minareru*, to get used to seeing, to be familiar (with)

眼	丨	冂	目	GAN; *manako*, eye
	目	目	目	肉眼 *nikugan*, naked eye 近眼 *kingan*, near-sightedness 双眼鏡 *sōgankyō*, binoculars
669 11 strokes	眼	眼	眼	

基	一	十	艹	KI; *motoi*, foundation, basis; *moto(zuku)*, to be based on
	廿	甘	其	基本　*kihon*, foundation, basis, standard 基地　*kichi*, (air, etc.) base 基礎　*kiso*, foundation, basis
670 11 strokes	其	其	基	

寄	丶	宀	宀	KI; *yo(ru)*, to approach, to drop in, to gather (v.i.); *yo(seru)*, to draw up (a chair), to push (a desk) aside
	宀	宇	安	寄港　*kikō*, call at a port 寄付　*kifu*, contribution 寄与　*kiyo*, contribution, service
671 11 strokes	宝	客	寄	

規	一	二	丰	KI compass
	夫	刦	刞	規律　*kiritsu*, order, discipline 規模　*kibo*, scale, scope 規準　*kijun*, standard
672 11 strokes	刞	刬	規	

技	一	十	扌	GI art, skill
	扌	扑	扙	技師　*gishi*, engineer 競技　*kyōgi*, sporting events, contest 技術　*gijutsu*, art, technique
673 7 strokes	技			

義	丶	丷	丷	GI, justice, morality, loyalty, relationship; prefix for "in-law," "artificial"
	羊	羊	羊	主義　*shugi*, principle, ~ism 講議　*kōgi*, lecture 義兄　*gikei*, elder brother-in-law
674 13 strokes	羊	莠	義	

逆	丶	丷	丷
	丷	屵	屵
675 9 strokes	屵	逆	逆

GYAKU, inverse, reverse; *gyaku(ni)*, inversely, reversely; *saka(rau)*, to oppose, to go against

逆転　　*gyakuten*, reversal, going backward
逆境　　*gyakkyō*, adversity
反逆　　*hangyaku*, treason

久	ノ	ク	久
676 3 strokes			

KYŪ, KU; *hisa(shii)*, long (time), lasting; *hisa(shiku)*, for a long time

永久　　　*eikyū*, permanence, eternity
久しぶり　*hisashiburi*, after a long time
久遠　　　*kuon*, eternity

旧	｜	｜｜	丨冂
	旧	旧	
677 5 strokes			

KYŪ, old

旧式　*kyūshiki*, old-style
旧跡　*kyūseki*, place of historic interest
旧暦　*kyūreki*, lunar calendar

居	｀	ㄱ	尸
	尸	尸	尼
678 8 strokes	居	居	

KYO dwelling place; *i(ru)*, to be, to be present, to dwell

住居　　*jūkyo*, dwelling
居眠り　*inemuri*, napping, dozing (n.)
居間　　*ima*, living room

許	丶	二	亠
	言	言	訁
679 11 strokes	訐	訐	許

KYO; *yuru(shi)*, permission, pardon, approval; *yuru(su)*, to permit, to forgive, to approve

許可　*kyoka*, permission, license, admission, approval
特許　*tokkyo*, patent, concession
免許　*menkyo*, license, certificate

境 680 14 strokes	土	圹	垆
	坍	培	培
	培	堷	境

KYŌ, KEI; *sakai*, border, boundary, border line

境遇　*kyōgū*, circumstances, surroundings
国境　*kokkyō*, frontier
境内　*keidai*, precincts

均 681 7 strokes	一	十	土
	圠	均	均
	均		

KIN level, equality

平均　*heikin*, average, balance
均等　*kintō*, equality, identity

禁 682 13 strokes	一	十	才
	木	林	埜
	埜	禁	禁

KIN; *kin~*, prefix for "forbidden" or "prohibited"; *kin(jiru)*, to forbid, to abstain from

禁止　*kinshi*, prohibition, ban
禁煙　*kin'en*, "No Smoking"
禁酒　*kinshu*, abstinence from alcoholic beverages

| 句 683 5 strokes | ノ | 勹 | 勹 |
| | 句 | 句 | |

KU, clause, phrase, verse, line

文句　*monku*, words, objection
語句　*goku*, words and phrases
句読点　*kutōten*, punctuation marks

群 684 13 strokes	ヨ	尹	君
	君	君′	君″
	群	群	群

GUN; *mu(re)*, group, flock, herd; *mu(reru)*, *mura(garu)*, to throng (v.i.)

魚群　*gyogun*, school of fish
群島　*guntō*, group of islands
群衆　*gunshū*, crowd (of people)

経	㇑	幺	幺	KEI, circles of longitude; KYŌ, the sutras, (law, reason, way, ordinary course of things); *he(ru)*, to pass, to pass through
	糸	糸	糸	経費　*keihi*, expenditure 経由　*keiyu*, by way of, through 神経　*shinkei*, nerve
685 11 strokes	紀	級	経	

潔	氵	氵	汁	KETSU; *isagiyo(i)*, manly, brave, pure
	浐	泄	淐	清潔　*seiketsu*, clean 潔白　*keppaku*, innocent, pure, upright 簡潔　*kanketsu*, concise
686 15 strokes	潔	潔	潔	

件	ノ	イ	イ	KEN, matter
	仁	仁	件	事件　*jiken*, event, matter 用件　*yōken*, business 条件　*jōken*, condition, terms
687 6 strokes				

券	丶	㇏	㇍	KEN, bond, ticket
	丷	半	关	定期券　*teikiken*, commutation ticket 旅券　*ryoken*, passport 入場券　*nyūjō-ken*, admission ticket, platform ticket
688 8 strokes	券	券		

険	㇋	了	阝	KEN; *kewa(shii)*, steep, fierce
	阝	阝	阶	危険　*kiken*, danger 保険　*hoken*, insurance 冒険　*bōken*, adventure
689 11 strokes	陉	険	険	

検	一	十	オ	**KEN to examine** 探検　*tanken*, exploration 検診　*kenshin*, medical examination 検定　*kentei*, official approval
	木	朴	朴	
690 **12 strokes**	朴	柃	検	

限	⁊	⁊	⻖	**GEN;** *kagi(ri)*, limit, end, as far as possible; *kagi(ru)*, to limit, to restrict 制限　*seigen*, limitation 期限　*kigen*, term 無限　*mugen*, infinity
	阝⁊	阝ㅋ	阝ヨ	
691 **9 strokes**	阻	限	限	

現	一	丁	干	**GEN present, now;** *ara(wareru)*, to show oneself, to come into sight, to be found (out); *ara(wasu)*, to manifest, to expose, to express 実現　*jitsugen*, realization 表現　*hyōgen*, expression 現代　*gendai*, present age
	王	玑	珇	
692 **11 strokes**	珇	玥	現	

減	丶	氵	氵	**GEN;** *he(ru)*, to decrease (v.i.), to wear out; *he(rasu)*, to decrease (v.t.) 加減　*kagen*, state of health, degree, adjustment, influence, addition and subtraction 減少　*genshō*, diminution, decrease 減退　*gentai*, decline, failing
	氵	沪	洉	
693 **12 strokes**	減	減	減	

故	一	十	十	**KO old, former times; reason;** *yue* reason, cause 事故　*jiko*, accident, hindrance 故郷　*kokyō*, one's native place 故障　*koshō*, mishap, trouble, accident, hindrance
	古	古	古	
694 **9 strokes**	苦	故	故	

139

個	ノ	イ	们
	们	侗	佩
695 10 strokes	佩	個	個

KO individual, suffix for enumeration

個人   *kojin,* individual
個性   *kosei,* individual character, personality
数個   *sūko,* several

護	言	言	言
	訙	詳	詳
696 20 strokes	謹	護	護

GO to protect, to defend

保護   *hogo,* protection
看護婦   *kangofu,* trained nurse
弁護士   *bengoshi,* lawyer

効	丶	二	亠
	六	方	交
697 8 strokes	効	効	

KŌ, efficacy, effect; *ki(ku),* to be effective

効果   *kōka,* effect, efficacy, result, sound effects
効力   *kōryoku,* effect, efficacy
有効   *yūkō,* valid, effective, efficacious

厚	一	厂	厂
	厇	戽	厚
698 9 strokes	厚	厚	厚

KŌ; *atsu(i),* thick, cordial

厚紙   *atsugami,* thick paper, cardboard
厚意   *kōi,* kindness
厚生   *kōsei,* public welfare

耕	一	三	丰
	耒	耒	耒
699 10 strokes	耒	耕	耕

KŌ; *tagaya(su),* to till

耕地   *kōchi,* arable (cultivated) land
耕作   *kōsaku,* cultivation
農耕   *nōkō,* farm labor

鉱 700 13 strokes	ハ 金 鈩	午 釒 鉱	釒 釒 鉱	**KŌ** ore 鉱山　*kōzan*, mine 鉱物　*kōbutsu*, mineral 鉄鉱　*tekkō*, iron ore
構 701 14 strokes	木 栉 構	栉 構 構	栉 構 構	**KŌ**; *kama(e)*, structure, posture; *kama(eru)*, to put oneself in a posture, to build 構成　*kōsei*, composition 構造　*kōzō*, structure, construction 心構え　*kokorogamae*, mental attitude, preparation
興 702 16 strokes	⺦ 卬 佣	⺧ 卬 興	日 佣 興	**KŌ, KYŌ**; interest; *oko(ru)*, to prosper; *oko(su)*, to restore 興味　*kyōmi*, interest, appeal 興奮　*kōfun*, excitement 復興　*fukkō*, revival, reconstruction
講 703 17 strokes	言 諅 講	言 講 講	言 講 講	**KŌ** investigation, lecture; to think out, to study, to explain 講演　*kōen*, lecture 講堂　*kōdō*, auditorium 講習　*kōshū*, short training course
混 704 11 strokes	丶 汜 泥	氵 汜 混	氵 浘 混	**KON**; *ma(zeru)*, to mix, to mingle; *ma(jiru)*, to be mixed, to be mingled; *ma(zaru)* (= *majiru*) 混乱　*konran*, confusion 混雑　*konzatsu*, congestion, confusion 混合　*kongō*, mixture

査	一	十	才	**SA** to examine, to investigate
	木	木	杏	検査 *kensa,* inspection, examination 巡査 *junsa,* policeman 審査 *shinsa,* screening
705 9 strokes	杏	杳	査	

再	一	丆	冂	**SAI** re- (prefix); *futata(bi),* again
	币	再	再	再建 *saiken,* reconstruction 再会 *saikai,* meeting again 再三 *saisan,* again and again
706 6 strokes				

災	㇑	㇓㇑	㇓㇓㇑	**SAI;** *wazawa(i),* disaster, misfortune
	巛	巛	災	災害 *saigai,* disaster, calamity 災難 *sainan,* misfortune, calamity 火災 *kasai,* fire, conflagration
707 7 strokes	災			

妻	一	ㄱ	彐	**SAI,** my wife; *tsuma,* wife
	彐	圭	妻	夫妻 *fusai,* husband and wife 妻子 *saishi,* wife and children 妻君 *saikun,* wife
708 8 strokes	妻	妻		

採	一	十	扌	**SAI;** *to(ru),* to gather (fruit, etc.), to employ (a person), to adopt (a measure)
	扌	扩	扩	採集 *saishū,* collection 採用 *saiyō,* employment, adoption 採掘 *saikutsu,* mining
709 11 strokes	扩	抨	採	

際	７	３	阝	SAI, occasion; *kiwa*, verge, occasion
	阝	阹	阹	実際　*jissai*, actual state, truth, reality 国際　*kokusai*, international 交際　*kōsai*, intercourse, acquaintance, association
710 14 strokes	際	際	際	

在	一	ナ	ナ	ZAI, country, suburbs, to exist; *a(ru)*, to be, to exist
	在	存	在	存在　*sonzai*, existence, being 滞在　*taizai*, sojourn 現在　*genzai*, present time, present tense
711 6 strokes				

財	l	冂	月	ZAI treasure
	目	貝	貝	財産　*zaisan*, property, fortune 財政　*zaisei*, finance(s) 私財　*shizai*, private property
712 10 strokes	財	財	財	

罪	、	冖	罒	ZAI; *tsumi*, crime, sin
	罒	罒	罪	犯罪　*hanzai*, crime 罪悪　*zaiaku*, sin, crime 謝罪　*shazai*, apology
713 13 strokes	罪	罪	罪	

雑	ノ	九	卆	ZATSU, rough; ZŌ miscellaneous, rough
	杂	杂	新	複雑　*fukuzatsu*, complexity, complication 雑誌　*zasshi*, magazine 雑きん　*zōkin*, floorcloth, mopping cloth
714 14 strokes	新	雑	雑	

143

酸	丆	酉	酉′	SAN, acid; *su(ppai)*, sour
	酉′	酉′	酉′	酸素　　*sanso*, oxygen
				塩酸　　*ensan*, hydrochloric acid
715 **14 strokes**	酸′	酸′	酸	酸化　　*sanka*, oxidization

賛	一	二	夫	SAN to praise, to assist, to agree
	夫	夫夫	替	賛成　　*sansei*, approval, support
				賛助　　*sanjo*, support, help
716 **15 strokes**	替	賛	賛	協賛　　*kyōsan*, cooperation

支	一	十	亅	SHI branch; to branch off, to support; *sasa(eru)*, to support, to hold
	支			支配　　*shihai*, rule, management
				支払う　*shiharau*, to pay
717 **4 strokes**				支店　　*shiten*, a branch (store, office)

志	一	十	士	SHI; *kokorozashi*, will intention, ambition, aim, kindness; *kokoroza(su)*, to intend, to aim at
	士	志	志	意志　　*ishi*, will
				志望　　*shibō*, desire
718 **7 strokes**	志			同志　　*dōshi*, comrade

枝	一	十	才	SHI; *eda*, branch, twig
	才	朾	朾	枝隊　　*shitai*, detachment (troops)
				枝葉　　*shiyō*, minor details, side issues
719 **8 strokes**	枝	枝		枯れ枝　*kare-eda*, dead branch

師	´	亻	宀	SHI, teacher, expert; army
	戶	戶	自	牧師　　*bokushi*, pastor 教師　　*kyōshi*, teacher 師団　　*shidan*, division (army)
720 10 strokes	師	師	師	

資	`			SHI wealth, help, nature
	冫	汐	次	資源　　*shigen*, resource 資格　　*shikaku*, capacity, qualification 物資　　*busshi*, goods, materials
721 13 strokes	資	資	資	

飼		𠆢	今	SHI; *ka(u)*, to raise/keep/feed (animals)
	食	食	飼	飼料　　*shiryō*, fodder, animal-feed 飼い主　*kainushi*, animal owner 飼育　　*shi-iku*, breeding, rearing
722 13 strokes	飼	飼	飼	

示	一	二	亓	JI, SHI; *shime(su)*, to show, to point out
	示	示		示唆　　*shisa*, suggestion 掲示　　*keiji*, notice 指示　　*shiji*, instructions, indication
723 5 strokes				

似	ノ	亻	仈	JI; *ni(ru)*, to resemble
	仏	似	似	類似　　*ruiji*, similarity 似顔　　*nigao*, portrait, likeness 不似合　*funiai*, unbecoming
724 7 strokes	似			

	二	言	言	**SHIKI** to know, to write down, to distinguish
識	言	訐	諳	知識　*chishiki*, knowledge 標識　*hyōshiki*, mark 常識　*jōshiki*, common sense
725 19 strokes	識	識	識	

	′	宀	斤	**SHITSU**, quality, substance; to inquire; simple and honest; **SHICHI**, pawn
質	斤	斦	斦	質問　*shitsumon*, question 素質　*soshitsu*, makings, quality 質屋　*shichiya*, pawnshop
726 15 strokes	質	質	質	

	ノ	人	入	**SHA** house, lodging
舎	仐	全	全	校舎　*kōsha*, school building 牛舎　*gyūsha*, cowshed 宿舎　*shukusha*, lodging
727 8 strokes	舎	舎		

	、	亠	言	**SHA**; *sha(suru)*, to apologize, to thank; *ayama(ru)*, to apologize
謝	言	言	訃	感謝　*kansha*, thanks 謝絶　*shazetsu*, refusal 謝礼　*sharei*, remuneration, thanks
728 17 strokes	訃	謝		

	一	扌	扌	**JU**; *sazu(keru)*, to grant, to instruct; *sazu(karu)*, to be blessed with
授	扌	扌	扌	授業　*jugyō*, lesson(s), teaching 教授　*kyōju*, teaching, professor 受賞　*jushō*, awarding a prize
729 11 strokes	扌	授	授	

146

修 730 10 strokes	ノ 亻 仈	亻 仃 仃	亻 攸 攸	SHŪ, SHU; *osa(meru),* to study, to finish, to practice; *osa(maru),* to behave well 修理　*shūri,* repair 改修　*kaishū,* improvement, repair 修正　*shūsei,* amendment
述 731 8 strokes	一 朮 述	十 朮 述	才 求	JUTSU; *no(beru),* to speak, to express, to state 著述　*chojutsu,* writing (of books), one's writings 口述　*kōjutsu,* oral statement 述語　*jutsugo,* predicate (gram.)
術 732 11 strokes	彳 朮 休	彳 术 術	彳 休 術	JUTSU, art, artifice, means, magic 手術　*shujutsu,* surgical operation 技術　*gijutsu,* technique 美術　*bijutsu,* art
準 733 13 strokes	氵 氵 淮	氵 汁 進	氵 汁 準	JUN, water level; rule; to imitate; prefix denoting "semi-," "associate" 標準　*hyōjun,* standard 基準　*kijun,* standard 準急　*junkyū,* semi-express
序 734 7 strokes	丶 庐 序	亠 庐	广 庐	JO, preface 順序　*junjo,* order, method 秩序　*chitsujo,* public order, discipline 序文　*jobun,* preface

| 招 735 8 strokes | 一 才 才 扌 | 扌 扩 招 | 才 扩 招 | **SHŌ**; *mane(ku),* to invite, to beckon 招待　　*shōtai,* invitation 招待状　*shōtaijō,* invitation card |

| 承 736 8 strokes | 了 了 了 了 承 | 了 孑 孑 承 | 了 矛 承 | **SHŌ**; *uketamawa(ru),* to hear 承知　　*shōchi,* consent, knowledge 承認　　*shōnin,* approval 了承　　*ryōshō,* acknowledgment |

| 証 737 12 strokes | 丶 言 訂 | 言 言 訌 証 | 言 訂 証 | **SHŌ** evidence, testimony 証明，*shōmei,* proof, certification 証人，*shōnin,* witness (law), surety 保証，*hoshō,* guarantee, security |

| 条 738 7 strokes | 丿 冬 条 | 夕 夂 条 | 夂 条 | **JŌ** clause in a law or treaty, logic, stripe 条件　　*jōken,* terms, conditions 条約　　*jōyaku,* treaty 無条件　*mujōken,* unconditional |

| 状 739 7 strokes | 一 丬 状 | 丬 丬 状 | 丬 状 | **JŌ** state, condition, letter 状態，*jōtai,* state (of things), condition 現状，*genjō,* existing state of affairs, present condition 礼状，*reijō,* letter of thanks |

常	ヽ	⺌	⺌	JŌ; *tsune*, usual, ordinary; *toko-*, everlasting
	⺌	些	尚	非常に　*hijō-ni*, very (much) 正常　　*seijō*, normal 日常　　*nichijō*, everyday
740 11 strokes	常	常	常	

情	ヽ	忄	忄	JŌ, feeling, sympathy; *nasa(ke)*, feeling, sympathy, love, mercy
	忄	忄	忄	愛情　　　*aijō*, affection 情け深い　*nasakebukai*, compassionate 情勢　　　*jōsei*, state of things
741 11 strokes	忄	情	情	

織	糸	糸	紒	SHOKU, SHIKI; *ori*, textile; *o(ru)*, to weave
	紵	紒	絟	織物　*orimono*, textile fabric 織機　*shokki*, weaving machine 組織　*soshiki*, organization
742 18 strokes	織	織	織	

職	一	厂	耳	SHOKU, employment, duties
	耳	耴	聄	職業　*shokugyō*, occupation, business 内職　*naishoku*, side job 職場　*shokuba*, place of work
743 18 strokes	職	職	職	

制	ノ	⺊	乍	SEI law, rule; *sei(suru)*, to restrain, to control
	午	缶	制	制度　*seido*, system, institution 制服　*seifuku*, uniform 制限　*seigen*, restriction
744 8 strokes	制	制		

性	`	ハ	忄
	忄	忄	忄生
745 8 strokes	忄生	性	

SEI, sex, nature; SHŌ, nature, temperament

性質　*seishitsu,* nature, property
習性　*shūsei,* habit
気性　*kishō,* temper

政	一	丁	下
	疋	正	正
746 9 strokes	政	政	政

SEI, SHŌ; *matsurigoto,* government

政府　*seifu,* government
政治　*seiji,* administration, politics
政策　*seisaku,* policy

勢	土	去	夫
	幸	刦	執
747 13 strokes	執	勢	勢

SEI; *ikio(i),* force, vigor, power, influence

勢力　*seiryoku,* power, influence
大勢　*taisei,* general trend; *ōzei,* large number of people
軍勢　*gunzei,* number of soldiers, troops

精	`	⺌	半
	米	米	米
748 14 strokes	精	精	精

SEI, spirit, vitality, essence; SHŌ

精神　*seishin,* spirit, mind, soul
精巧　*seikō,* exquisite (workmanship)
精進　*shōjin,* diligence

製	`	⺊	仁
	告	朱	制
749 14 strokes	制	製	製

SEI to manufacture, suffix for "make" or "manufacture"

製品　*seihin,* manufactured goods
銀製　*ginsei,* made of silver
米国製　*Beikokusei,* of American make

税	ノ	ニ	千	ZEI, tax
	禾	禾	利	税金　　*zeikin*, tax 納税　　*nōzei*, tax payment 税関　　*zeikan*, custom house
750 12 strokes	秤	秒	税	

責	一	十	主	SEKI; *se(meru)*, to blame, to urge, to torture
	圭	青	青	責任　　　*sekinin*, responsibility 責任者　*sekininsha*, person responsible 無責任　*musekinin*, irresponsibility
751 11 strokes	青	責	責	

績	く	幺	糸	SEKI to spin; meritorious deed
	紅	紆	結	成績　　*seiseki*, result, record 功績　　*kōseki*, meritorious deeds 紡績　　*bōseki*, spinning
752 17 strokes	績	績	績	

接	扌	扩	扩	SETSU; *ses(suru)*, to come in contact with, to receive, to adjoin; *tsu(gu)*, to join together, to splice, to set (a broken bone)
	扩	护	拉	直接　　*chokusetsu*, directly 接待　　*settai*, reception 接続　　*setsuzoku*, junction
753 11 strokes	接	接	接	

設	、	ニ	言	SETSU; *mō(keru)*, to establish
	言	言	言	設備　　*setsubi*, equipment 設計　　*sekkei*, plan, design (for construction) 建設　　*kensetsu*, construction
754 11 strokes	訳	設	設	

151

舌 755 6 strokes	ノ 千	二 舌	千 舌	ZETSU; *shita*, tongue 舌打ち *shita-uchi*, click of the tongue, smacking one's lips 舌鼓 *shita-tsuzumi*, smacking of the lips
絶 756 12 strokes	㇗ 紀 絡	幺 糺 絎	糸 糺 絶	ZETSU; *ta(eru)*, to cease, to become extinct; *ta(tsu)*, to sever, to discontinue 絶対 *zettai*, absoluteness 絶頂 *zetchō*, peak, zenith, summit 気絶 *kizetsu*, fainting
銭 757 14 strokes	ノ 牛 釒	𠆢 金 銭	今 金 銭	SEN, former unit of money (a hundredth part of a yen); *zeni*, money 金銭 *kinsen*, money こづかい銭 *kozukaisen*, pocket money
祖 758 9 strokes	丶 ネ 祀	ラ 礻 祖	ネ 初 祖	SO, ancestor, founder 祖国 *sokoku*, fatherland 祖母 *sobo*, grandmother 先祖 *senzo*, ancestor
素 759 10 strokes	一 圭 素	十 丰 素	主 丰 素	SO, SU white, origin, source 素朴 *soboku*, simple 要素 *yōso*, element, important factor 素顔 *sugao*, unpainted face

総	く	幺	糸	SŌ whole, general
	紋	紀	絵	総理大臣　　*sōri-daijin*, prime minister 総員　　　　*sōin*, entire staff, all hands, 　　　　　　full force
760 14 strokes	絵	総	総	総選挙　　　*sōsenkyo*, general election

造	ノ	⺊	牛	ZŌ; *tsuku(ri)*, structure, build (n.); *tsuku(ru)*, to make, to create, to build; ~*zuku(ri)*, made of ~ (suffix denoting type of structure)
	生	牛	告	木造　　*mokuzō*, made of wood 人造　　*jinzō*, artificial
761 10 strokes	告	浩	造	石造り　*ishizukuri*, built of stone

像	ノ	イ	伫	ZŌ, image, figure
	仔	俘	伊	銅像　　*dōzō*, bronze statue 仏像　　*butsuzō*, image of Buddha 現像　　*genzō*, development (of a film)
762 14 strokes	傻	像	像	

増	一	十	土	ZŌ; *ma(su)*, to increase (v.i. & v.t.); *fu(eru)* (v.i.), to increase, to proliferate; *fu(yasu)* (v.t.), to increase, to add (to)
	圵	圵	坿	増加　　*zōka*, increase 増強　　*zōkyō*, reinforcement
763 14 strokes	坿	増	増	増進　　*zōshin*, promotion

則	l	⊓	月	SOKU law; to act on
	月	目	貝	法則　　*hōsoku*, law 規則　　*kisoku*, rule 原則　　*gensoku*, principle
764 9 strokes	貝	則	則	

153

測	`、`	`ミ`	`氵`	SOKU; *haka(ru)*, to fathom, to measure
	`氵フ`	`泪`	`泪`	観測　*kansoku*, observation 測量　*sokuryō*, surveying 測定　*sokutei*, measurement
765 12 strokes	`浿`	`測`	`測`	

属	`フ`	`コ`	`尸`	ZOKU, genus (biol.); *zoku(suru)*, to belong to
	`尸`	`戸`	`属`	金属　　　*kinzoku*, metal 所属　　　*shozoku*, one's position 付属病院　*fuzoku-byōin*, attached 　　　　　hospital
766 12 strokes	`属`	`属`	`属`	

率	`、`	`亠`	`𠂆`	SOTSU; *hiki(iru)*, to lead, to command; RITSU, rate
	`玄`	`玄`	`㳄`	能率　　*nōritsu*, efficiency 出席率　*shussekiritsu*, percentage of 　　　　attendance 統率　　*tōsotsu*, command, leadership
767 11 strokes	`㳄`	`㳄`	`率`	

損	`一`	`扌`	`扌`	SON, loss, disadvantage; *son(suru)*, to suffer a loss; *soko(nau)*, *soko(neru)*, to hurt, to damage
	`护`	`扪`	`損`	損害　*songai*, loss, damage 損失　*sonshitsu*, loss 破損　*hason*, damage, breakdown
768 13 strokes	`揁`	`損`	`損`	

退	`フ`	`ヲ`	`ヨ`	TAI; *shirizo(ku)*, to retreat, to withdraw, to retire (v.i.); *shirizo(keru)*, to drive back, to keep away, to refuse (v.t.)
	`艮`	`艮`	`艮`	退場　*taijō*, leaving, walk-out, exit 退治　*taiji*, stamping out, subjugation 後退　*kōtai*, retreat
769 9 strokes	`退`	`退`	`退`	

貸	ノ	イ	仁	TAI; *ka(shi)*, loan; *ka(su)*, to lend, to loan, to hire out
	代	代	俗	貸家　　　*kashiya*, house for rent 貸ボート　*kashibōto*, boat for hire 貸借　　　*taishaku*, borrowing and
770 12 strokes	俗	貸	貸	lending

態	ム	ム	宀	TAI appearance, state of affairs
	台	自	自	態度　　*taido*, attitude 状態　　*jōtai*, state (of things) condition 容態　　*yōdai*, condition (of a patient)
771 14 strokes	能	能	態	

団	｜	冂	冂	DAN, group, party
	団	団	団	団体　　*dantai*, party, organization 楽団　　*gakudan*, band (musical) 団結　　*danketsu*, unity
772 6 strokes				

断	⺍	⺍	半	DAN; *kotowa(ru)*, to decline, to refuse, to give notice, to ask leave; *ta(tsu)*, to sever, to give up (drinking), to exterminate
	米	迷	迷	断食　　*danjiki*, a fast 油断　　*yudan*, negligence, carelessness,
773 11 strokes	幽	断	断	unpreparedness 判断　　*handan*, judgment

築	⺮	⺮	竹	CHIKU; *kizu(ku)*, to build
	竹	笁	笁	建築　　*kenchiku*, building 築造　　*chikuzō*, construction 新築　　*shinchiku*, new building
774 16 strokes	筑	筑	築	

張	⁷	⁷	弓	CHŌ; *ha(ri)*, tension, expansion; *ha(ru)*, to stretch, to spread, to cover
	引	引	張	見張り　　*mihari*, lookout 引っ張る　*hipparu*, to pull 主張　　　*shuchō*, insistence, opinion
775 **11 strokes**	張	張	張	

提	一	十	扌	TEI *sa(geru)*, to carry in one's hand
	押	押	捍	提出　*teishutsu*, presentation (of a thesis), filing (of an application) 提供　*teikyō*, offer, tender (law) 提案　*teian*, suggestion, proposition
776 **12 strokes**	捍	捍	提	

程	⁷	⁼	千	TEI degree, rule; *hodo*, extent, limit
	禾	和	和	程度　*teido*, degree, standard, limit 日程　*nittei*, day's program, schedule 行程　*kōtei*, distance
777 **12 strokes**	秆	程	程	

適	、	⁻	亠	TEKI; *teki(suru)*, to be fit for
	广	市	产	適当　*tekitō*, suitable, moderate 適任　*tekinin*, fitness 快適　*kaiteki*, agreeable
778 **14 strokes**	商	商	適	

敵	亠	方	产	TEKI, *kataki*, enemy, opponent
	商	商	商	強敵　*kyōteki*, formidable enemy 敵意　*teki-i*, hostile feeling 敵国　*tekikoku*, enemy country
779 **15 strokes**	敵	敵	敵	

統	ノ	幺	糸	**TŌ**; *su(beru)*, to control
	糸	糸	糸	統計 *tōkei*, statistics 大統領 *daitōryō*, president (of a country) 伝統 *dentō*, tradition
780 **12 strokes**	糸	糸	統	

銅	ノ	ト	牟	**DŌ**, copper
	牟	金	釒	青銅 *seidō*, bronze 銅線 *dōsen*, copper wire 銅山 *dōzan*, copper mine
781 **14 strokes**	釘	銅	銅	

導	`	```	丷	**DŌ**; *michibi(ki)*, guidance; *michibi(ku)*, to guide, to lead
	丷	首	道	指導 *shidō*, guidance 指導者 *shidōsha*, leader 補導 *hodō*, guidance
782 **15 strokes**	道	導	導	

徳	彳	彳	彳	**TOKU**, virtue, power of commanding love and respect
	彳	徔	徔	道徳 *dōtoku*, morality 徳望 *tokubō*, moral influence 人徳 *jintoku*, natural virtue
783 **14 strokes**	徳	徳	徳	

独	ノ	犭	犭	**DOKU**; *hito(ri)*, one person; Germany
	犭	犭	犭	独立 *dokuritsu*, independence 独特 *dokutoku*, peculiar, unique 独唱 *dokushō*, vocal solo
784 **9 strokes**	独	独	独	

157

| 任 785 6 strokes | ノ | イ | 仁 | NIN, duty; *maka(seru)*, to entrust, to leave (v.t.) |
| | 仁 | 任 | 任 | 責任　　*sekinin*, responsibility 転任　　*tennin*, change of post 任務　　*ninmu*, duty |

燃 786 16 strokes	`	``	ソ	NEN; *mo(eru)*, to burn (v.i.); *mo(yasu)*, to burn (v.t.)
	火	炒	炒	燃料　　*nenryō*, fuel 燃焼　　*nenshō*, combustion 不燃性　*funensei*, incombustible
	炒	燃	燃	

能 787 10 strokes	㇗	㇛	㇑	NŌ, ability, the *Noh*
	肖	肖	肖	能力　　*nōryoku*, ability, capacity, faculty 才能　　*sainō*, talent 能率　　*nōritsu*, efficiency
	肖	能	能	

破 788 10 strokes	一	㇆	石	HA; *yabu(re)*, a tear (rent); *yabu(ru)*, to tear, to break (a promise)
	石	石	矼	破損　　*hason*, breakdown 破産　　*hasan*, bankruptcy 難破　　*nanpa*, shipwreck
	矼	破	破	

| 犯 789 5 strokes | ノ | 犭 | 犭 | HAN; *oka(su)*, to commit, to violate, to rape |
| | 犭 | 犯 | | 犯罪　　*hanzai*, crime 犯人　　*hannin*, criminal 防犯　　*bōhan*, crime prevention |

判	丶	丷	半	HAN to decide; seal for stamping; BAN, size
	半	半	半	判断　*handan*, judgment, divinatiion 裁判　*saiban*, justice, trial, judgment 大判　*ō-ban*, large size (paper, book)
790 7 strokes	判			

版	丿	丿	片	HAN, plate, printing, edition
	片	片	版	版画　*hanga*, woodblock print 版権　*hanken*, copyright 出版　*shuppan*, publication
791 8 strokes	版	版		

比	一	上	比	HI, ratio, comparison; *kura(beru)*, to compare
	比			比較　*hikaku*, comparison 比率　*hiritsu*, ratio 比例　*hirei*, proportion
792 4 strokes				

肥	丿	刀	月	HI; *ko(eru)*, to grow fat; *ko(yasu)*, to fertilize, to fatten, to enrich (oneself)
	月	肥	肥	肥料　*hiryō*, manure, fertilizer たい肥　*taihi*, compost
793 8 strokes	肥	肥		

非	丿	丿	扌	HI, fault, wrong; non-, un-
	扌	非	非	非常に　*hijō-ni*, very 非常口　*hijōguchi*, emergency door 非難　*hinan*, censure
794 8 strokes	非	非		

備 795 12 strokes	ノ 个 伊	イ 伊 併	仁 伴 備	BI; *sona(e)*, preparation(s); *sona(eru)*, to furnish, to prepare; *sona(waru)*, to be possessed of, to be furnished with 準備　*junbi*, preparation(s) 守備　*shubi*, defense 予備　*yobi*, reserve
俵 796 10 strokes	ノ 什 俵	イ 佳 俵	仁 伊 俵	HYŌ; *tawara*, straw bag 土俵　*dohyō*, sandbag; sumō (wrestling) ring 一俵　*ippyō*, one straw bag 炭俵　*sumidawara*, charcoal sack
評 797 12 strokes	丶 言 訂	二 言 訂	言 言 評	HYŌ, criticism; *hyō(suru)*, to criticize, to comment 評判　*hyōban*, reputation, popularity, rumor 評価　*hyōka*, appraisal, appreciation 批評　*hihyō*, criticism
貧 798 11 strokes	ノ 分 貧	八 岔 貧	分 貧 貧	HIN, poverty; BIN; *mazu(shii)*, poor 貧弱　*hinjaku*, meager, poor 貧乏　*binbō*, poverty 貧困　*hinkon*, poverty, lack
布 799 5 strokes	ノ 右	ナ 布	才	FU; *nuno*, cloth 毛布　*mōfu*, blanket 配布　*haifu*, distribution 綿布　*menpu*, cotton cloth

婦	く	女	女¬
	女ァ	女ァ	女ョ
800 11 strokes	女帚	婦	婦

FU woman, wife

婦人　*fujin,* woman
主婦　*shufu,* housewife
夫婦　*fūfu,* husband and wife

富	`	` `	宀
	官	宀	宵
801 12 strokes	富	富	富

FU, FŪ; *tomi,* riches; *to(mu),* to be rich,
to abound (in)

豊富　*hōfu,* abundance
富貴　*fuki, fūki, fukki,* rich and noble
富裕　*fuyū,* riches, wealth

武	一	二	千
	千	疒	正
802 8 strokes	武	武	

BU, MU, military

武装　*busō,* arms, weapons
武器　*buki,* weapon
武力　*buryoku,* military power

復	'	ゟ	彳
	彳	彳	彴
803 12 strokes	復	復	復

FUKU re-, again, repeat

回復　*kaifuku,* recovery
復興　*fukkō,* revival, reconstruction
復活　*fukkatsu,* revival, resurrection

複	ゥ	ネ	ネ
	ネ	ネ	裆
804 14 strokes	褚	褙	複

FUKU to repeat; prefix for "double"

複雑　*fukuzatsu,* complication,
　　　complexity
複製　*fukusei,* reproduction
重複　*chōfuku, jūfuku,* duplication,
　　　repetition

仏	ノ	イ	仏	BUTSU; *hotoke*, Buddha; France
	仏			大仏　　*daibutsu*, colossal statue of Buddha
805 **4 strokes**				仏像　　*butsuzō*, image of Buddha 仏教　　*bukkyō*, Buddhism

編	纟	纟	纟	HEN; *a(mu)*, to knit, to edit
	纩	纩	絹	編集　　　*henshū*, editing 編集者　*henshūsha*, editor
806 **15 strokes**	絹	編	編	編成　　　*hensei*, formation

弁	厶	厶	厶	BEN, speech
	弁	弁		弁論　　　*benron*, debate 弁護人　*bengonin*, counsel
807 **5 strokes**				弁当　　　*bentō*, lunch

保	ノ	イ	仈	HO; *tamo(tsu)*, to keep, to maintain
	仈	仢	但	保護　　*hogo*, protection 保存　　*hozon*, preservation
808 **9 strokes**	伴	俣	保	保険　　*hoken*, insurance

墓	一	十	艹	BO; *haka*, grave
	苩	茸	莫	墓地　　*bochi*, graveyard 墓石　　*boseki*, *haka-ishi*, gravestone
809 **13 strokes**	莫	莫	墓	墓参　　*bosan*, visit to a grave

報	土	圭	吉	HŌ, report; *muku(i)*, retribution; *muku(iru)*, to reward, to return (a favor)
	坴	幸	幸	報告　*hōkoku*, report 時報　*jihō*, announcement of time 電報　*denpō*, telegram
810 12 strokes	幸ﾞ	報	報	

豊	口	曲	曲	HŌ; *yuta(ka)*, abundance
	曲	曲	曹	豊年　*hōnen*, year of abundance 豊作　*hōsaku*, good harvest
811 13 strokes	豊	豊	豊	

防	ﾞ	了	阝	BŌ; *fuse(gu)*, to defend, to keep off, to prevent
	阝	阝	防	予防　　*yobō*, prevention 消防　　*shōbō*, fire fighting 防波堤　*bōhatei*, breakwater
812 7 strokes	防			

貿	ﾞ	ﾑ	厶	BŌ to purchase, to exchange
	幻	幼	留	貿易商　　*bōekishō*, trader 貿易会社　*bōekigaisha*, trading firm 貿易風　　*bōekifū*, trade wind
813 12 strokes	留	貿	貿	

暴	日	旦	昱	BŌ, BAKU violent; to disclose; *aba(ku)*, to divulge; *aba(reru)*, to behave violently
	昱	昇	昪	暴力　*bōryoku*, violence, force 乱暴　*ranbō*, violence, unreasonableness 暴露　*bakuro*, disclosure
814 15 strokes	暴	暴	暴	

163

務	マ	予	矛	MU; *tsuto(meru)*, to discharge one's duties, to enact (a role)
	矛	矛	矛	事務所 *jimusho*, office 勤務 *kinmu*, service, duty 義務 *gimu*, duty
815 11 strokes	矜	務	務	

夢	一	艹	芍	MU; *yume*, dream, vision
	莤	芦	苎	悪夢 *akumu*, nightmare 夢中 *muchū*, unconsciousness; ecstasy, rapture 夢幻 *mugen*, dreams, visions
816 13 strokes	夢	夢	夢	

迷	、	゛	丷	MEI; *mayo(u)*, to be puzzled, to lose one's way, to go astray, to be tempted by; *mayo(wasu)*, to lead astray, to puzzle, to tempt
	半	米	米	迷信 *meishin*, superstition 迷惑 *meiwaku*, trouble, annoyance
817 9 strokes	米	迷	迷	

綿	く	幺	糸	MEN; *wata*, cotton
	糸	約	綃	綿屋 *wataya*, cotton shop (dealer) 綿密 *menmitsu*, minute, careful
818 14 strokes	絅	綿	綿	

輸	亘	車	車	YU to send
	軯	軩	軩	輸出 *yushutsu*, export 輸血 *yuketsu*, blood transfusion 輸送 *yusō*, transportation
819 16 strokes	輪	輸	輸	

余 820 7 strokes	ノ	人	人	YO, more (than), above; *ama(ri)*, the remainder, the balance; *~ama(ri)*, more than, over; *ama(ru)*, to remain, to be beyond (one's power); *ama(su)*, to leave over
	合	全	余	
	余			余分　*yobun*, surplus 余暇　*yoka*, spare time 余地　*yochi*, room, scope

預 821 13 strokes	フ	マ	ヌ	YO; *azu(karu)*, to keep, to take charge of, to refrain from, to receive; *azu(keru)*, to deposit, to put into the charge of
	予	予	予	預金　*yokin*, money on deposit 預り物　*azukarimono*, item left in someone's charge
	預	預	預	預り証　*azukarishō*, deposit receipt

容 822 10 strokes	、	ハ	宀	YŌ figure; to admit
	宀	灾	灾	形容詞　*keiyōshi*, adjective 内容　*naiyō*, content, substance 容積　*yōseki*, capacity, cubic measure
	突	灾	容	

略 823 11 strokes	｜	冂	冊	RYAKU, abbreviation, omission, outline; *ryaku(suru)*, to omit
	田	田	田	計略　*keiryaku*, stratagem, plan, plot 省略　*shōryaku*, omission 略称　*ryakushō*, abbreviation
	畔	畍	略	

留 824 10 strokes	ノ	ᄃ	ᄯ	RYŪ, RU; *to(meru)*, to fasten, to stop (v.t.)
	幻	幼	幼	停留所　*teiryūjo*, streetcar (bus) stop 留学　*ryūgaku*, studying abroad 留守　*rusu*, absence
	留	留	留	

165

| 領 | 令 令一 令 | RYŌ chief point; to control |
| 825 14 strokes | 令 領 領 領 領 領 | 要領 *yōryō,* the point, knack 領土 *ryōdo,* territory 領事 *ryōji,* consul |

| 異 | 丶 口 田 田 甲 畀 | I; *koto(naru),* to be different, to be unusual |
| 826 11 strokes | 畢 異 異 | 異常 *ijō,* unusual 異論 *iron,* different opinion, objection 異様 *iyō,* strange, odd, extraordinary |

| 遺 | 口 中 虫 虫 肀 書 貴 | I, YUI to leave behind, to bequeath |
| 827 15 strokes | 潰 潰 遺 | 遺族 *izoku,* bereaved family 遺跡 *iseki,* remains, relics 遺言 *yuigon,* will, testament |

| 域 | 一 土 士 圬 圷 域 | IKI, region, limits |
| 828 11 strokes | 域 域 | 地域 *chi-iki,* region, area 区域 *kuiki,* domain, zone, limits 領域 *ryōiki,* territory, sphere |

| 宇 | 丶 八 宀 宀 宀 宇 | U canopy of heaven, space, eaves |
| 829 6 strokes | | 宇宙 *uchū,* universe, cosmos 宇宙服 *uchūfuku,* space suit 堂宇 *dō-u,* hall, temple, edifice |

| 映 830 9 strokes | 丨 丨丨 日 日 日 旷 旷 映 映 | EI; *utsu(ru)*, to be reflected, match, come out (of photos); *utsu(su)*, to project, reflect; *ha(eru)*, to shine (v.i.) 映画 *eiga*, film, movie 上映 *jōei*, screening 反映 *han'ei*, reflection, influence |

| 延 831 8 strokes | ノ 千 千 正 正 延 延 | EN; *no(biru)*, to be postponed, to be extended; *no(basu)*, to postpone, to extend; *no(be)*, total 延長 *enchō*, prolongation, extension 延着 *enchaku*, late arrival 延期 *enki*, postponement |

| 沿 832 8 strokes | 丶 冫 氵 沿 沿 沿 | EN; *so(u)*, to run along, lie along 沿岸 *engan*, coast, shore 沿道 *endō*, roadside 川沿い *kawazoi*, riverside |

| 我 833 7 strokes | ノ 二 千 手 我 我 我 | GA; *ware*, self, oneself, I 我々 *ware-ware*, we 無我 *muga*, selflessness, ecstasy 我流 *garyū*, one's own way, self-taught method |

| 灰 834 6 strokes | 一 厂 灰 灰 灰 灰 | KAI; *hai*, ash, ashes 石灰 *sekkai*, lime 灰色 *hai-iro*, grey 火山灰 *kazanbai*, volcanic ash |

| 拡 835 8 strokes | 一 ー | 十 扌 | 扌 扩 | KAKU to extend, to unfold, to spread

拡大　*kakudai*, magnification
拡張　*kakuchō*, extension, expansion
拡声機　*kakuseiki*, loud-speaker |
| | 扌 拡 | 扩 拡 | 扩 | |

拡 835 8 strokes — strokes: 一, 十, 扌, 扌, 扩, 扩, 拡, 拡

| 革 836 9 strokes | 一 | 十 | 廿 | KAKU leather; to reform

革命　*kakumei*, revolution
革新　*kakushin*, innovation, reform
改革　*kaikaku*, reform |
| | 廿 苦 | 苎 芏 | 苦 革 | |

| 閣 837 14 strokes | 丨 | 冂 | 冃 | KAKU tower, pavilion, the Cabinet

内閣　*naikaku*, the Cabinet
閣僚　*kakuryō*, Cabinet member
閣下　*kakka*, Your Excellency |
| | 門 閔 | 門 閣 | 門 閣 | |

| 割 838 12 strokes | 丶 | 丷 | 宀 | KATSU; *wa(ru)*, to split, divide, separate (v.t.); *wa(reru)*, to break, split (v.i.); *wa(ri)* proportion, rate; *sa(ku)*, to cut, spare

分割　*bunkatsu*, division, partition
割合　*wariai*, rate, ratio
割引　*waribiki*, discount, rebate |
| | 宀 害 | 守 害 | 宔 割 | |

| 株 839 10 strokes | 一 | 十 | 才 | *kabu*, shares, stocks, speculation in shares; stub

切り株　*kirikabu*, stump
株式会社　*kabushiki-kaisha*, joint-stock corporation
株券　*kabuken*, share certificate |
| | 木 杵 | 朮 株 | 朾 株 | |

干	一	二	干	KAN to dry, to drain, shield, thrust; *ho(su)*, to dry, to drain (v.t.); *hi(ru)*, to dry, to ebb (v.i.)
840 **3 strokes**				干し草　*hoshikusa*, dry grass, hay 干潮　*kanchō/hishio*, ebb tide 干渉　*kanshō*, interference, intervention

巻	丶	ヽ丶	半	KAN; *ma(ki)*, volume, manuscript roll; *ma(ku)*, to roll, wind (v.t.)
	半	半	关	巻頭　*kantō*, the beginning part of a book 巻物　*makimono*, a scroll
841 **9 strokes**	关	巻	巻	竜巻　*tatsumaki*, whirlwind, tornado

看	一	二	三	KAN see, observe, examine
	手	丢	看	看護　*kango*, nursing, caring for 看守　*kanshu*, warder, jailer
842 **9 strokes**	看	看	看	看板　*kanban*, signboard, sign, placard

簡	ノ	ゟ	ゟゟ	KAN simple, brief; document
	篸	篸	箚	簡単　*kantan*, simple, easy 簡易　*kan'i*, easy, elementary
843 **18 strokes**	節	簡	簡	書簡　*shokan*, letter, correspondence

危	ノ	ゟ	ク	KI; *abu(nai)*, dangerous, critical (of condition), doubtful; *aya(ui)*, dangerous, doubtful
	产	产	危	
844 **6 strokes**				危険　*kiken*, danger 危篤　*kitoku*, critical condition (illness) 危機　*kiki*, crisis

机	一	十	才	KI; *tsukue*, desk
				机上の *kijō no*, theoretical, impractical
	木	朾	机	事務机 *jimuzukue*, office desk
				机一杯 *tsukue-ippai*, a deskful
845 6 strokes				

揮	一	十	扌	KI wield, brandish
				指揮 *shiki*, command; conducting (of music)
	扩	护	护	発揮 *hakki*, display, exhibition
				揮発性 *kihatsusei*, volatility
846 12 strokes	揖	揖	揮	

貴	口	中	虫	KI noble, dear, precious; *tatto(bu)*, to esteem, to prize; *tatto(i)*, valuables, precious
	虫	貴	青	貴重 *kichō*, precious
				貴金属 *kikinzoku*, precious metals
847 12 strokes	貴	貴	貴	貴重品 *kichōhin*, valuables

疑	ノ	ヒ	上	GI; *utaga(i)*, doubt, suspicion; *utaga(u)*, to doubt, to suspect
	矣	矣	鲜	疑問 *gimon*, question, doubt
				質疑 *shitsugi*, question
				疑惑 *giwaku*, suspicion, doubt
848 14 strokes	鲜	疑	疑	

吸	丶	口	口	KYŪ; *su(u)*, to sip, breathe in, suck, smoke (tobacco)
	叮	吸	吸	吸収 *kyūshū*, absorption
				吸血鬼 *kyūketsuki*, vampire
849 6 strokes				呼吸 *kokyū*, breathing, respiration

供 850 8 strokes	ノ イ 仁 什 伴 供 供 供	KYŌ; *tomo,* attendant; *sona(eru),* to offer (to a god) 供給　*kyōkyū,* supply, provision 提供　*teikyō,* offer 供出　*kyōshutsu,* quota delivery
胸 851 10 strokes	) 刀 月 月 肑 肑 胸 胸 胸	KYŌ; *mune,* chest, heart, mind 度胸　*dokyō,* courage 胸焼け　*muneyake,* heartburn 胸囲　*kyōi,* chest measurement
郷 852 11 strokes	く 幺 纟 幻 纟 組 組 組 郷	KYŌ, GŌ country, village, native place 郷土　*kyōdo,* one's native place; local 近郷　*kingō,* neighbouring districts 郷愁　*kyōshū,* nostalgia, homesickness
勤 853 12 strokes	一 十 艹 苫 苹 菫 菫 勤 勤	KIN; *tsuto(me),* duties, service; *tsuto(meru),* to serve (in an office) 勤務　*kinmu,* service, duty 勤勉　*kinben,* diligence 出勤　*shukkin,* attendance
筋 854 12 strokes	ノ 亻 竹 竹 竹 竹 竹 筋 筋	KIN; *suji,* muscle, sinew; thread, plot, line; sources 筋肉　*kinniku,* muscle 筋道　*sujimichi,* reason, logic 筋書き　*sujigaki,* outline, plan

171

系	一	ㄥ	幺	**KEI system, family line** 系統　*keitō,* system, family line 系図　*keizu,* genealogical table 家系　*kakei,* family line
	玄	幺	系	
855 7 strokes	系			

敬	一	卄	艹	**KEI; *uyama(u),* to respect** 尊敬　*sonkei,* respect 敬語　*keigo,* honorific word 敬意　*kei-i,* respects
	芍	苟	苟	
856 12 strokes	苟	敬	敬	

警	一	卄	芍	**KEI warn, caution** 警察　*keisatsu,* police 警告　*keikoku,* warning, caution 警報　*keihō,* alarm, warning
	苟	苟ㄅ	敬	
857 19 strokes	警	警	警	

劇	ㅏ	广	虍	**GEKI, drama, play; intense, severe** 劇場　*gekijō,* theater 演劇　*engeki,* play, theatrical performance 劇薬　*gekiyaku,* powerful medicine
	虍	虏	虜	
858 15 strokes	虜	豦	劇	

激	氵	氵	泊	**GEKI; *geki(suru),* to become excited/ agitated; *hage(shii),* violent, intense, passionate** 感激　*kangeki,* deep emotion 急激　*kyūgeki,* sudden, abrupt 激烈　*gekiretsu,* severe, intense, violent
	渲	滂	滂	
859 16 strokes	滂	激	激	

172

穴	丶	八	宀	KETSU; *ana*, cave, hole
	穴	穴		墓穴　*boketsu*, a grave 穴埋め　*ana-ume*, stopgap 穴居　*kekkyo*, cave-dwelling
860 5 strokes				

絹	〈	么	幺	KEN; *kinu*, silk
	糸	糸	糸	絹糸　*kinu-ito*, silk thread 絹織物　*kinu-orimono*, silk fabrics 人絹　*jinken*, artificial silk, rayon
861 13 strokes	絹	絹	絹	

権	木	朾	朾	KEN weight, authority, power; GON
	朾	朾	朾	人権　*jinken*, human rights 版権　*hanken*, copyright 政権　*seiken*, political power
862 15 strokes	栌	栌	権	

憲	丶	八	宀	KEN law, regulation
	宀	宀	宝	憲法　*kenpō*, constitution 憲兵　*kenpei*, military police, shore patrol 憲章　*kenshō*, charter, constitution
863 16 strokes	害	憲	憲	

源	氵	沪	沪	GEN; *minamoto*, origin, source
	沪	沪	沪	資源　*shigen*, resources 源氏　*Genji*, Minamoto Clan 水源　*suigen*, head of a stream/river
864 13 strokes	源	源	源	

厳	`	``	``
	``	厂	厂
865 17 strokes	厂	厃	厳

GEN, GON severe, strict, austere; *kibi(shii),* strict, harsh; *ogoso(ka),* solemn, severe

厳禁　　*genkin,* strict prohibition
厳格　　*genkaku,* stern, austere
荘厳　　*sōgon,* sublime, solemn

己	ㄱ	コ	己
866 3 strokes			

KO, KI myself, oneself, I

自己　　　　*jiko,* one's self, self
利己主義　　*rikoshugi,* egoism
知己　　　　*chiki,* acquaintance, appreciative friend

呼	l	口	口
	口'	口'	口''
867 8 strokes	呼	呼	

KO call, breathe; *yo(bu),* to call, to invite, to name

点呼　　*tenko,* roll call
呼び物　*yobimono,* drawcard, attraction
呼気　　*koki,* exhalation

誤	`	亠	亖
	言	訂	誤
868 14 strokes	誤	誤	誤

GO; *ayama(ri)* fault, mistake, error; *ayama(ru),* to err, to mistake

誤解　*gokai,* misunderstanding
誤字　*goji,* wrong word
誤訳　*goyaku,* mistranslation

后	一	厂	斥
	斥	后	后
869 6 strokes			

KŌ empress, queen

皇后　　*kōgō,* Empress (of Japan)
皇太后　*kōtaikō,* Empress Dowager (of Japan), Queen Mother (of England)

孝	一	十	土	**KŌ**, filial duty
	尹	耂	孝	孝行　*kōkō*, filial piety 孝心　*kōshin*, filial affection
870 7 strokes	孝			孝養　*kōyō*, discharge of filial duties

皇	`	´	白	**KŌ, Ō** monarch, emperor
	白	白	白	皇太子　*kōtaishi*, Crown Prince (of Japan) 皇室　*kōshitsu*, Imperial Family (of Japan)
871 9 strokes	皐	皐	皇	天皇　*tennō*, Emperor (of Japan)

紅	㇝	幺	幺	**KŌ, KU**; *kurenai*, crimson; *beni*, lipstick, rouge
	糸	糸	糸	口紅　*kuchibeni*, lipstick 紅茶　*kōcha*, black tea 紅葉　*kōyō*, crimson foliage; *momiji*,
872 9 strokes	紅	紅	紅	maple

降	㇆	了	阝	**KŌ**; *fu(ru)*, to fall (of rain/snow); *o(riru)*, to come down, to get off (a vehicle, etc.); *o(rosu)*, to lower
	阝	阞	阼	(三日)以降　*(mikka) ikō*, (falling) on and after (the 3rd)
873 10 strokes	陉	隆	降	乗り降り　*noriori*, getting on and off 降雨　*kō-u*, rainfall

鋼	ハ	亽	全	**KŌ**; *hagane*, steel
	金	金	釒	鋼鉄　*kōtetsu*, steel 鋼色　*hagane-iro*, steel-blue 製鋼　*seikō*, steelmaking
874 16 strokes	釦	鋼	鋼	

刻	、	二	亠	KOKU engrave; short period of time; *kiza(mu)*, to cut fine, to carve, engrave
	亥	亥	亥	時刻　*jikoku*, time 深刻　*shinkoku*, grave, serious 彫刻　*chōkoku*, carving, engraving, sculpture
875 8 strokes	刻	刻		

穀	士	吉	吉	KOKU grain, cereals
	吉	幸	莩	穀物　*kokumotsu*, grain, cereals 雑穀　*zakkoku*, minor cereals 穀類　*kokurui*, cereals, grain
876 14 strokes	莩	穀	穀	

骨	丨	冂	冎	KOTSU; *hone*, bone, frame, 'backbone'
	冎	冎	咼	骨折り　*hone-ori*, pains, trouble, effort 骨折　*kossetsu*, a fracture 気骨　*kikotsu*, spirit, grit, mettle
877 10 strokes	骨	骨	骨	

困	丨	冂	冂	KON; *koma(ru)*, to be in trouble/in a fix
	用	困	困	困難　*konnan*, difficulty, adversity 困窮　*konkyū*, destitution 貧困　*hinkon*, poverty, indigence
878 7 strokes	困			

砂	一	厂	石	SA, SHA; *suna*, sand
	石	石	砂	砂糖　*satō*, sugar 砂金　*sakin*, gold dust 砂利　*jari*, gravel
879 9 strokes	砂	砂	砂	

座 880 10 strokes	丶	二	广
	广	疒	庆
	应	座	座

ZA, seat, gathering, constellation; *suwa(ru)*, to sit

座席　*zaseki*, seat
星座　*seiza*, constellation
銀座　*Ginza*, the Ginza (major street/district in Tokyo)

済 881 11 strokes	氵	氵	汸
	汸	汸	済
	済	済	済

SAI; *su(mu)*, to end, to be settled; *su(masu)*, to finish, to pay back (a debt), to manage with (little money, etc.)

経済　　*keizai*, economics, thrift
不経済　*fukeizai*, bad economy
返済　　*hensai*, repayment

裁 882 12 strokes	十	土	圭
	圭	圭	表
	裁	裁	裁

SAI; *saba(ku)*, to judge; *ta(tsu)*, to cut (cloth etc.)

裁判　*saiban*, trial
裁縫　*saihō*, needlework
独裁　*dokusai*, dictatorship

策 883 12 strokes	ノ	ト	⺮
	⺮	竿	竿
	第	第	策

SAKU, policy, scheme, measure, plan

政策　*seisaku*, policy
策略　*sakuryaku*, stratagem
対策　*taisaku*, counterplan

| 冊 884 5 strokes | 丨 | 冂 | 冂 |
| | 冊 | 冊 | |

SATSU, SAKU; counter for books and magazines

一冊　*issatsu*, one volume
冊子　*sasshi*, booklet, pamphlet, brochure
別冊　*bessatsu*, separate volume

	一	二	丆	SAN; *kaiko*, silkworm
蚕	天	天	吞	養蚕　　*yōsan*, sericulture 蚕室　　*sanshitsu*, silkworm rearing room 養蚕地　*yōsanchi*, silkworm raising district
885 10 strokes	吞	蚕	蚕	

	一	工	云	SHI; *ita(ru)*, to reach, to go so far (as to), to come, to lead to, to be brought to
至	굿	쪽	至	至急　　*shikyū*, urgency 冬至　　*tōji*, winter solstice
886 6 strokes				

	一	二	千	SHI; *watakushi*, I, personal (affairs), privacy
私	禾	禾	利	私用　　*shiyō*, private use (business) 私物　　*shibutsu*, private property 私有　　*shiyū*, private ownership
887 7 strokes	私			

	、	冫	丷	SHI; *sugata*, shape, figure; appearance, condition
姿	沙	沙	次	姿勢　　*shisei*, posture, pose, stance 容姿　　*yōshi*, one's form, appearance 後ろ姿　*ushirosugata*, view from the back
888 9 strokes	次	姿	姿	

	、	ラ	ネ	SHI to look at carefully
視	ネ	礻	初	視界　　*shikai*, field of vision 視力　　*shiryoku*, eyesight, vision 無視　　*mushi*, disregard
889 11 strokes	袒	視	視	

詞	、	二	言
	言	訂	訂
890 12 strokes	詞		

SHI speech, words

歌詞　　*kashi*, words (of a song)
名詞　　*meishi*, noun
形容詞　*keiyōshi*, adjective

誌	、	二	言
	言	言	計
891 14 strokes	計	誌	誌

SHI document, magazine, record

雑誌　　　*zasshi*, magazine
週刊誌　　*shūkanshi*, weekly magazine
地誌　　　*chishi*, a topography

磁	一	厂	石
	矿	矿	矿
892 14 strokes	磁	磁	磁

JI magnet; porcelain

磁石　　*jishaku*, magnet, compass
磁気　　*jiki*, magnetism
磁器　　*jiki*, porcelain ware

射	′	亻	勹
	勻	身	身
893 10 strokes	射	射	

SHA; *i(ru)*, to shoot (an arrow); to strike (one's eyes)

射撃　　　*shageki*, firing, shooting
発射　　　*hassha*, discharge, fire
日射病　　*nisshabyō*, sunstroke, heatstroke

捨	一	扌	扌
	扩	拎	抾
894 11 strokes	捨	捨	捨

SHA; *su(teru)*, to throw away, abandon

捨て子　　*sutego*, abandoned child
喜捨　　　*kisha*, charity, alms
取捨　　　*shusha*, adoption or rejection; choice

179

尺

895
4 strokes

SHAKU old unit of length (approx 30 cm); length

尺度　*shakudo,* linear measure, scale, gauge
尺貫法　*shakkanhō,* Japanese system of weights and measures
尺八　*shakuhachi,* shakuhachi flute

若

896
8 strokes

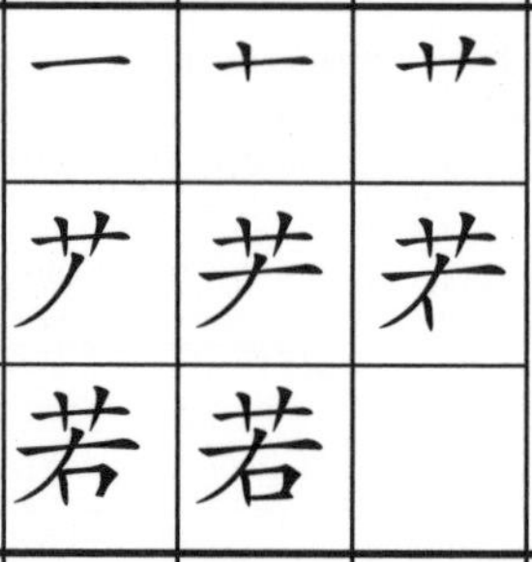

JAKU; *waka(i),* young; immature; *mo(shikuwa),* or

若者　*wakamono,* young people
若々しい　*wakawakashii,* youthful, young-looking
若干　*jakkan,* some, a few, a little

樹

897
16 strokes

JU tree, plant; *ki,* tree

樹木　*jumoku,* trees and shrubs
樹脂　*jushi,* resin
樹立　*juritsu,* establishment, founding

収

898
4 strokes

SHŪ; *osa(meru),* to obtain, to pay (taxes), to accept, to store, to seize; *osa(maru),* to be restored, contented

収穫　*shūkaku,* harvest
収容　*shūyō,* admission, accommodation
収入　*shūnyū,* income

宗

899
8 strokes

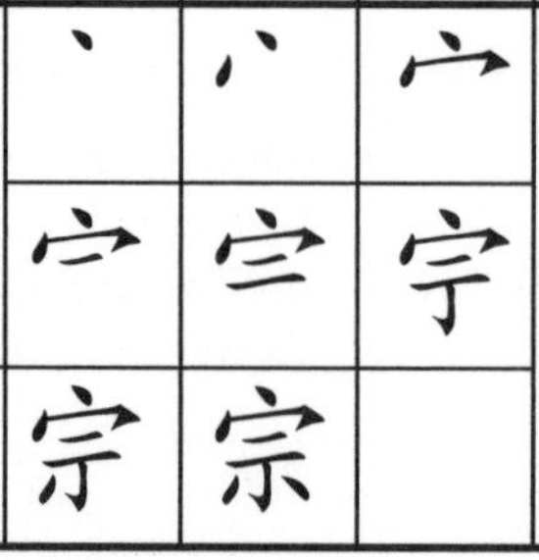

SHŪ, SŌ foundation, source, origin

宗教　*shūkyō,* religion
宗派　*shūha,* sect
宗匠　*sōshō,* master (in an art), teacher

就	ヽ	亠	亨
	京	京	京
900 12 strokes	刻	就	就

SHŪ, JU to sit, to engage in, to be completed; *tsu(ku)*, to engage in, to set about (a job)

就学 *shūgaku*, entering school
就職 *shūshoku*, finding employment
成就 *jōju*, accomplishment, realization

衆	宀	血	血
	卆	卆	卆
901 12 strokes	衆	衆	衆

SHŪ many

衆議院 *Shūgi-in*, House of Representatives
観衆 *kanshū*, spectators
民衆 *minshū*, the masses

従	ノ	彳	彳
	彳	彳	彳
902 10 strokes	徉	従	従

JŪ; *shitaga(u)*, to obey, to comply with, to observe (rules), to yield to, to follow

服従 *fukujū*, obedience
従事 *jūji*, engaging in (business)
従業員 *jūgyōin*, employee

縦	く	幺	幺
	糸	糸	紵
903 16 strokes	絆	縦	縦

JŪ; *tate*, length, height; warp

操縦 *sōjū*, handling, operation
縦書き *tategaki*, vertical script
縦横 *tateyoko*, length and breadth

縮	く	幺	幺
	糸	糸	紵
904 17 strokes	紵	紵	縮

SHUKU; *chiji(meru)*, to shrink (v.t.); *chiji(mu)*, *chiji(maru)*, to shrink (v.i.); *chiji(reru)*, to be frizzy, wavy

縮小 *shukushō*, reduction, curtailment, retrenchment
縮れ毛 *chijirege*, curly hair
軍縮 *gunshuku*, arms reduction

181

熟	亠	吉	亨	**JUKU**; *juku(suru)*, *u(reru)*, to ripen, mature
	享	剹	孰	成熟　　*seijuku*, ripeness, maturation 未熟　　*mijuku*, immature 熟練　　*jukuren*, skill, dexterity, mastery
905 15 strokes	孰	熟	熟	

純	く	幺	幺	**JUN** purity, innocence
	糸	糸	糸	単純　　　　*tanjun*, simple 純粋　　　　*junsui*, pure, genuine 純日本風　　*jun-nihonfū*, purely Japanese 　　　　　　　style
906 10 strokes	紀	紬	純	

処	ノ	ク	久	**SHO**; *sho(suru)*, to manage, to deal with, to sentence, to conduct oneself
	処	処		処理　　*shori*, management, transaction 処置　　*shochi*, measure, treatment 　　　　　　(medical) 処分　　*shobun*, disposal, punishment
907 5 strokes				

署	冂	罒	罒	**SHO** station (police, fire, etc.); (public) office; write, sign
	罒	罗	罗	警察署　　*keisatsusho*, police station 署長　　　*shochō*, head of a government 　　　　　　　office 署名　　　*shomei*, signature
908 13 strokes	署	署	署	

諸	言	言	計	**SHO** many
	計	訣	訣	諸国　　*shokoku*, various countries 諸君　　*shokun*, gentlemen, you 諸島　　*shotō*, group of islands
909 15 strokes	諸	諸	諸	

除	⁷	³	⻖	JO, JI division (math.); *nozo(ku)*, to take off, to remove, to exclude, to omit
	⻖	阝合	险	除幕式 *jomakushiki*, unveiling ceremony
910 10 strokes	除	除	除	除名 *jomei*, dismissal from membership 駆除 *kujo*, extermination

将	丶	⸍	丬	SHŌ to lead; about to
	丬	丬	丬	大将 *taishō*, a general, leader 将棋 *shōgi*, Japanese chess 将来 *shōrai*, the future
911 10 strokes	丬	将	将	

傷	ノ	イ	仁	SHŌ; *kizu*, wound, injury, cut; *kizu(tsukeru)*, to injure; *kizu(tsuku)*, to get injured; *ita(mu)*, to be painful
	伯	佢	伃	傷害 *shōgai*, wound, injury, accident 死傷者 *shishōsha*, casualties
912 13 strokes	傷	傷	傷	傷跡 *kizuato*, scar

障	阝	阝	阝	SHŌ hinder; separate; *sawa(ru)*, to hinder, interfere with, harm
	陟	陪	陪	障害 *shōgai*, obstacle, impediment 故障 *koshō*, obstacle, impediment, breakdown
913 14 strokes	障	障	障	障子 *shōji*, paper sliding door

城	一	十	土	JŌ; *shiro*, castle
	圵	圹	圹	城跡 *shiroato*, castle ruins/site 城下町 *jōkamachi*, castle town 姫路城 *Himeji-jō*, Himeji Castle
914 9 strokes	城	城	城	

蒸 915 13 strokes	一 艹 芐 芐 菡	艹 艹 芐 菡	艹 茈 莁 蒸	**JŌ**; *mu(su)*, to steam, be steamy; *mu(rasu)*, to steam (v.t.); *mu(reru)*, to be steamed, steamy, stuffy, musty (v.i.) 蒸気　　*jōki*, steam, vapour 蒸し暑い　*mushiatsui*, hot and muggy 蒸発　　*jōhatsu*, evaporation, strange disappearance
針 916 10 strokes	ノ 牛 金	人 仐 金	仝 余 針	**SHIN**; *hari*, needle, pin, pointer 針金　　*harigane*, wire 方針　　*hōshin*, policy, line 秒針　　*byōshin*, second-hand (of a watch)
仁 917 4 strokes	ノ 仁	イ	仁	**JIN**, perfect virtue, benevolence, humanity 仁徳　　*jintoku*, benevolence 仁義　　*jingi*, humanity and justice, humanity, duty, gamblers' moral code 仁愛　　*jin'ai*, benevolence
垂 918 8 strokes	一 舌 垂	二 乒 垂	三 岳	**SUI**; *ta(reru)*, to hang down, dangle (v.i.); *ta(rasu)*, to drip, dribble, spill (v.t.) 垂直の　*suichoku*, vertical, perpendicular 雨垂れ　*amadare*, raindrops, eavesdrops 垂れ飾り　*tarekazari*, pendant
推 919 11 strokes	一 扗 扗	扌 扩 推	扌 扩 推	**SUI**; *o(su)*, to infer, to guess, to recommend, to boost (a candidate) 推理　*suiri*, reasoning 推定　*suitei*, inference, presumption 推薦　*suisen*, recommendation

寸	一	寸	寸	SUN, old unit of length (approx. 3 cm) 寸法　　*sunpō*, measurements; plan 寸分　　*sunbun*, a little 寸前　　*sunzen*, just before
920 **3 strokes**				

盛	ノ	厂	厈	SEI, JŌ abundant, plentiful; *mo(ru)*, to pile up; *saka(n)*, prosperous; *saka(ri)*, prime, heyday
	厎	成	成	盛大　　*seidai*, splendid, prosperous 大盛り　*ōmori*, large serve, helping 繁盛　　*hanjō*, prosperity, success
921 **11 strokes**	盛	盛	盛	

聖	一	丆	下	SEI sage, saint
	王	耳	耵	聖人　　*seijin*, sage, saint 聖書　　*seisho*, the Bible 神聖　　*shinsei*, sacred, holy
922 **13 strokes**	聖	聖	聖	

誠	二	言	言	SEI; *makoto*, sincerity, truth
	言	訂	訪	誠実　　*seijitsu*, sincerity, faithfulness 誠意　　*sei-i*, sincerity, good faith 至誠　　*shisei*, sincerity, one's true heart
923 **13 strokes**	誠	誠	誠	

宣	、	丷	宀	SEN to promulgate, to state
	宀	宁	宁	宣言　　*sengen*, declaration 宣伝　　*senden*, propaganda 宣教師　*senkyōshi*, missionary
924 **9 strokes**	宦	宦	宣	

185

専	一	厂	戸	SEN sole, exclusive; *moppa(ra)*, wholly, exclusively
	戸	亘	叀	専門　　*senmon*, specialty 専用　　*sen'yō*, exclusive use 専売　　*senbai*, monopoly
925 9 strokes	叀	専	専	

泉	ノ	ハ	白	SEN; *izumi*, spring, fountain, source
	白	白	臼	温泉　　*onsen*, hot spring 泉水　　*sensui*, garden pond, fountain 源泉　　*gensen*, source, origin
926 9 strokes	泉	泉	泉	

洗	丶	冫	氵	SEN; *ara(u)*, to wash, cleanse
	氵	汁	汁	洗濯　　*sentaku*, washing, laundry 洗剤　　*senzai*, washing powder 洗練　　*senren*, polishing, refinement
927 9 strokes	汁	泩	洗	

染	丶	冫	氵	SEN; *so(meru)*, to dye; *shi(miru)*, to pierce, penetrate, soak into; to smart; *shi(mi)*, a stain
	氵	氿	氿	染料　　　　*senryō*, dyestuffs, dyes 染み抜き　　*shiminuki*, stain remover 汚染　　　　*osen*, pollution
928 9 strokes	染	染	染	

善	丶	丷	䒑	ZEN, good, goodness, virtue; *yo(i)*, virtuous, goodnatured
	䒑	羊	羊	親善　　*shinzen*, amity, friendship 最善　　*saizen*, the best 慈善　　*jizen*, charity
929 12 strokes	羊	盖	善	

奏 930 9 strokes	一	二	三	SŌ; kana(deru), to play/perform on (an instrument)
	丰	夫	表	演奏　ensō, (musical) performance, recital
	秦	奏	奏	伴奏　bansō, (musical) accompainment 合奏　gassō, concert, ensemble

窓 931 11 strokes	`	`	宀	SŌ; mado, window
	宀	空	空	窓口　madoguchi, service window 同窓会　dōsōkai, alumni association 窓際　madogiwa, by the window
	空	窓	窓	

創 932 12 strokes	ノ	ト	卜	SŌ origin, beginning
	今	今	介	創立　sōritsu, establishment 創作　sōsaku, literary creation, original work
	倉	創	創	独創的　dokusōteki, original, creative

装 933 12 strokes	ゝ	⺆	壮	SŌ, SHŌ; yoso-o(u), to dress, wear; to pretend
	壮	壮	壮	装置　sōchi, equipment, device 衣装　ishō, clothes, costume
	装	装	装	変装　hensō, disguise

層 934 14 strokes	⼀	⼀	尸	SŌ, layer, stratum
	尸	屄	屄	高曽ビル　kōsō-biru, high-rise building 下層階級　kasōkaikyū, the lower classes
	層	層	層	断層　dansō, (geological) fault

操	一	十	扌	SŌ grasp, manage, principle; *misao*, chastity, virtue; *ayatsu(ru)*, to operate (machine), manipulate
	扌	护	损	操作　　　*sōsa*, manipulation, operation 操り人形　*ayatsuri-ningyō*, puppet 貞操　　　*teisō*, chastity
935 16 strokes	搖	撍	操	

蔵	一	十	艹	ZŌ; *kura*, warehouse; *zō(suru)*, to own, to have
	广	芦	萈	冷蔵庫　*reizōko*, refrigerator 貯蔵　　*chozō*, storage 蔵書　　*zōsho*, one's library
936 15 strokes	蔵	蔵	蔵	

臓	丿	几	月	ZŌ entrails
	肝	肵	肵	肝臓　*kanzō*, the liver 内臓　*naizō*, internal organs 心臓　*shinzō*, the heart
937 19 strokes	旷	臁	臓	

存	一	ナ	才	SON, ZON to exist; *zon(jiru)*, to know, to think
	存	存	存	保存　*hozon*, preservation 生存　*seizon*, existence, life, survival 存在　*sonzai*, existence, being
938 6 strokes				

尊	丷	兰	台	SON; *tatto(i)*, noble, valuable; *tatto(bu)*, to respect, to value
	酋	酋	酋	尊敬　*sonkei*, respect 尊重　*sonchō*, respect, deference 本尊　*honzon*, principal image, idol
939 12 strokes	酋	尊	尊	

宅

940
6 strokes

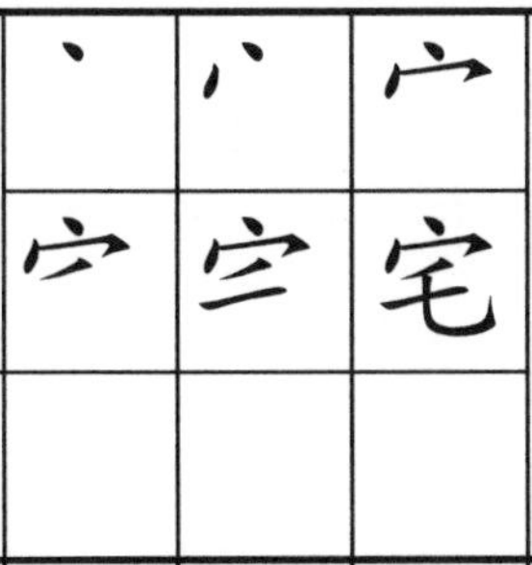

TAKU home; dwell

住宅 *jūtaku,* a dwelling, housing
自宅 *jitaku,* one's own home
宅地 *takuchi,* residential land

担

941
8 strokes

TAN; *katsu(gu),* to carry on the shoulder; *nina(u),* to carry; take upon oneself

担架 *tanka,* a stretcher
担当 *tantō,* being in charge (of)
負担 *futan,* burden

探

942
11 strokes

TAN; *sagu(ru),* to search, look for, explore; *saga(su),* to search

探求 *tankyū,* search, enquiry, research
探検 *tanken,* exploration, expedition
探知 *tanchi,* detection

誕

943
15 strokes

TAN be born, give birth

誕生日 *tanjōbi,* birthday
降誕 *kōtan,* holy birth
生誕 *seitan,* birth, nativity

段

944
9 strokes

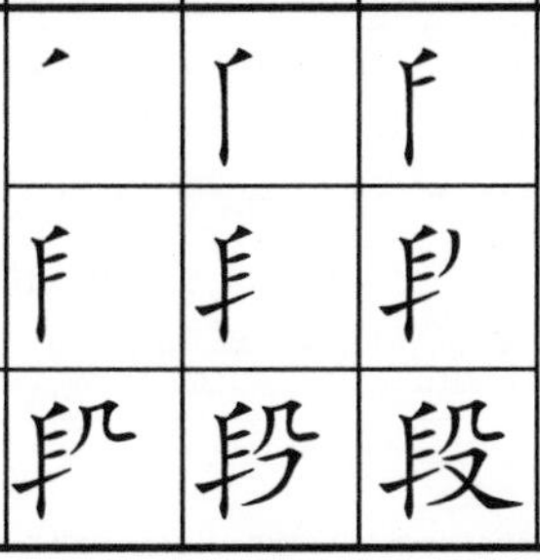

DAN, platform, step, grade

階段 *kaidan,* steps, stairs
段階 *dankai,* stage, phase, grade
手段 *shudan,* a means, way

暖	一	日	日	DAN; *atata(kai)*, warm; *atata(meru)*, to warm (v.t.); *atata(maru)*, to warm up (v.i.)
	旷	盰	盰	暖房　*danbō*, heating 暖流　*danryū*, warm current 温暖　*ondan*, warm, mild, temperate
945 13 strokes	旷	暖	暖	

値	亻	仁	仁	CHI; *ne*, price; *atai*, price, value, merit
	仁	佶	佶	値段　*nedan*, price 価値　*kachi*, value, worth, merit 数値　*sūchi*, numerical value
946 10 strokes	佶	値	値	

宙	丶	丷	宀	CHŪ, heaven, sky, space, air
	宀	宀	审	宇宙　*uchū*, the universe, space 宙返り　*chūgaeri*, somersault 航宙　*kōchū*, space flight
947 8 strokes	宙	宙		

忠	丶	冖	口	CHŪ, loyalty, faithfulness
	中	中	忠	忠告　*chūkoku*, (friendly) advice 忠義　*chūgi*, loyalty 忠実　*chūjitsu*, faithful
948 8 strokes	忠	忠		

著	一	十	艹	CHO; *ichijiru(shii)*, remarkable, notable, conspicuous; *ara(wasu)*, to write (a book)
	艹	芋	苹	著書　*chosho*, book, work 著者　*chosha*, writer, author 著名　*chomei*, famous
949 11 strokes	莘	莙	著	

190

庁	`	ハ	广
	庐	庁	
950 5 strokes			

CHŌ hall, government office

官庁	*kanchō*, government office
環境庁	*Kankyōchō*, Environment Agency
庁令	*chōrei*, official ordinance

頂	丁	厂	厂
	圹	疠	頂
951 11 strokes	頂	頂	頂

CHŌ; *itada(ku)*, to receive (humble), be capped; *itadaki*, top, summit

頂点	*chōten*, zenith, peak
頂き物	*itadakimono*, a gift one has received
絶頂	*zetchō*, summit (of mountain); zenith

潮	氵	汁	泸
	泔	渣	淖
952 15 strokes	潮	潮	潮

CHŌ; *shio*, tide, seawater

潮流	*chōryū*, tide, current; trend
満潮	*manchō*, high tide
潮風	*shiokaze*, sea breeze

賃	ノ	イ	仁
	仁	仟	任
953 13 strokes	侇	賃	賃

CHIN wages, rent

賃金	*chingin*, wages
家賃	*yachin*, house rent
電車賃	*denshachin*, carfare

痛	`	广	疒
	疒	疒	疖
954 12 strokes	疡	痛	痛

TSŪ; *ita(mu)*, to feel pain, ache; *ita(i)*, painful

頭痛	*zutsū*, headache
苦痛	*kutsū*, pain, anguish
痛烈	*tsūretsu*, severe, bitter, scathing

展	⁻	⁻	尸	**TEN** to open, to exhibit
	尸	屏	屏	展望車 *tenbōsha*, observation car
				発展 *hatten*, expansion, development, prosperity
955 10 strokes	屏	展	展	展示会 *tenjikai*, exhibition

討	、	ニ	言	**TŌ**; *u(tsu)*, to subjugate, to attack
	言	言	討	検討 *kentō*, examination, investigation
				討論 *tōron*, debate
956 10 strokes	討			討議 *tōgi*, discussion

党	'	''	'''	**TŌ**, party, faction
	少	当	当	政党 *seitō*, political party
				党派 *tōha*, party, faction, clique
957 10 strokes	当	党	党	

糖	'	ソ	半	**TŌ** sugar
	米	米	料	砂糖 *satō*, sugar
				糖分 *tōbun*, sugar content
958 16 strokes	料	糖	糖	糖尿病 *tōnyōbyō*, diabetes

届	⁻	⁻	尸	*todo(ku)*, to reach; *todo(keru)*, to forward, to send, to report
	尸	屇	届	欠席届け *kessekitodoke*, notice of one's absence
				届け先 *todokesaki*, receiver's address
959 8 strokes	届	届		行き届く *yukitodoku*, to be attentive (to details), to be careful

難	一	サ	苫	NAN, disaster, difficulty; *kata(i),* difficult, impossible; *muzuka(shii),* difficult
	苣	革	莫	難破　　*nanpa,* shipwreck 非難　　*hinan,* (adverse) criticism, censure 困難　　*konnan,* difficulty, trouble, suffering
960 18 strokes	斳	斳	難	

乳	⼂	⼂	⼂	NYŪ; *chi-, chichi,* milk, breasts
	⼂	⼂	孚	牛乳　　*gyūnyū,* milk 乳製品　*nyūseihin,* dairy products 乳首　　*chikubi/chichikubi,* nipple
961 8 strokes	孚	乳		

認	⼀	⼀	言	NIN; *mito(meru),* to see, to recognize; to approve of, to judge, to regard (as)
	訂	訒	訒	承認　　*shōnin,* approval, consent, recognition 公認　　*kōnin,* official recognition 認識　　*ninshiki,* cognition
962 14 strokes	認	認	認	

納	⼂	⼂	⼂	NŌ, NA, TŌ; *osa(meru),* to put away, to pay, to supply, to dedicate, to obtain, to accept, to put back
	⼂	糸	紅	納入　　*nōnyū,* payment, delivery 納屋　　*naya,* barn 出納　　*suitō,* receipts and disbursements
963 10 strokes	紂	納	納	

脳	⼁	⼌	月	NŌ, brain(s)
	月	肜	肜	頭脳　　*zunō,* brain(s) 主脳　　*shunō,* head (of group), leader 脳障害　*nōshōgai,* brain injury
964 11 strokes	肜	脳	脳	

派	、	‥	氵	HA, group, party, school
	氵	氵	汈	左派　　*saha*, left wing, radical
965 **9 strokes**	沂	泝	派	派遣　　*haken*, dispatch

拝	一	十	扌	HAI; *oga(mu),* to worship, to pray to
	扌	扌	扌	拝見　　*haiken*, inspection, looking over 　　　　(polite speech)
966 **8 strokes**	扞	拝		拝啓　　*haikei,* Dear Sir, Dear Madam, 　　　　etc. (salutation in a letter) 参拝　　*sanpai,* worship

背	丿	⺻	土	HAI; *se,* the back, stature, behind; *sei,* stature, height; *somu(ku),* to disobey, rebel; *somu(keru),* to turn one's back
	北	北	背	背景　　　　*haikei*, background, setting; 　　　　　　affiliations
967 **9 strokes**	背	背	背	背中　　　　*senaka,* the back 背が高い　　*se/sei ga takai,* be tall

肺	丿	刀	月	HAI, lung(s)
	月	月	肝	肺臓　　*haizō,* the lungs 肺病　　*haibyō,* lung disease
968 **9 strokes**	肝	肺	肺	肺炎　　*haien,* pneumonia

俳	丿	亻	伃	HAI amusement; actor
	伃	伃	佴	俳句　　*haiku,* 17-syllable Japanese verse 俳味　　*haimi,* refined taste
969 **10 strokes**	俳	俳	俳	俳優　　*haiyū,* actor

班	一	丁	王	HAN, squad, group
	王	刵	玒	救護班 *kyūgohan,* relief squad 作業班 *sagyōhan,* work squad 班長 *hanchō,* squad leader
970 10 strokes	玥	玹	班	

晩	日	日′	日′′	BAN, evening, night
	日″	晘	晘	今晩 *konban,* this evening, tonight 晩御飯 *bangohan,* evening meal, dinner 晩年 *bannen,* late in life, evening
971 12 strokes	晘	晩	晩	years

否	一	フ	不	HI; *ina,* no
	不	否	否	否定 *hitei,* denial 拒否 *kyohi,* refusal, rejection 安否 *anpi,* safety, well-being
972 7 strokes	否			

批	一	十	才	HI criticise, comment on; strike
	才	扎	批	批難 *hinan,* (adverse) criticism 批評 *hihyō,* commentary 批判 *hihan,* comment, criticism
973 7 strokes	批			

秘	ノ	二	千	HI secret, mysterious; *hi(meru),* to conceal
	禾	禾	利	秘密 *himitsu,* a secret 神秘 *shinpi,* mystery 秘書 *hisho,* secretary
974 10 strokes	秘	秘	秘	

腹	月	肝	肝	FUKU; *hara*, abdomen, belly; heart, mind
	肑	胪	胪	満腹　　*manpuku*, full stomach 腹立ち　*haradachi*, anger 腹切り　*harakiri*, suicide by disembowelment
975 13 strokes	肪	腹	腹	

奮	大	六	奋	FUN; *furu(u)*, to rouse oneself
	奋	奋	奋	興奮　　*kōfun*, excitement 奮闘　　*funtō*, hard fighting, strenuous efforts 発奮　　*happun*, being inspired, rousing oneself
976 16 strokes	奞	奞	奮	

並	丶	ソ	丷	HEI; *nami(no)*, common, ordinary; *nara(beru)*, to place in order; *nara(bu)*, to form a line/be in line; *nara(bi ni)*, and
	丬	屮	竝	並列　　*heiretsu*, a row 月並み　*tsukinami (no)*, commonplace 並木　　*namiki*, row of trees
977 8 strokes	並	並		

陛	⁊	彐	阝	HEI stairs of a palace
	阝	阼	阼	陛下　　　　*heika*, His (Her) Majesty, Your Majesty 天皇陛下　*tennō-heika*, His Majesty the Emperor (of Japan) 皇后陛下　*kōgō-heika*, Her Majesty the Empress (of Japan)
978 10 strokes	陛	陛	陛	

閉	丨	冂	門	HEI; *to(jiru)*, to shut/close (v.t.); *shi(meru)*, to shut/close (v.t.); *shi(maru)*, to shut/close (v.i.)
	門	門	門	閉店　　*heiten*, closing a shop 閉口　　*heikō (suru)*, be dumbfounded 閉鎖　　*heisa*, closing, lockout
979 11 strokes	門	閉	閉	

| 片 980 4 strokes | ノ | ノ゛ | 丿 |
| | 片 | | |

HEN; *kata*, piece, scrap; incomplete; one side

断片　*danpen*, fragment, scrap
破片　*hahen*, broken piece, splinter (of glass, etc.)
片手　*katate*, one hand

補 981 12 strokes	⼀	ネ	衤
	衤	衤	補
	補	補	補

HO; *ogina(u)*, to supply, to compensate (for), to supplement

候補　*kōho*, candidacy, candidate
補助　*hojo*, assistance, supplement, subsidy
補給　*hokyū*, supply

暮 982 14 strokes	一	艹	艹
	苎	苩	莗
	莫	莫	暮

BO; *ku(re)*, nightfall, year-end; end; *ku(reru)*, to grow dark, end; *ku(rasu)*, to make a living

歳暮　　　*seibo*, end of year, end-of-year present
夕暮れ　　*yūgure*, evening
一人暮らし　*hitorigurashi*, single life, celibacy

宝 983 8 strokes	、	ハ	宀
	宀	宁	宇
	宝	宝	

HŌ; *takara*, treasure, riches

宝石　*hōseki*, precious stone, gem
国宝　*kokuhō*, a national treasure
宝箱　*takarabako*, treasure chest

訪 984 11 strokes	、	二	言
	言	言	言
	訂	訪	訪

HŌ; *otozu(reru)*, *tazu(neru)*, to visit, call on

訪問　*hōmon*, visit
来訪　*raihō*, visit
訪米　*hōbei*, visiting America

亡	`	亠	亡	**BŌ, MŌ** perish, flee; *na(ki)*, the late (of deceased persons); *na(kunaru)*, to pass away, die; *na(kusu)*, to lose (a loved one) 亡命 　　 *bōmei*, exile 死亡 　　 *shibō*, death 亡き森氏 *naki Mori-shi*, the late Mr Mori
985 3 strokes				
忘	`	亠	亡	**BŌ**; *wasu(reru)*, to forget, leave behind 忘年会 *bōnenkai*, year-end party 忘れ物 *wasuremono*, a forgotten item 物忘れ *monowasure*, forgetfulness
	亡	忘	忘	
986 7 strokes	忘			
棒	一	十	木	**BŌ**, stick, club 鉄棒 　　 *tetsubō/kanabō*, iron bar, crowbar 棒グラフ *bōgurafu*, bar graph 編み棒 *amibō*, knitting needle
	杧	杧	栏	
987 12 strokes	桙	棒	棒	
枚	一	十	才	**MAI** counter for thin or flat objects 枚数 　　 *maisū*, number of pages 数枚 　　 *sūmai*, a few (sheets of paper, shirts, etc.) 枚挙 　　 *maikyo*, enumerate, count
	才	朾	枚	
988 8 strokes	枚	枚		
幕	一	艹	苫	**MAKU**, curtain; act (of a play); **BAKU** 幕切れ *makugire*, fall of the curtain 幕内 　　 *makunouchi*, high-ranking sumo wrestlers 幕府 　　 *bakufu*, Shogunate
	草	莫	莫	
989 13 strokes	莫	幕	幕	

密	丶	宀	宀	MITSU dense, fine (of texture); secret
990 11 strokes	少	宓	宓	綿密　menmitsu, detailed, meticulous 密度　mitsudo, density 秘密　himitsu, a secret
	宓	密	密	

盟	冂	日	明	MEI to swear, to pledge
991 13 strokes	明	明	明	連盟　renmei, league 同盟　dōmei, alliance 加盟　kamei, joining (an alliance), 　　　participation
	明	盟	盟	

模	一	十	木	MO, BO mould; model after
992 14 strokes	朾	朾	槽	模範　　　mohan, model, paragon 縮尺模型　shukushakumokei, scale 　　　　　model 規模　　　kibo, scale, scope
	槽	模	模	

訳	丶	言	言	YAKU, translation; wake, reason, meaning, circumstances; yaku(suru), to translate
993 11 strokes	言	言	訂	翻訳　　hon'yaku, translation 通訳　　tsūyaku, interpretation, 　　　　interpreter 言い訳　iiwake, excuse, apology
	訂	訳	訳	

郵	一	二	三	YŪ posthouse, mail
994 11 strokes	垂	垂	垂	郵便　　　yūbin, mail, post 郵便局　　yūbinkyoku, post office 郵送　　　yūsō, transport, transportation
	垂	郵	郵	

優 995 17 strokes	イ	イ	俥	YŪ excellent; abundant; actor; *yasa(shii)*, gentle, graceful, kindly; *sugu(reru)*, to excel, be superior
	俥	傓	傓	優越 *yūetsu*, superiority, supremacy
	優	優	優	優先 *yūsen*, priority 俳優 *haiyū*, actor

| 幼 996 5 strokes | ㄑ | 幺 | 幺 | YŌ; *osana(i)*, young, childish, immature |
| | 幻 | 幼 | | 幼児 *yōji*, baby, infant
幼虫 *yōchū*, larva
幼稚園 *yōchien*, kindergarten |

欲 997 11 strokes	ノ	ハ	ク	YOKU, avarice, desire; *hos(suru)* to desire, to wish; *ho(shii)*, want, desire
	夕	谷	谷	欲ばり *yokubari*, greedy person, miser
	谷	欲	欲	欲望 *yokubō*, desire 食欲 *shokuyoku*, appetite

翌 998 11 strokes	ヿ	ヨ	ヨヿ	YOKU the next, the following (day, etc.)
	羽	羽	翌	翌日 *yokujitsu*, the next day 翌年 *yokunen*, the next year
	翌	翌	翌	翌々年 *yokuyokunen*, two years later

乱 999 7 strokes	ノ	二	千	RAN; *mida(reru)*, to fall into disorder/disarray, be corrupt; *mida(su)*, to throw into disorder/disarray, disturb, agitate
	千	舌	舌	混乱 *konran*, confusion
	乱			乱雑 *ranzatsu*, disorderly, confused 反乱 *hanran*, rebellion, revolt

卵

1,000
7 strokes

RAN; *tamago,* egg, spawn; budding, emergent

卵黄 *ran'ō,* egg yolk
卵白 *ranpaku,* albumen, egg white
生卵 *namatamago,* raw egg

覧

1,001
17 strokes

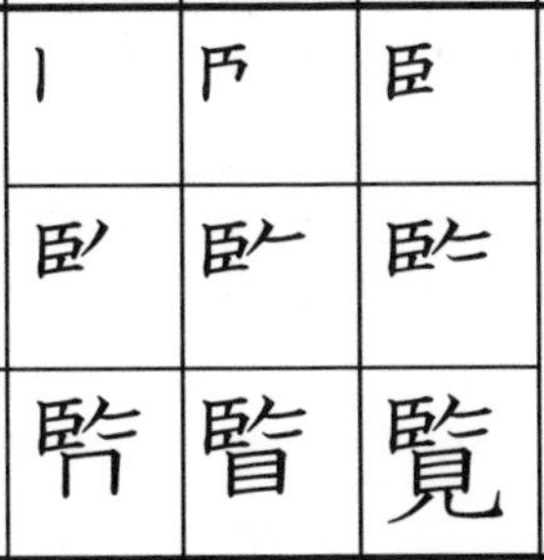

RAN see, look at

遊覧 *yūran,* sightseeing, excursion
展覧会 *tenrankai,* exhibition
一覧 *ichiran,* a look, check, summary

裏

1,002
13 strokes

RI; *ura,* reverse side, back, opposite, inner, lining

裏面 *rimen,* back, inside, 'behind the scenes'
裏付け *urazuke,* backing, support
裏打ち *urauchi,* backing, lining

律

1,003
9 strokes

RITSU law, degree

法律 *hōritsu,* law
規律 *kiritsu,* order, discipline, regulations
旋律 *senritsu,* melody

臨

1,004
18 strokes

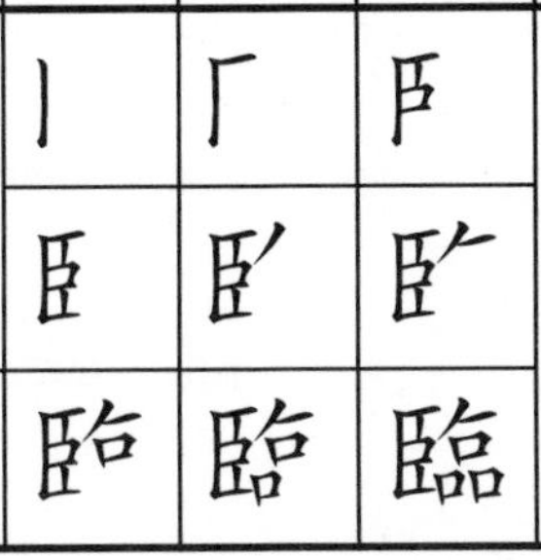

RIN; *nozo(mu),* to face, to meet, to be present at

臨終 *rinjū,* the hour of death
臨時 *rinji,* special, extra, temporary
臨席 *rinseki,* attendance

朗	丶	㇇	㇕	RŌ; *hogaraka,* clear, bright, cheerful, melodious
	自	良	郎	朗読　*rōdoku,* reading aloud, recitation 朗報　*rōhō,* glad tidings 明朗　*meirō,* bright, clear, open-hearted
1,005 10 strokes	朗	朗	朗	
論	言	言	訁	RON, argument, opinion, essay
	訡	訡	訡	結論　*ketsuron,* conclusion 討論　*tōron,* debate, discussion 理論　*riron,* theory
1,006 15 strokes	論	論	論	

202

The 1,945

GENERAL-USE CHARACTERS

1 STROKE

一	1 page 1	乙	OTSU, second in a series, grade B; chic, witty; strange

2 STROKES

丁	367 page 74	入	28 page 6
七	7 page 2	八	8 page 2
九	9 page 2	刀	198 page 40
了	RYŌ to come to an end, to understand	力	38 page 8
二	2 page 1	十	10 page 3
人	39 page 8	又	*mata,* and, again, also

3 STROKES

丈	JŌ, old unit of length (3.316 yd.), length; *take*, height, stature	千	12 page 3
三	3 page 1	及	KYŪ; *oyo(bi)*, and; *oyo(bu)*, to reach, to equal, to extend
上	23 page 5	口	34 page 7
下	24 page 5	土	19 page 4
丸	101 page 21	士	521 page 105
久	676 page 136	夕	54 page 11
亡	985 page 198	大	25 page 6
凡	BON generally, all; roughly, ordinary	女	41 page 9
刃	JIN; *ha*, edge (of a knife, sword, etc.), blade	子	40 page 9
勺	SHAKU, old unit of capacity (0.152 gi.), old unit of area (0.355 sq. ft.)	寸	920 page 185

小	27 page 6	干	840 page 169
山	58 page 12	弓	107 page 22
川	59 page 12	才	139 page 28
工	125 page 26	与	YO; *ata(eru)*, to give, to award, to supply, to cause (damage), to assign (a task)
己	866 page 174	万	227 page 46

4 STROKES

不	600 page 121	五	5 page 2
中	26 page 6	井	SEI, SHŌ; *i* (lit.), well (n.)
丹	TAN cinnabar, red; elixir of life	仁	917 page 184
乏	BŌ; *tobo(shii)*, scanty, short (of food, money)	仏	805 page 162
互	GO; *taga(i)*, each other, one another, mutual	介	KAI to come between, to aid; *kai(shite)*, through the good offices of

今	138 page 28	化	258 page 52
元	117 page 24	匹	HITSU an equal; HIKI suffix for counting small animals, rolls of cloth
内	207 page 42	区	282 page 57
公	126 page 26	升	SHŌ, old unit of capacity (3.81 pt.); *masu,* a unit of measure
六	6 page 2	午	122 page 25
冗	JŌ waste, uselessness, surplus	厄	YAKU, misfortune, disaster
凶	KYŌ evil, calamity	友	234 page 47
分	218 page 44	反	393 page 79
切	173 page 35	円	50 page 11
刈	*ka(ru),* to mow, to reap, to prune, to shear, to cut (hair)	天	67 page 14
匁	*monme,* old unit of weight (2.117 dr.)	太	181 page 37

夫	601 page 121	収	898 page 180
孔	KŌ hole; extremely; to pass	文	77 page 16
少	160 page 33	斗	TO old unit of capacity (19.04 qt.), one-*to* measure
尺	895 page 180	斤	KIN old unit of weight (1.323 lb.)
幻	GEN; *maboroshi*, vision, phantom	方	223 page 45
弔	CHŌ; *tomura(i)*, funeral, condolence; *tomura(u)*, to condole, to mourn	日	13 page 3
引	81 page 17	月	14 page 3
心	164 page 33	木	17 page 4
戸	120 page 25	止	143 page 29
手	35 page 8	比	792 page 159
支	717 page 144	毛	230 page 47

氏	522 page 105	牛	108 page 22
水	16 page 4	犬	73 page 15
火	15 page 4	王	47 page 10
屯	TON barracks	欠	496 page 100
父	216 page 44	予	425 page 86
片	980 page 197	双	SŌ, both, pair; to rival; *futa-*, a pair

5 STROKES

且	*ka(tsu)*, besides, moreover, at the same time	主	315 page 64
世	344 page 69	仕	301 page 61
丘	KYŪ; *oka*, hill	他	354 page 71
丙	HEI, third class, the third in a series, grade	付	602 page 121

仙	SEN hermit, wizard	包	611 page 123
代	358 page 72	北	224 page 45
令	633 page 127	半	214 page 43
以	443 page 89	占	SEN; *urana(i),* divination; *urana(u),* to divine; *shi(meru),* to occupy, to hold (a seat)
兄	114 page 23	去	276 page 56
冊	884 page 177	古	121 page 25
冬	199 page 40	句	683 page 137
出	29 page 6	召	SHŌ; *me(su),* honorific for "to wear," "to summon"
刊	666 page 134	可	655 page 132
功	502 page 101	史	523 page 105
加	453 page 91	右	22 page 5

司	524 page 105	巧	KŌ; *taku(mi)*, skill
囚	SHŪ to capture; captivity, slavery, prisoner	巨	KYO many, much, huge, gigantic
四	4 page 1	市	144 page 29
圧	641 page 129	布	799 page 160
外	96 page 20	平	411 page 83
央	254 page 51	幼	996 page 200
失	529 page 106	広	127 page 26
奴	DO manservant, fellow, guy	庁	950 page 191
写	313 page 63	必	597 page 120
尼	NI; *ama*, nun	打	355 page 72
左	21 page 5	払	FUTSU; *hara(u)*, to pay, to clear away, to lop off (branches), to dispose

斥	SEKI to drive away, to keep away, to refuse	犯	789 page 158
未	617 page 124	玄	GEN dark, black, abstruse; heaven; quiet
末	615 page 124	玉	48 page 10
本	76 page 16	甘	KAN; ama(i), sweet, indulgent, flattering, over-optimistic, easy to deal with
札	513 page 103	生	44 page 9
正	79 page 16	用	235 page 48
母	222 page 45	田	60 page 13
民	619 page 124	由	421 page 85
氷	401 page 81	甲	KŌ, grade A, the former; back (of the hand); shell (of a tortoise); KAN
永	644 page 129	申	338 page 68
汁	JŪ; shiru, soup, juice, gravy	白	53 page 11

皮	396 page 80	台	183 page 37
皿	300 page 61	旧	677 page 136
目	30 page 7	処	907 page 182
矛	MU; *hoko*, halberd	号	297 page 60
矢	145 page 30	弁	807 page 162
石	72 page 15	込	*ko(mu)*, to be crowded; *ko(meru)*, to load (a gun), to include; to concentrate (on)
示	723 page 145	辺	608 page 122
礼	436 page 88	凸	TOTSU convex
穴	860 page 173	凹	Ō concave
立	37 page 8		

6 STROKES

交	128 page 26	伝	580 page 117
仰	GYŌ, KŌ; *ao(gu)*, to look up at (to), to ask for; *ō(se)*, another's word or instructions	充	JŪ to fill; *a(teru)*, to allot, to appropriate
仲	571 page 115	兆	573 page 115
件	687 page 138	先	43 page 9
任	785 page 158	光	129 page 26
企	KI; *kuwada(te)*, attempt, plan, intrigue; *kuwada(teru)*, to attempt, to plan	全	347 page 70
伏	FUKU; *fu(seru)*, to turn over (v.t.), to cover, to conceal, to lay (an ambush)	両	434 page 87
伐	BATSU to attack, to fell; to boast	共	484 page 97
休	80 page 17	再	706 page 142
仮	656 page 132	刑	KEI, punishment, penalty

列	437 page 88	后	869 page 174
劣	RETSU; *oto(ru)*, to be inferior	吏	RI an official
匠	SHŌ carpenter, artisan	吐	TO; *ha(ku)*, to vomit, to spew, to emit, to confess, to express
印	448 page 90	向	294 page 59
危	844 page 169	吸	849 page 170
叫	KYŌ; *sake(bu)*, to exclaim, to shout, to cry for	回	92 page 19
各	462 page 93	因	643 page 129
合	134 page 27	団	772 page 155
吉	KICHI, good luck, good omen; KITSU	在	711 page 143
同	204 page 41	地	184 page 37
名	55 page 12	壮	SŌ powerful, influential, brave

多	180 page 37	寺	149 page 30
好	503 page 101	州	320 page 65
如	JO, NYO as if, looking like; to equal, to reach	巡	JUN; *megu(ru),* to go one's rounds, to patrol, to travel about
妃	HI empress, married princess	帆	HAN; *ho,* sail, canvas
妄	MŌ, BŌ arbitrary, reckless	年	20 page 5
字	78 page 16	式	311 page 63
存	938 page 188	忙	BŌ; *isoga(shii),* busy
宅	940 page 189	成	545 page 110
宇	829 page 166	扱	*atsuka(u),* to deal with, to receive, to manage, to deal in, to work (manipulate)
守	316 page 64	旨	SHI; *mune,* purport, effect, principle, command
安	242 page 49	早	56 page 12

旬	JUN period of ten days	気	68 page 14
曲	279 page 56	汗	KAN; *ase*, sweat
会	93 page 19	汚	O; *kega(su)*, *yogo(su)*, to soil; *kega(reru)*, *yogo(reru)*, to get dirty; *kitana(i)*, dirty
有	423 page 85	江	KŌ; *e*, inlet, bay
朱	SHU, cinnabar, vermilion	池	185 page 38
朴	BOKU simple, plain	灯	583 page 117
机	845 page 170	灰	874 page 167
朽	KYŪ; *ku(chiru)*, to rot, to perish, to remain in obscurity	争	558 page 112
次	308 page 62	当	200 page 41
死	302 page 61	百	11 page 3
毎	225 page 46	尽	JIN; *tsu(kusu)*, to render service to; to exhaust, to use up; *tsu(kiru)*, to be used up

竹	71 page 15	自	150 page 31
米	220 page 45	至	886 page 178
糸	75 page 16	舌	755 page 152
缶	KAN a can	舟	SHŪ; *fune*, boat, ship
羊	426 page 86	色	162 page 33
羽	82 page 17	芋	*imo*, taro, Irish potato, sweet potato, etc.
老	638 page 128	芝	*shiba*, turf, grass
考	130 page 27	虫	74 page 15
耳	32 page 7	血	288 page 58
肉	209 page 42	行	131 page 27
肌	*hada*, skin	衣	444 page 89

西	169 page 34	迅	JIN swift, quick, fast
弐	NI, two (used in legal documents)		

7 STROKES

乱	999 page 200	位	445 page 90
亜	A, sub~, near~ (used as prefix); Asia	低	575 page 116
伯	HAKU a count, a chief, elder brother	住	325 page 66
伴	HAN, BAN; *tomo(nau)*, to accompany, to take with	佐	SA to help
伸	SHIN; *no(biru)*, to extend, to grow; to collapse (v.i.); *no(basu)*, to lengthen, to stretch	何	86 page 18
伺	SHI; *ukaga(u)*, to visit, to ask, to hear	作	141 page 29
似	724 page 145	来	237 page 48
但	*tada(shi)*, but, provided (that)	克	KOKU to be able to do, to conquer

児	526 page 106	却	KYAKU to reject, to withdraw
兵	606 page 122	卵	1,000 page 201
冷	634 page 127	即	SOKU at once; namely, nothing but; accession
初	535 page 108	君	285 page 58
判	790 page 159	吟	GIN; *gin(jiru)*, to recite (a poem)
別	607 page 122	否	972 page 195
利	626 page 126	含	GAN; *fuku(mu)*, to contain, to include, to keep in one's mouth, to harbor, to cherish
助	330 page 67	呈	TEI; *tei(suru)*, to offer (congratulations), to present (a tragic sight)
努	582 page 117	呉	GO ancient province of China
労	639 page 128	吹	SUI; *fu(ku)*; to blow, to breathe out, to play (a wind instrument), to talk big
励	REI; *hage(mu)*, to strive, to make an effort	告	507 page 102

困	878 page 176	妥	DA peaceful, calm
囲	446 page 90	妨	BŌ; *samata(geru)*, to obstruct, to disturb, to prevent
図	167 page 34	孝	870 page 175
坂	394 page 79	完	464 page 93
均	681 page 137	対	356 page 72
坊	BŌ, sonny, boy, priest, priest's lodge	尾	BI suffix for counting fish; *o*, tail, ridge, trail (of a shooting star)
坑	KŌ hole, mine pit, cave	尿	NYŌ, urine
壱	ICHI, one (used in legal documents)	局	280 page 57
寿	JU; *kotobuki*, congratulations; longevity	岐	KI fork of a road
妊	NIN to conceive, to become pregnant	希	470 page 95
妙	MYŌ, strange, mysterious; clever, admirable	床	SHŌ; *toko*, bed, alcove; *yuka*, floor

序	734 page 147	我	833 page 167
廷	TEI public office	戒	KAI; *imashi(meru)*, to admonish, to warn; *imashi(me)*, admonition, warning, lesson
弟	194 page 39	戻	REI; *modo(ru)*, to return, go back; *modo(su)*, to give back, restore
形	115 page 24	扶	FU to help
役	419 page 84	批	973 page 195
忌	KI; *i(mu)*, to abhor, to detest, to avoid, to taboo; *i(mawashii)*, odious, offensive	技	673 page 135
忍	NIN; *shino(bu)*, to endure (pain); *shino(baseru)*, to conceal	抄	SHŌ to excerpt; extract, excerpt
志	718 page 144	把	HA bundle, sheaf, to grasp
忘	986 page 198	抑	YOKU to restrain, to hold down, to stop; *osa(eru)*, to hold down, to restrain
快	661 page 133	投	378 page 76
応	651 page 131	抗	KŌ to resist, to confront

折	551 page 111	求	478 page 96
抜	BATSU; *nu(ku)*, to pull out, to outstrip, to omit, to remove, to capture	決	289 page 58
択	TAKU to choose, to select, to sort out	汽	104 page 21
改	458 page 92	沈	CHIN; *shizu(mu)*, to sink, to feel depressed
攻	KŌ; *se(meru)*, to attack, to assault; *se(me)*, attack	没	BOTSU, rejection (of a manuscript); *bos(suru)*, to sink, to set (sun), to die
更	KŌ to renew, reform; *sara (ni)*, again, still more; *fu(keru)*, to grow late	沖	CHŪ; *oki*, offing, open sea
杉	*sugi*, cryptomeria, a Japanese cedar	沢	TAKU; *sawa*, marsh, swamp
材	511 page 103	災	707 page 142
村	62 page 13	状	739 page 148
束	561 page 113	狂	KYŌ ~addict; *kuru(i)*, disorder, warp; *kuru(u)*, to go mad, to get out of order
条	738 page 148	男	42 page 9

町	61 page 13	花	70 page 15
社	153 page 31	芳	HŌ; *kanba(shii)*, fragrant
秀	SHŪ excellent; to surpass, to excel; *hii(deru)*, to surpass, to excel	芸	495 page 100
私	887 page 178	見	31 page 7
究	271 page 55	角	97 page 20
系	855 page 172	言	118 page 24
声	170 page 35	谷	135 page 28
肖	SHŌ to resemble, to pattern after, to copy after	豆	379 page 76
肝	KAN vital point; *kimo*, the liver; pluck, mind	貝	49 page 10
臣	543 page 109	売	211 page 43
良	628 page 126	赤	51 page 11

走	179 page 36	邦	HŌ country, land, Japan
足	36 page 8	医	244 page 49
身	339 page 68	里	238 page 48
車	63 page 13	防	812 page 163
辛	SHIN bitter, hard, severe; *kara(i)*, pungent, spicy, hot, salty	余	820 page 165
迎	GEI; *muka(eru)*, to meet, to welcome, to invite; *muka(e)*, meeting, greeter	体	182 page 37
近	113 page 23	麦	213 page 43
返	412 page 83		

8 STROKES

| 乳 | 961
page 193 | 事 | 309
page 62 |
| 延 | 831
page 167 | 享 | KYŌ to receive, to enjoy |

京	110 page 23	具	284 page 57
佳	KA, good, beautiful	典	579 page 116
使	303 page 61	到	TŌ to reach, to go or come to
例	635 page 128	制	744 page 149
侍	JI samurai; *ji(suru)*, to attend on	刷	514 page 103
供	850 page 171	券	688 page 138
依	I, E to depend on	刺	SHI name card; thorn, splinter; *sa(su)*, to sting, to pierce, to stab
侮	BU; *anado(ru)*, to look down upon, to hold in contempt	刻	875 page 176
併	HEI; *awa(seru)*, to amalgamate, to combine	効	697 page 140
価	657 page 132	劾	GAI to investigate thoroughly
免	MEN exempt; *manuka(reru)*, to avoid, to be exempt	卒	564 page 113

卓	TAKU to excel, to surpass; table, desk	固	501 page 101
協	485 page 98	国	136 page 28
参	517 page 104	坪	*tsubo*, old unit of area (3.952 sq. yd.)
叔	SHUKU younger brother of one's parent	垂	918 page 184
取	317 page 64	夜	232 page 47
受	319 page 64	奇	KI unusual, rare, surpassing, strange, mysterious
周	532 page 107	奉	HŌ; *hō(jiru)*, to serve, to obey; *tatematsu(ru)*, to dedicate, to offer
味	415 page 84	奔	HON to run, to rush
呼	867 page 174	妹	226 page 46
命	416 page 84	妻	708 page 142
和	440 page 89	姉	146 page 30

始	304 page 61	宝	983 page 197
姓	SEI, surname, family name; SHŌ	尚	SHŌ; *nao*, furthermore, yet
委	245 page 50	居	678 page 136
季	471 page 95	届	959 page 192
学	45 page 10	屈	KUTSU; *kus(suru)*, to yield to, to be daunted, to bend
宗	899 page 180	岩	102 page 21
官	465 page 94	岬	*misaki*, cape, promontory
宙	947 page 190	岸	267 page 54
定	371 page 75	岳	GAKU; *take* (lit.), peak, mountain
宜	GI all right, good, just, proper, natural	幸	295 page 60
実	312 page 63	底	576 page 116

店	195 page 40	怪	KAI, mystery, apparition; *aya(shii)*, suspicious; *aya(shimu)*, to doubt, to suspect
府	603 page 121	房	BŌ chamber, house; *fusa*, cluster, tuft, fringe
弦	GEN, *tsuru*, string (for musical instruments), bowstring, chord	所	328 page 66
彼	HI; *kare*, he; *ka(no)*, that	承	736 page 148
往	652 page 131	披	HI open
征	SEI to subjugate	抱	HŌ; *da(ku)*, to hug; *ida(ku)*, to hold (a belief); *kaka(eru)*, to employ, hold
径	492 page 99	抵	TEI to touch, to go against
忠	948 page 190	押	Ō; *o(su)*, to push, to press; *o(shi)*, influence, audacity; *osa(eru)*, to repress
念	590 page 119	抽	CHŪ to draw out, to pull
怖	FU to fear, to be afraid; *kowa(i)*, frightening, afraid	抹	MATSU to erase, to rub
性	745 page 150	拐	KAI to falsify, kidnap

拍	HAKU, HYŌ to clap; musical time, beat	昆	KON elder brother, posterity; sometimes used for its sound value
拒	KYO; *koba(mu),* to refuse, to decline, to resist, to deny	昇	SHŌ to rise, to go up; *nobo(ru),* to ascend, to rise
拓	TAKU clearing, reclamation; production of copies by rubbing	明	228 page 46
拘	KŌ to catch, to affect, to adhere to	易	647 page 130
拙	SETSU, clumsy, unskillful, inexpert	昔	346 page 70
招	735 page 148	服	408 page 82
拝	966 page 194	杯	HAI, suffix for counting cupfuls, glassfuls, etc.; *sakazuki,* sake cup
担	941 page 189	東	201 page 41
拠	KYO, KO to depend on, to be based on, to hold; foundation, ground, authority	松	536 page 108
拡	835 page 168	板	395 page 80
放	414 page 83	析	SEKI to divide, to tear, to break

林	64 page 13	河	658 page 132
枚	988 page 198	沸	FUTSU; *wa(ku)*, to boil, to seethe, to ferment (v.i.)
枠	*waku*, frame, spindle, limit	油	422 page 85
枝	719 page 144	治	527 page 106
枢	SŪ pivot, vital point, center	沼	SHŌ; *numa*, swamp, marsh, bog
果	454 page 91	沿	832 page 167
欧	Ō Europe	況	KYŌ state of things; still more
殴	Ō to beat, to strike; *nagu(ru)*, to strike, to beat	泊	HAKU; *to(maru)*, to stay overnight, to stop over; *to(meru)*, to lodge (v.t.)
歩	221 page 45	泌	HITSU, HI to ooze out
武	802 page 161	法	612 page 123
毒	588 page 118	泡	HŌ; *awa*, foam, bubbles

波	387 page 78	画	91 page 19
泣	479 page 96	的	578 page 116
泥	DEI; *doro,* mud	盲	MŌ; *mekura,* blindness, blind person; ignorance
注	365 page 74	知	186 page 38
泳	252 page 51	祈	KI; *ino(ru),* to pray, to invoke, to wish; *ino(ri),* prayer, wish
炊	SUI; *ta(ku),* to cook, to boil	祉	SHI blessing, happiness
炎	EN to burn; *hono-o,* flame, blaze	空	66 page 14
炉	RO, fireplace, hearth, smelting furnace	突	TOTSU sudden; *tsu(ku),* to pierce, to thrust, to strike, to attack
版	791 page 159	並	977 page 196
牧	614 page 123	者	314 page 63
物	410 page 83	肢	SHI limbs

肥	793 page 159	茂	MO; *shige(ru)*, to grow thick, to grow rank
肩	KEN; *kata*, shoulder	茎	KEI; *kuki*, stalk, stem
肪	BŌ fat, grease, tallow	表	402 page 81
肯	KŌ to consent, to agree; daringly, boldly	迫	HAKU; *sema(ru)*, to press, to urge, to draw near
育	247 page 50	迭	TETSU to change places with; by turns
舎	727 page 146	述	731 page 147
苗	BYŌ; *nae*, seedling, sapling	邸	TEI mansion, residence
若	896 page 180	邪	JA, wrong, injustice, evil
苦	283 page 57	直	192 page 39
英	449 page 90	金	18 page 4
芽	457 page 92	長	189 page 38

門	231 page 47	青	52 page 11
阻	SO steep; to separate, to obstruct; *haba(mu)*, to obstruct, to hinder	非	794 page 159
附	FU to stick to, to adhere to	斉	SEI equal, similar
雨	69 page 14		

9 STROKES

乗	336 page 68	促	SOKU; *unaga(su)*, to urge
亭	TEI, restaurant, pavilion	俊	SHUN to be excellent, to surpass, to be high
侯	KŌ feudal lord; marquis	俗	ZOKU customs, manners; vulgar
侵	SHIN; *oka(su)*, to invade, to violate	保	808 page 162
係	286 page 58	信	544 page 109
便	610 page 123	冒	BŌ; *oka(su)*, to brave, to defy, to attack, to damage, to profane

冠	KAN; *kanmuri,* crown	咲	*sa(ku),* to bloom, to blossom
則	764 page 153	哀	AI; *awa(re),* pathos, misery, pity; *awa(remu),* to feel pity for
削	SAKU; *kezu(ru),* to shave (wood), to sharpen, to delete, to curtail	品	405 page 82
前	177 page 36	単	569 page 114
勅	CHOKU Imperial edict	型	493 page 99
勇	622 page 125	垣	*kaki,* fence, hedge
卑	HI; *iya(shii),* base, vulgar, low-lived; *iya(shimeru),* to despise	城	914 page 183
南	208 page 42	奏	930 page 187
巻	841 page 169	契	KEI; *chigi(ru),* to pledge, to promise
厘	RIN, old unit of money (0.001 yen); old unit of length (about 0.0119 in.)	姻	IN to get married
厚	698 page 140	姿	888 page 178

威	I majestic, solemn; to threaten	帥	SUI to command an army
孤	KO orphan; solitary, alone	幽	YŪ faint, profound, quiet
客	270 page 55	度	377 page 76
宣	924 page 185	建	498 page 100
室	152 page 31	弧	KO, arc
封	FŪ, seal; fū(jiru), to prevent, to enclose, to blockade, to seal; HŌ fief	待	357 page 72
専	925 page 186	律	1,003 page 201
屋	256 page 52	後	123 page 25
峠	tōge, mountain pass, ridge, peak, crisis	怒	DO; ika(ru) (lit.), to get angry; oko(ru), to get angry
峡	KYŌ gorge, ravine	思	147 page 30
帝	TEI emperor, sovereign, Mikado	怠	TAI; okota(ru), to neglect, nama(keru), to be lazy

急	272 page 55	政	746 page 150
恒	KŌ always, eternal	故	694 page 139
恨	KON; *ura(mi)*, spite, grudge; *ura(mu)*, to bear a grudge; *ura(meshii)*, hateful	叙	JO, preface; *jo(suru)*, to describe, to confer (a rank) upon
悔	KAI; *ku(iru)*, to regret; *kuya(mi)*, condolence; *kuya(mu)*, to mourn, to repent	施	SHI, SE; *hodoko(su)*, to give in charity; to perform, to administer
括	KATSU to fasten, to bind, to tie up	星	171 page 35
拷	GŌ to beat, to strike	映	830 page 167
拾	321 page 65	春	158 page 32
持	310 page 63	昨	512 page 103
指	305 page 62	昭	331 page 67
挑	CHŌ; *ido(mu)*, to challenge, to strive	是	ZE right, just
挟	KYŌ; *hasa(mu)*, to put (hold) between; *hasa(maru)*, to be sandwiched between	昼	188 page 38

県	291 page 59	栄	450 page 91
枯	KO; *ka(reru)*, to wither, to mature (v.i.); *ka(rasu)*, to blight	段	944 page 189
架	KA; *ka(suru)*, to build, to span (a river with a bridge, etc.)	泉	926 page 186
柄	HEI; *e*, handle; *gara*, pattern, design, build, character, nature	洋	427 page 86
某	BŌ, a certain person, Mr. So-and-so; one, a, a certain~ (used as prefix)	洗	927 page 186
染	928 page 186	洞	DŌ; *hora*, cave, excavation
柔	JŪ, NYŪ; *yawa(rakai)*, soft, tender, mild, mellow	津	*tsu*, harbor, ferry
査	705 page 142	洪	KŌ flood, vast
柱	366 page 74	活	99 page 20
柳	RYŪ, *yanagi*, willow tree	派	965 page 194
相	348 page 70	海	94 page 19

浄	JŌ pure, innocent	畑	391 page 79
浅	554 page 111	疫	EKI epidemic
炭	361 page 73	発	392 page 79
為	I to do, to make, to think; benefit, reason, cause, purpose	皆	KAI; *mina, minna*, all, everything, everyone
牲	SEI sacrifice, victim	皇	871 page 175
狩	SHU; *ka(ri)*, hunting, gathering, (maple- etc.) viewing; *ka(ru)*, to hunt	盆	BON, tray; the Bon Festival (Buddhist celebration held in Japan in mid-July)
挟	KYŌ; *sema(i)*, narrow, small; *seba(meru)* (v.t.), to narrow, to reduce	盾	JUN; *tate*, shield
独	784 page 157	省	546 page 110
珍	CHIN; *mezura(shii)*, rare, novel, unusual	看	842 page 169
甚	JIN; *hanaha(da)*, extremely, immensely; *hanaha(dashii)*, extreme, enormous	砂	879 page 176
界	260 page 53	研	290 page 59

砕	SAI; *kuda(ku)* (v.t.), to smash, simplify; *kuda(keru)* (v.i.), to be broken, softened	紅	872 page 175
祖	758 page 152	級	273 page 55
祝	533 page 107	美	398 page 80
神	340 page 69	耐	TAI; *ta(eru)*, to endure, to bear, to stand (v.t.)
秋	156 page 32	肺	968 page 194
科	87 page 18	胃	447 page 90
秒	403 page 81	背	967 page 194
窃	SETSU to steal, to rob	胎	TAI to conceive; womb, fetus
糾	KYŪ to investigate, to examine, to twist, to twine around	胞	HŌ placenta
紀	472 page 95	胆	TAN liver; spirit, courage
約	621 page 125	臭	SHŪ smell, stink; *kusa(i)*, ill-smelling, suspicious; *~kusa(i)*, smelling of ~

茶	187 page 38	赴	FU to go; *omomu(ku)*, to proceed (towards)
草	57 page 12	軌	KI space between two wheels, print of a wheel
荒	KŌ; *ara(i)*, violent, wild; *a(reru)*, to be rough, dilapidated; *a(rasu)*, to lay waste	軍	490 page 99
荘	SŌ majestic, solemn; villa	迷	817 page 164
虐	GYAKU to treat harshly, to spoil; *shiita(geru)*, to oppress, to persecute	追	370 page 75
要	623 page 125	退	769 page 154
訂	TEI to correct, to establish	送	349 page 70
計	116 page 24	逃	TŌ; *ni(geru)*, to flee; *noga(reru)*, to escape, avoid; *ni(gasu)*, to set free
変	609 page 122	逆	675 page 136
貞	TEI right, just, chaste	郊	KŌ suburbs, the country
負	406 page 82	郎	RŌ man, male — used as suffix in men's given names

重	326 page 66	食	163 page 33
限	691 page 139	首	155 page 32
面	417 page 84	香	KŌ, incense; *ka* (lit.), perfume, fragrance; *kao(ri)*, fragrance; *kao(ru)* to be fragrant
革	836 page 168	点	196 page 40
音	33 page 7	衷	CHŪ heart, sincerity
風	217 page 44	卸	*oro(su),* to sell wholesale; *oroshi*, wholesale
飛	595 page 120		

10 STROKES

修	730 page 147	倉	559 page 112
俳	969 page 194	俸	HŌ salary
俵	796 page 160	値	946 page 190

個	695 page 140	剖	BŌ to divide, to distinguish
倍	389 page 78	剛	GŌ inflexible, stubborn, stiff, hard
倒	TŌ; *tao(reru)*, to fall, to break down, to go to ruin; *tao(su)*, to fell, to overthrow	剤	ZAI medicine, drug
候	504 page 101	剣	KEN, *tsurugi*, sword
借	530 page 107	勉	413 page 83
倣	HŌ; *nara(u)*, to model after, to imitate	匿	TOKU to give refuge to, to conceal, to hide, to keep secret
倫	RIN principles, duty, rules	原	119 page 24
倹	KEN frugal, modest, humble	員	248 page 50
兼	KEN, and, in addition, concurrently; *ka(neru)*, to combine, be unable to (suffix)	哲	TETSU wise, sagacious
准	JUN rule; to imitate, to approve	唆	SA; *sosonoka(su)*, to tempt, to instigate
凍	TŌ; *kō(ru)*, to freeze (v.i.); *kogo(eru)*, to be benumbed with cold	唇	SHIN; *kuchibiru*, lips

唐	TŌ, Tang, (an ancient Chinese dynasty); *kara*, China (old name used in Japan)	宴	EN, feast, banquet
埋	MAI; *u(meru)*, to bury, to fill up; *u(maru)*, to be buried, to be filled up	宵	SHŌ; *yoi*, evening
夏	88 page 18	家	89 page 18
姫	*hime*, princess, young lady of birth; also used as prefix for "small" or "dainty"	容	822 page 165
娘	*musume*, girl, daughter	射	893 page 179
娯	GO to enjoy, to take pleasure in	将	911 page 183
娠	SHIN to conceive, to become pregnant	展	955 page 192
孫	565 page 114	峰	HŌ; *mine*, peak, back (of a sword)
宮	274 page 55	島	380 page 77
宰	SAI to administer, to manage, to take charge of; chief, head	差	508 page 102
害	460 page 93	師	720 page 145

席	549 page 110	恩	654 page 131
帯	566 page 114	恭	KYŌ respectful, reverent; *uyauya(shii)*, reverent
座	880 page 177	息	351 page 71
庫	292 page 59	悦	ETSU to be glad, to rejoice
庭	372 page 75	悟	GO; *sato(ru)*, to be spiritually awakened, to perceive, to comprehend
弱	154 page 31	恵	KEI, E; *megu(mi)*, grace, blessing; *megu(mu)*, to give in charity
徐	JO slowly, gently	悩	NŌ; *naya(mi)*, affliction, trouble, pain; *naya(mu)*, to be troubled with
徒	581 page 117	恋	REN; *koi*, love; *koi(shii)*, dear, beloved
従	902 page 181	扇	SEN; *ōgi*, folding fan
恐	KYŌ; *oso(re)*, fear, anxiety; *oso(reru)*, to fear; *oso(roshii)*, fearful, fierce, awful	振	SHIN; *fu(ru)*, to wave, shake, wield, discard; *fu(ruu)*, to brandish, master, prosper
恥	CHI; *haji*, shame, disgrace; *ha(jiru)*, to be ashamed of; *ha(zukashii)*, embarrassing	挿	SŌ; *sa(su)*, to insert, to put into

捕	HO; *tora(eru), to(ru)*, to catch, to seize; *tsuk(maeru)*, to catch, to arrest	栓	SEN, bolt, plug, faucet
捜	SŌ; *saga(su)*, to hunt for, to search for	校	46 page 10
挙	482 page 97	株	839 page 168
敏	BIN clever, quick	核	KAKU, nucleus, kernel, core, stone (of a fruit)
料	629 page 126	根	298 page 60
旅	433 page 87	格	663 page 133
既	KI; *sude(ni)*, already, previously	桟	SAN, crosspiece, jetty
時	151 page 31	桃	TŌ; *momo*, peach
書	159 page 32	梅	592 page 119
朕	CHIN, We, Our (formerly used by the Emperor of Japan in Imperial rescripts)	桜	653 page 131
朗	1,005 page 202	案	442 page 89

桑	SŌ; *kuwa*, mulberry	浮	FU; *u(ku)*, to float, to be merry, to be left over; *u(kabu)*, to float, to come to mind
栽	SAI to plant	浴	625 page 126
帰	106 page 22	浸	SHIN; *hita(su)*, to soak, to wet; *hita(ru)*, to be immersed, to indulge
殉	JUN; *jun(jiru)*, to follow even to death, to sacrifice oneself	消	332 page 67
殊	SHU especially; to be different; *koto(ni)*, especially	涙	RUI; *namida*, tear (from the eye)
残	520 page 105	浜	HIN; *hama*, beach, shore
殺	515 page 104	烈	RETSU valiant, violent, brave, strong
泰	TAI peaceful, great, extravagant, extremely	特	586 page 118
流	432 page 87	珠	SHU pearl
浦	HO; *ura*, inlet, beach	班	970 page 195
浪	RŌ billow; to wander about	畔	HAN vicinity; footpath between rice fields, edge

留	824 page 165	破	788 page 158
畜	CHIKU to raise cattle, to cultivate	秘	974 page 195
畝	*se*, old unit for measuring land (3.92 sq. rd.); *une*, furrow, groove	祥	SHŌ good fortune, omen
疲	HI; *tsuka(re)*, fatigue; *tsuka(reru)*, to get tired, to become fatigued	租	SO tribute
疾	SHITSU sickness; to fall ill; quick, swift	秩	CHITSU order, rank
病	404 page 81	称	SHŌ to praise; *shō(suru)*, to call, to name, to pretend
症	SHŌ nature of a disease	笑	537 page 108
益	648 page 130	粉	605 page 122
真	341 page 69	粋	SUI, essence, elegance; delicate, smart, stylish
眠	MIN; *nemu(ri)*, sleep; *nemu(ru)*, to sleep; *nemu(i)*, sleepy	紋	MON, family insignia, crest, figures (in cloth)
砲	HŌ, gun, cannon	納	963 page 193

純	906 page 182	能	787 page 158
紙	148 page 30	脂	SHI; *abura*, fat, grease, tallow
紛	FUN; *magi(reru)*, to be obscure, to be diverted, to be confused	脅	KYŌ; *obiya(kasu)*, *odo(su)*, *odo(kasu)*, to threaten, to menace, to intimidate
素	759 page 152	脈	618 page 124
紡	BŌ; *tsumu(gu)*, to spin (thread)	致	CHI, to do, to bring about; taste, appearance; *ita(su)*, to do (humbly)
索	SAKU cable, rope; to seek for, to search for	航	505 page 102
翁	Ō, old man, honorific title for an old man	般	HAN generally; to carry, to turn; to enjoy
耕	699 page 140	荷	259 page 52
耗	MŌ, KŌ to decrease, to spend	華	KA flower, showiness, China; *hana(yaka)*, showy, splendid
胴	DŌ, trunk (of the body), body armor	蚊	*ka*, mosquito
胸	851 page 171	蚕	885 page 178

衰	SUI; *otoro(eru)*, to become weak, to decline	透	TŌ penetrate; *su(ku)*, to be transparent, leave gaps; *su(kasu)*, to make transparent, thin out
被	HI; *kōmu(ru)*, to suffer (damage, etc.), to receive (a favor, etc.)	逐	CHIKU to chase, to pursue
討	956 page 192	途	TO way, road
訓	489 page 98	通	193 page 39
託	TAKU to entrust to a person, to make a pretext of	逝	SEI; *yu(ku)*, to pass away, to die
記	105 page 22	速	352 page 71
財	712 page 143	造	761 page 153
貢	KŌ tribute, contribution; *mitsu(gu)*, to give financial support	連	637 page 128
起	268 page 54	逓	TEI alternately, by turns; to convey
軒	KEN suffix for counting houses; *noki*, eaves	郡	491 page 99
辱	JOKU to put to shame, to disgrace; *hazukashi(meru)*, to humiliate, to violate	酌	SHAKU; *ku(mu)*, to ladle, to drink together, to consider

配	388 page 78	隻	SEKI suffix for counting ships
酒	318 page 64	飢	KI; *u(e)*, hunger, starvation; *u(eru)*, to be hungry, to starve
針	916 page 184	馬	210 page 43
降	873 page 175	骨	877 page 176
陛	978 page 196	高	132 page 27
院	249 page 50	鬼	KI; *oni*, ogre, fiend, demon
陣	JIN, camp, position (military), battle array	党	957 page 192
除	910 page 183	竜	RYŪ; *tatsu*, dragon
陥	KAN; *ochii(ru)*, to fall into, to yield, to cave in, to fall (to surrender to a siege)		

11 STROKES

| 乾 | KAN to dry, to be thirsty; *kawa(ku)* (v.i.), *kawa(kasu)* (v.t.), to dry | 偵 | TEI spy |

偏	HEN, left-hand radical; one-sided, biased; *kata(yoru)*, to be biased	喝	KATSU scold, get hoarse
停	577 page 116	唯	YUI merely, only, alone
健	499 page 100	唱	538 page 108
側	562 page 113	商	333 page 67
偶	GŪ even number; by chance, accidentally	問	418 page 84
偽	GI; *itsuwa(ru)* to tell a lie, to pretend, to deceive	啓	KEI to enlighten, to open
剰	JŌ surplus; moreover	域	828 page 166
副	604 page 121	執	SHITSU, SHŪ; *to(ru)*, to do (business, etc.), to manage, to take, to grasp
動	384 page 77	培	BAI; *tsuchika(u)*, to cultivate, to foster
勘	KAN, perception, intuition	基	670 page 135
務	815 page 164	堀	*hori*, ditch, moat

堂	584 page 117	崩	HŌ; *kuzu(reru)*, to collapse; *kuzu(su)*, to destroy, reduce, write in simplified form
婆	BA old woman, old mother	巣	560 page 113
婚	KON marriage	帳	368 page 74
婦	800 page 161	常	740 page 149
宿	327 page 66	庶	SHO various, all, many
寂	JAKU, SEKI; *sabi(shii)*, lonesome, lonely, solitary; *sabi(reru)*, to mature, to mellow	康	506 page 102
寄	671 page 135	庸	YŌ moderate, ordinary, mediocre
密	990 page 199	張	775 page 156
尉	I military rank	強	111 page 23
崇	SŪ lofty, noble; to respect, to worship	彩	SAI coloration; to color; *irodo(ru)*, to paint, to color
崎	*saki*, cape, promontory	彫	CHŌ; *ho(ru)*, to carve, to engrave

得	587 page 118	授	729 page 146
悠	YŪ distance, leisure	排	HAI to reject; to display, to push open
患	KAN sickness, anxiety, trouble	掘	KUTSU; *ho(ru)*, to dig, to dig up
悼	TŌ; *ita(mu)*, to mourn over, to lament, to feel pity for	掛	*ka(keru)*, to hang (v.t.), to sit on (a chair, etc.), to cover with
情	741 page 149	採	709 page 142
惜	SEKI; *o(shii)*, regrettable; precious; wasteful; *o(shimu)*, to begrudge, to regret	探	942 page 189
悪	241 page 49	接	753 page 151
惨	SAN cruel, horrible, appalling; *miji(me)*, wretched, cruel	控	KŌ; *hika(eru)*, to write down; to refrain from, to be moderate in, to wait
捨	894 page 179	推	919 page 184
据	*su(eru)*, to lay (a foundation), to install (a person); *su(waru)*, to become set/fixed	措	SO to put aside, to except, to dispose of; to place
掃	SŌ; *ha(ku)*, to sweep	描	BYŌ; *ega(ku)*, to picture, to describe

揭	KEI; *kaka(geru)*, to put up, to hoist, to carry	殻	KAKU; *kara*, husk, shell
教	112 page 23	渉	SHŌ to wade, to cross over, to walk about; to be related to
救	480 page 97	涯	GAI shore
敗	591 page 119	液	649 page 130
斜	SHA; *nana(me)*, slanting, oblique	涼	RYŌ, (lit.) coolness; *suzu(shii)*, cool
断	773 page 155	淑	SHUKU graceful, gentle
旋	SEN to rotate, to return	淡	TAN; *awa(i)*, light (color, taste, etc.), transitory (love, joy, etc.)
族	353 page 71	深	342 page 69
望	613 page 123	混	704 page 141
械	459 page 92	清	547 page 110
欲	997 page 200	添	TEN; *so(eru)*, to annex (to), to add (to), to garnish (cooking); *so(u)*, to accompany

渇	KATSU, thirst; to be thirsty, to dry up *kawa(ku)*, to feel thirsty	瓶	BIN, bottle, vase
渓	KEI valley	産	518 page 104
渋	JŪ; *shibu*, astringent juice; *shibu(i)*, astringent, refined, sober; *shibu(ru)*, to demur	略	823 page 165
済	881 page 177	異	826 page 166
猛	MŌ strong, valiant, brave, fierce, wild	盛	921 page 185
猫	BYŌ; *neko*, cat	盗	TŌ; *nusu(mu)*, to steal, to rob
猟	RYŌ, hunting, shooting	眺	CHŌ; *naga(meru)*, to gaze at, to watch
率	767 page 154	眼	669 page 134
現	692 page 139	票	598 page 120
球	275 page 56	祭	299 page 60
理	239 page 48	移	642 page 129

窒	CHITSU to block up, to obstruct; nitrogen	細	140 page 29
窓	931 page 187	紳	SHIN ceremonial sash; man of high birth
章	334 page 67	紹	SHŌ to introduce a person; to succeed to
笛	373 page 75	紺	KON, dark blue
符	FU tally, mark, sign, good omen, charm, talisman	終	322 page 65
第	359 page 72	組	178 page 36
粒	RYŪ; *tsubu,* grain, drop	経	685 page 138
粗	SO rough, loose, coarse, humble; *ara(i),* coarse, rugged	翌	998 page 200
粘	NEN; *neba(ru),* to be sticky; to persevere	習	323 page 65
紫	SHI; *murasaki,* purple, violet	粛	SHUKU to be respectful, to be modest, to admonish, to be severe
累	RUI, trouble, involvement; to pile up, to trouble; to be acquainted with	脚	KYAKU leg, lower part, position, suffix for counting furniture with legs

脱	DATSU to omit, to escape; *nu(gu),* to take off shoes, coat, etc.	蛍	KEI; *hotaru,* firefly
脳	964 page 193	術	732 page 147
舶	HAKU ocean-going ship	袋	TAI; *fukuro,* bag, sack, pouch
船	175 page 36	規	672 page 135
菊	KIKU, chrysanthemum	視	889 page 178
菌	KIN, germ, fungus	訟	SHŌ to sue, to go to law
菓	KA fruit, nut, berry	訪	984 page 197
菜	509 page 102	設	754 page 151
著	949 page 190	許	679 page 136
虚	KYO, KO empty, vain	訳	993 page 199
蛇	JA, DA; *hebi,* snake	豚	TON; *buta,* pig

貧	798 page 160	逸	ITSU to excel, to be lost, to be rash, to run off, to enjoy oneself
貨	455 page 92	部	407 page 82
販	HAN to sell, to deal in	郭	KAKU enclosure, red-light district
貫	KAN, old unit of weight (8.27 lb.); *tsuranu(ku)*, to pierce, to carry out, to attain	郵	994 page 199
責	751 page 151	都	376 page 76
赦	SHA to forgive, to pardon	郷	852 page 171
軟	NAN soft, weak, feeble; *yawa(rakai)* soft, tender, mild, yellow	酔	SUI; *yo(u)*, to get drunk, to become sick (sea, car, air), to be in ecstasy
転	375 page 76	曹	SŌ an official, friend
逮	TAI to catch, to arrest, to overtake, to pursue	釈	SHAKU to interpret, to explain
週	157 page 32	野	233 page 47
進	343 page 69	釣	CHŌ; *tsu(ru)*, to fish, to entice; *tsu(ri)*, fishing, change (of money)

閉	979 page 196	雪	174 page 35
陪	BAI to attend upon; attendant	頂	951 page 191
陰	IN, gloom, negative, the female principle (yin); *kage,* shadow, shade, back	魚	109 page 22
隆	RYŪ high, prosperous, flourishing	鳥	190 page 39
陳	CHIN to state, to display; to be old	麻	MA; *asa,* hemp, flax
陵	RYŌ; *misagagi,* Imperial mausoleum	黄	133 page 27
陶	TŌ pottery, porcelain	黒	137 page 28
陸	627 page 126	斎	SAI religious purification; a room
険	689 page 138		

12 STROKES

偉	I; *era(i),* great, admirable	傍	BŌ side, neighborhood

傘	SAN; *kasa,* umbrella	喪	SŌ to lose, to ruin; *mo,* mourning
備	795 page 160	喫	KITSU to eat, to drink
割	838 page 168	圏	KEN, sphere, range
創	932 page 187	堅	KEN; *kata(i),* hard, tough, tight, firm, solid, strict, sound
勝	335 page 68	堤	TEI; *tsutsumi,* bank (of a river, etc.)
募	BO; *tsuno(ru),* to collect, to raise (troops, etc.); to grow intense	堪	KAN; *ta(eru),* to endure, to bear, to withstand, to resist
勤	853 page 171	報	810 page 163
博	593 page 119	場	161 page 33
善	929 page 186	堕	DA to fall, to get into, to let fall, to lose
喚	KAN to call, to cry, to summon	塔	TŌ, tower, pagoda, steeple
喜	473 page 95	塚	*tsuka,* mound, hillock

塀	HEI, wall, fence	帽	BŌ headgear, headdress
塁	RUI, base (in baseball), fort	幅	FUKU, scroll, suffix for counting scrolls; *haba*, width, difference in price
奥	OKU, Ō interior; *oku*, interior, depths, heart	幾	KI; *iku~*, how many?, how much?, some (used as prefix)
婿	SEI; *muko*, son-in-law, bridegroom	廊	RŌ corridor, passage
媒	BAI intermediation, matchmaking, intermediary, go-between	廃	HAI to abolish, abandon; *suta(ru)*, *suta(reru)*, to fall into disuse
富	801 page 161	弾	DAN; *hi(ku)*, to play a musical instrument; *hazu(mu)*, to spring back; *tama*, bullet
寒	263 page 53	復	803 page 161
尊	939 page 188	御	GYO, GO; *on*, honorific prefix; *gyo(suru)*, to drive (a horse)
尋	JIN; *tazu(neru)*, to ask, to look for	循	JUN to obey, to observe, to follow; to revolve
就	900 page 181	悲	397 page 80
属	766 page 154	惑	WAKU; *mado(u)*, to be puzzled, to go astray, to be captivated by

惰	DA to be idle, to neglect	揮	846 page 170
愉	YU to rejoice, to enjoy oneself	揺	YŌ; *yu(reru)*, to shake (v.i.), to swing, to flicker
慌	KŌ, busy, flustered; *awa(teru)*, to be in a hurry, confused; *awa(tadashii)*, bustling, hurried	敢	KAN daring, boldly
扉	HI; *tobira*, door, page	散	519 page 104
掌	SHŌ palm of the hand; to control, to preside over	敬	856 page 172
提	776 page 156	晩	971 page 195
揚	YŌ; *a(geru)*, to raise, to send up, to hoist; to fry	普	FU wide, universal, general
搭	TŌ load (a vehicle), ride	景	494 page 99
換	KAN; *ka(eru)*, to exchange, to change (v.t.); *ka(waru)*, to change (v.i.)	晴	172 page 35
握	AKU; *nigi(ru)*, to grasp, to clasp, to hold, to seize	晶	SHŌ bright; crystal
援	EN to help, to rescue, to pull	暑	329 page 66

暁	GYŌ; *akatsuki,* dawn, daybreak	棚	*tana,* shelf
替	TAI; *ka(eru),* to exchange, to replace; *ka(waru),* to be replaced, to take turns	極	488 page 98
最	510 page 103	検	690 page 139
朝	191 page 39	欺	GI; *azamu(ku),* to deceive, to cheat
期	269 page 54	款	KAN sincerity, goodwill; article in a legal document
棋	KI chessman, Japanese chess	減	693 page 139
棒	987 page 198	渡	TO; *wata(ru),* to go over; *wata(su),* to hand over, span
棟	TŌ; *mune,* ridge (of a roof)	渦	KA; *uzu,* whirlpool, eddy
森	65 page 14	測	765 page 154
棺	KAN, casket, coffin	港	296 page 60
植	337 page 68	湖	293 page 59

湯	381 page 77	営	645 page 130
温	257 page 52	猶	YŪ to hesitate; moreover, even, still; as if
滋	JI nourishing; to flourish, to be luxuriant	琴	KIN; *koto*, Japanese harp
満	616 page 124	番	215 page 44
湿	SHITSU; *shime(ru),* to become damp, to moisten; *shime(su),* to dampen	畳	JŌ, suffix for counting mats; *tatami,* mat; *tata(mu),* to fold (up)
湾	WAN, bay, gulf	疎	SO estranged, sparse; *uto(i),* estranged, ignorant of; *uto(mu),* to neglect, to shun
無	620 page 125	痘	TŌ smallpox
焦	SHŌ; *ko(geru)* (v.i.), *ko(gasu)* (v.t.), scorch, burn; *ko(gareru),* yearn; *ase(ru),* be impatient	痛	954 page 191
然	557 page 112	痢	RI diarrhoea
煮	SHA; *ni(ru),* to cook (v.t.); *ni(eru)* (v.i.), to be boiled, to be cooked	登	382 page 77
焼	539 page 108	短	362 page 73

硝	SHŌ niter, gunpowder	策	883 page 177
硫	RYŪ sulfur	粧	SHŌ to paint and powder, to embellish
硬	KŌ; *kata(i)*, hard, tough, stiff, firm	結	497 page 100
税	750 page 151	絶	756 page 152
程	777 page 156	絞	KŌ; *shibo(ru)*, to wring, to squeeze, to extort, to scold; *shi(meru)*, to strangle
童	385 page 78	絡	RAKU to twine around, to surround; *kara(mu)*, to get entangled, to pick a fight
筆	400 page 81	給	481 page 97
等	383 page 77	統	780 page 157
筋	854 page 171	絵	95 page 20
筒	TŌ; *tsutsu*, pipe, tube	着	364 page 73
答	202 page 41	脹	CHŌ to swell

腕	WAN; *ude,* arm, talent, ability	補	981 page 197
落	431 page 87	覚	463 page 93
菓	428 page 86	訴	SO; *utta(e),* lawsuit, appeal, complaint; *utta(eru),* to sue, to resort to, to appeal
葬	SŌ; *hōmu(ru),* to bury, to consign to oblivion, to shelve	診	SHIN to examine, to diagnose; *mi(ru),* to examine (a patient)
蛮	BAN barbarian	詐	SA to tell a lie, to pretend, to deceive
衆	901 page 181	詔	SHŌ; *mikotonori,* Imperial edict
街	461 page 93	評	797 page 160
裁	882 page 177	詞	890 page 179
裂	RETSU; *sa(ku),* to tear, to rend (v.t.); *sa(keru),* to tear, to rend (v.i.)	詠	EI poem, ode, recitation of poetry; *yo(mu),* to compose a poem
装	933 page 187	証	737 page 148
裕	YŪ abundant, broad-minded, at ease	象	540 page 109

貯	572 page 115		軽	287 page 58
貴	847 page 170		遂	SUI at last; *to(geru),* to accomplish, to attain
買	212 page 43		遇	GŪ to treat, to deal with, to meet with, to come across
貸	770 page 155		遊	424 page 85
費	596 page 120		運	251 page 51
貿	813 page 163		遍	HEN wide, universal
賀	660 page 133		過	659 page 132
超	CHŌ, to exceed, super-; *ko(eru)* (v.i.), *ko(su)* (v.t.), to exceed, to transcend		道	205 page 42
越	ETSU; *ko(eru),* to go over, to exceed; *ko(su),* to cross, to exceed, to move (to)		達	568 page 114
距	KYO to separate, to be distant, to reach		遅	CHI late, slow; *oku(reru),* to be late; *oso(i),* late
軸	JIKU, axis, axle, scroll picture, holder, stalk		酢	SAKU; *su,* vinegar

殖	SHOKU; *fu(eru)* (v.i.), *fu(yasu)* (v.t.), to increase, multiply, grow	雄	YŪ strong, valiant, brave, surpassing; *osu, o-*, male animal
量	630 page 127	雅	GA elegant, graceful
鈍	DON; *nibu(i)*, dull, slow, blunt, dim; *nibu(ru)*, to become blunt, to weaken	集	324 page 65
開	261 page 53	雇	KO; *yato(u)*, to hire, to employ
閑	KAN quiet, tranquil, leisure, time to spare	雰	FUN atmosphere
間	100 page 21	雲	83 page 17
陽	429 page 86	項	KŌ, clause, paragraph, item
隅	GŪ; *sumi*, corner	順	534 page 107
隊	567 page 114	飲	250 page 51
階	262 page 53	飯	594 page 119
随	ZUI to follow, to accompany; freely; as one pleases	歯	306 page 62

13 STROKES

傑	KETSU to excel, to surpass; man of great caliber	嘆	TAN; *nage(ku)*, to bewail, to deplore, to sigh
催	SAI; *moyo-o(shi)*, meeting, auspices; *moyo-o (su)*, to hold (a meeting), to feel	園	84 page 17
債	SAI debt, loan	塊	KAI clod, lump
傷	912 page 183	塑	SO earthen figure
傾	KEI; *katamu(ki)*, inclination; *katamu(ku)* (v.i.), *katamu(keru)* (v.t.), to incline	塗	TO; *nu(ru)*, to paint, to plaster, to coat, to lacquer, to smear
働	585 page 118	墓	809 page 162
僧	SŌ, Buddhist priest, bonze	夢	816 page 164
勢	747 page 150	奨	SHŌ to encourage, to promote
勧	KAN; *susu(meru)*, to advise, to persuade, to encourage	嫁	KA; *yome*, daughter-in-law, young wife, bride; *totsu(gu)*, to marry
嗣	SHI to succeed to, to inherit; heir, succession	嫌	KEN; *kira(u)*, to dislike; *iya*, unpleasant, repugnant

寝	SHIN; *ne(ru)*, to go to bed, to sleep, to lie down	感	264 page 53
寛	KAN generous, easy	慈	JI; *itsuku(shimu)*, to love, to cherish, to pity
幕	989 page 198	慎	SHIN; *tsutsushi(mu)*, to be discreet, to refrain from
幹	667 page 134	慨	GAI to deplore, to lament
廉	REN noble, lofty, pure; cheap	戦	555 page 112
微	BI slight, little, faint, dim	損	768 page 154
想	350 page 71	搬	HAN to carry, to transport, to remove
愁	SHŪ grief, sorrow, distress; *ure(eru)*, to lament, to grieve; *ure(i)*, grief, sorrow	携	KEI; *tazusa(eru)*, to carry in one's hand, to take with one
意	246 page 50	搾	SAKU to squeeze, to compress; *shibo(ru)*, to press, to extract, to reprimand
愚	GU; *oro(ka)*, foolish, stupid, silly	摂	SETSU to take, to cultivate, to act in place of
愛	441 page 89	数	168 page 34

新	165 page 34	準	733 page 147
暇	KA; *hima,* time, leisure, dismissal	溝	KŌ; *mizo,* ditch
暖	945 page 190	溶	YŌ; *to(keru),* to melt, to dissolve (v.i.); *to(kasu),* to melt (v.t.)
暗	243 page 49	滅	METSU; *horo(biru),* to go to ruin, to die out; *horo(bosu),* to ruin, to destroy
棄	KI to throw away, to abandon, to reject	滑	KATSU smooth, even; to slide; *sube(ru),* to slide
業	278 page 56	滞	TAI; *todokō(ru),* to stagnate, to fall into arrears, to be left undone
楽	98 page 20	漠	BAKU a desert, vague
楼	RŌ (lit.), stately mansion with two or more stories, watchtower	漢	265 page 54
歳	SAI ~ years old (used as suffix); SEI year, age, time	滝	*taki,* waterfall, cataract, cascade
殿	DEN, TEN; *~dono,* Mr., Mrs., etc. (used in formal letters); *tono,* lord, my lord	煙	EN; *kemuri,* smoke; *kemu(ru),* to smoulder; *kemu(i),* smoky
源	864 page 173	照	541 page 109

煩	HAN; *wazura(u)*, to be worried, ill; *wazura(wasu)*, to trouble; *wazura(washii)*, troublesome	禅	ZEN, Dhyāna, the Zen sect of Buddhism, religious meditation
猿	EN; *saru*, monkey	稚	CHI infant, young, childish, raw
献	KEN, KON to dedicate, to offer, to present	節	552 page 111
痴	CHI foolish, stupid	絹	861 page 173
盟	991 page 199	継	KEI; *tsu(gi)* a patch; *tsu(gu)*, to inherit, to succeed to, to come into (property, etc.)
睡	SUI to sleep, to doze	続	563 page 113
督	TOKU to control, to supervise, to urge	罪	713 page 143
碁	GO, the Japanese game of *go*	置	570 page 115
禁	682 page 137	署	908 page 182
禍	KA, misfortune, disaster, evil	群	684 page 137
福	409 page 82	義	674 page 135

聖	922 page 185	褐	KATSU woolen kimono, dark brown
腰	YŌ; *koshi*, waist, loins	解	662 page 133
腸	574 page 115	触	SHOKU; *fu(reru)*, to touch, to mention; to conflict with; to proclaim
腹	975 page 196	試	525 page 106
艇	TEI boat	詩	307 page 62
蒸	915 page 184	詰	KITSU; *tsu(meru)*, to cram; *tsu(maru)*, to be blocked; *tsu(maranai)*, trifling; *tsu(mari)*, in short
蓄	CHIKU to store, to save; *takuwa(eru)*, to save, to store up	話	240 page 49
虜	RYO, captive, prisoner of war	該	GAI that, the very, the ~ in question (used as prefix)
虞	*osore*, anxiety, apprehension	詳	SHŌ; *kuwa(shii)*, detailed, minute, well-informed
裏	1,002 page 201	誇	KO; *hoko(ri)*, pride; *hoko(ru)*, to be proud of, to boast of
裸	RA; *hadaka*, nakedness, nude	誠	923 page 185

誉	YO; *homa(re),* honor, credit, glory, reputation	載	SAI; *no(seru),* to load, place on, put in print; *no(ru),* to be put in print
豊	811 page 163	辞	528 page 106
賃	953 page 191	農	386 page 78
賄	WAI wealth, bribe; to cater for; *makana(u),* to provide (meals, etc.), expenses	違	I; *chiga(u),* to differ from, to be wrong; *chiga(eru),* to change, to break
資	721 page 145	遠	85 page 18
賊	ZOKU, thief, robber, burglar	遣	KEN to send, to dispatch, to bestow; *-zukai,* use of
跡	SEKI; *ato,* mark, trace, trail, wake, ruins	酬	SHŪ to reward, to recompense, to return, to repay
路	439 page 88	酪	RAKU dairy products
跳	CHŌ to jump, to leap, to flee; *ha(neru), to(bu),* to jump, to leap	鈴	REI; RIN, *suzu,* small bell
践	SEN to step on, to go, to carry out	鉛	EN; *namari,* lead (metal)
較	KAKU to compare	鉢	HACHI, bowl, pot

鉄	374 page 75	頑	GAN stubborn, foolish
鉱	700 page 141	頒	HAN to distribute, to divide
隔	KAKU; *heda(teru)*, to separate, to screen, to estrange; *heda(taru)*, to be distant from	飼	722 page 145
零	REI, zero, to fall, to rain; fragment	飽	HŌ; *a(ki)*, weariness, tiresomeness; *a(kiru)*, to grow tired of, to become weary of
雷	RAI; *kaminari*, thunder, thunderbolt	飾	SHOKU; *kaza(ru)*, to ornament, to embellish, to exhibit, to affect
電	197 page 40	塩	451 page 91
靴	KA; *kutsu*, shoes	鼓	KO; *tsuzumi*, hand drum
預	821 page 165		

14 STROKES

像	762 page 153	僚	RYŌ an official; friend, colleague
僕	BOKU, manservant, I	塾	JUKU, cram school, private school

境	680 page 137	徳	783 page 157
増	763 page 153	態	771 page 155
墨	BOKU; *sumi,* India ink, ink stick	慕	BO; *shita(u),* to yearn for, to adore, to follow
奪	DATSU; *uba(u),* to take by force, to rob, to captivate	慢	MAN to be idle, to neglect; to despise, to be naughty, to be selfish
嫡	CHAKU heir, legitimate child	慣	668 page 134
察	516 page 104	憎	ZŌ; *niku(mu),* to hate, to detest; *niku(i), niku(rashii),* hateful, provoking; *niku(shimi),* hatred
寡	KA few, little, small, scanty; alone; widow	摘	TEKI to disclose, to reveal, to point out; *tsu(mu),* to pick, to pluck
寧	NEI quiet, peaceful, easy; kind; rather	旗	474 page 95
層	934 page 187	暮	982 page 197
彰	SHŌ manifest, clear, to elucidate	暦	REKI; *koyomi,* calendar, almanac
徴	CHŌ symptom, sign; effect, proof; to summon	構	701 page 141

概	GAI roughly, generally, as a rule	漫	MAN in spite of oneself, involuntarily, self-willfulness; vast, wide, lax
模	992 page 199	漬	*tsu(keru)* (v.t.), to pickle, to preserve, to soak; *tsu(karu)* (v.i.), to be soaked/steeped in
様	430 page 87	漸	ZEN gradually; to advance gradually; at last
歌	90 page 19	獄	GOKU, prison, jail
歴	636 page 128	疑	848 page 170
滴	TEKI; *shizuku,* a drop (of liquid); *shitata(ru),* to trickle, to drip	碑	HI, monument, tombstone
漁	483 page 97	磁	892 page 179
漂	HYŌ to wander about; to bleach; *tadayo(u),* to drift, to float	種	531 page 107
漆	SHITSU; *urushi,* lacquer	稲	TŌ; *ine,* rice plant
漏	RŌ; *mo(ru),* to leak; *mo(reru),* to leak, to get out (secret, etc.), to be omitted	穀	876 page 176
演	650 page 131	端	TAN right, correct, just; *hashi, hata, ha-,* end, tip, edge, border

箇	KA (used as auxiliary in counting)	総	760 page 153
算	142 page 29	罰	BATSU, BACHI, penalty, punishment; *bas(suru)*, to punish, to penalize
管	466 page 94	聞	219 page 44
精	748 page 150	腐	FU; *kusa(ru)*, to go bad, to rot; to be dejected, to lose heart
緑	435 page 88	膜	MAKU, membrane
維	I to keep; to fasten; fundamental principles	製	749 page 150
綱	KŌ basic principles; *tsuna*, rope, cable; last hope (of life, etc.)	複	804 page 161
網	MŌ; *ami*, net, netting	誌	891 page 179
綿	818 page 164	認	962 page 193
緒	SHO, beginning, lineage; clue; *o*, cord, string (of a musical instrument)	誓	SEI; *chika(i)*, oath, vow; *chika(u)*, to swear, to take a vow
練	438 page 88	誘	YŪ; *saso(i)*, invitation, temptation; *saso(u)*, to invite, to induce, to allure

語	124 page 25	酸	715 page 144
誤	868 page 174	銀	281 page 57
説	553 page 111	銃	JŪ, gun, rifle
読	206 page 42	銅	781 page 157
豪	GŌ to excel, to stand pre-eminent; strong, vigorous; Australia	銑	SEN pig iron
踊	YŌ; *odo(ri)*, dance; *odo(ru)*, to dance, to jump	銘	MEI, signature, inscription, appellation, motto
適	778 page 156	銭	757 page 152
遭	SŌ to encounter, to come across; *a(u)*, to encounter, to be confronted by	閣	837 page 168
遮	SHA; *saegi(ru)*, to interrupt, to obstruct	閥	BATSU, clique, faction, clan
酵	KŌ yeast, ferment, sake lees	関	467 page 94
酷	KOKU, severity, cruelty, harshness	際	710 page 143

障	913 page 183	駆	KU to drive a vehicle, to chase; *ka(keru)*, to run, to gallop
隠	IN; *kaku(reru)*, to hide (v.i.), to disappear; *kaku(su)*, to hide (v.t.), to conceal	駅	253 page 51
雑	714 page 143	髪	HATSU; *kami*, hair, hairdo
需	JU demand, request	魂	KON; *tamashii*, soul, spirit, ghost
静	548 page 110	鳴	229 page 46
領	825 page 166	鼻	399 page 80
駄	DA packhorse; sometimes used for its sound value	雌	SHI; *mesu, me-*, female (animal, bird; *me-* is also used in the case of plants)

15 STROKES

儀	GI, rule, ceremony, affair, matter	勲	KUN meritorious deed, distinguished service
億	452 page 91	器	475 page 96
劇	858 page 172	噴	FUN; *fu(ku)*, to emit, to spout, to belch out

嘱	SHOKU to entrust, to request	慮	RYO to consider, to deliberate, to plan, to be anxious
墜	TSUI to fall, to drop	慰	I; *nagusa(me)*, comfort; *nagusa(mi)*, pastime; *nagusa(meru)*, to comfort, to console
墳	FUN mound, tumulus, hillock, tomb	慶	KEI congratulation, happiness; to rejoice
審	SHIN detailed, full, clear, evident, obvious	憂	YŪ; *ure(i)*, grief, anxiety, affliction; *ure(eru)*, to fear, to lament, to be worried
寮	RYŌ, boarding house, dormitory	憤	FUN; *ikidō(ru)*, to be indignant, to resent
導	782 page 157	戯	GI fun, play, flirtation; *tawamu(reru)*, to joke, to play, to flirt with
履	RI footwear; to walk; to do, to experience; *ha(ku)*, to put on, to wear (footwear)	摩	MA to rub, to grind, to wear away; *ma(suru)* (lit.), to nearly touch, to scrape
幣	HEI pendant paper strips in a Shinto shrine; riches, offering, money	撤	TETSU; *tes(suru)*, to remove, to get rid of, to withdraw (an army, etc.)
弊	HEI, evil, abuse, vice, our (used as prefix denoting modesty)	撮	SATSU to pinch, to pick, to gather, to take a photograph; *to(ru)*, to photograph, to film
影	EI; *kage*, shadow, reflection, image, phantom, light	撲	BOKU to strike, to beat
徹	TETSU to pierce, to penetrate	撃	GEKI; *u(tsu)*, to fire (a gun, etc.), to attack, to strike, to fight

敵	779 page 156	潟	*kata*, lagoon
敷	FU; *shi(ku)*, to spread, to pave, to sit on (a cushion), to lay (a railway)	潤	JUN; *uruo(i)*, moisture; profit; charm; *uruo(su)* (v.t.), to moisten; to profit
暫	ZAN for a little while, for some time	潮	952 page 191
暴	814 page 163	澄	CHŌ; *su(mu)*, to become clear or serene (moon, stream, sky, mind, etc.)
槽	SŌ tank, vat	熟	905 page 182
標	599 page 120	熱	589 page 118
横	255 page 52	監	KAN to watch over, to keep control over, to supervise; prison, jail
権	862 page 173	盤	BAN, board (for chess, etc.), shallow basin, phonograph record, plate
歓	KAN to rejoice	確	664 page 133
潔	686 page 138	稼	KA; *kase(gu)*, to work, to earn
潜	SEN, dive, submerge, lurk; *hiso(mu)*, to lie concealed, *mogu(ru)*, to dive in, to crawl in	稿	KŌ, draft, rough copy, manuscript

穂	SUI; *ho*, ear (of wheat, etc.), head	縄	JŌ; *nawa*, rope
窮	KYŪ; *kiwa(meru)*, to carry to extremes; *kiwa(maru)*, to end, to reach the extreme	罷	HI to pause, to intermit, to dismiss, to release, to get tired
窯	YŌ; *kama*, kiln for baking tiles, ceramics, etc.	膚	FU; *hada*, skin (of the body)
箱	390 page 79	舗	HO store; to pave
範	HAN, example, model	舞	BU; *mai*, dancing, dance; *ma(u)*, to dance
緊	KIN to shrink, to become tight, to contract; severe, strict, hard, solid	蔵	936 page 188
線	176 page 36	衝	SHŌ, important position, focus; to attack, to strike against; to brave
締	TEI; *shi(maru)*, to be shut, to be tight; *shi(meru)*, to tie, to tighten, to shut (v.t.)	褒	HŌ; *ho(meru)*, to praise
縁	EN, relation, ties, blood relation; fate; veranda, porch; *fuchi*, edge, verge	課	456 page 92
編	806 page 162	調	369 page 74
緩	KAN slow, easy, slack, lenient; *yuru(i)*, loose, lenient	談	363 page 73

請	SEI, SHIN; *ko(u)*, to beg, to ask, to request; *u(keru)*, to receive, to undertake	質	726 page 146
論	1,006 page 202	賛	716 page 144
誕	943 page 189	趣	SHU; *omomuki*, taste, elegance, grace, air, appearance, purport, effect
諸	909 page 182	踏	TŌ; *fu(mu)*, to step on, to tread on; *fu(maeru)*, to step on, to be based on
諾	DAKU, consent, assent	輝	KI; *kagaya(ku)*, to shine, to be radiant
謁	ETSU, (Imperial) audience; audience with persons of high rank	輩	HAI fellows, companions
賓	HIN guest	輪	631 page 127
賜	SHI; *tamawa(ru)*, to deign to give, to grant, to award	遵	JUN to obey, to observe, to abide by
賞	542 page 109	遷	SEN to move from one location to another, to transfer
賠	BAI to make up for, to compensate for	選	556 page 112
賦	FU (lit.), ode, poetical prose; tribute, levy, allotment	遺	827 page 166

鋭	EI; *surudo(i)*, sharp, pointed, biting, acute, keen, smart	養	624 page 125
鋳	CHŪ; *i(ru)*, to cast (metal), to found	餓	GA to be hungry, to starve
閲	ETSU (lit.), inspection, examination; to examine, to inspect, to peruse, to elapse	駐	CHŪ to stop, to stay
震	SHIN; *furu(u)*, *furu(eru)*, to shake (v.i.), to tremble; *furu(waseru)*, to shake (v.t.)	魅	MI; *mi(suru)* (lit.), to fascinate, to enchant, to bewitch
霊	REI, *tama*, soul, spirit, ghost	黙	MOKU; *dama(ru)*, to become silent, to close one's lips

16 STROKES

儒	JU Confucianism, Confucianist, scholar; cowardice, tenderness	壇	DAN, platform, dais, raised floor
凝	GYŌ; *ko(ri)*, stiffness; *ko(ru)*, to be absorbed in, to elaborate, to grow stiff	壊	KAI to collapse, to be destroyed; to break, to destroy
墾	KON to cultivate, to farm, to reclaim	奮	976 page 196
壁	HEKI; *kabe*, wall	嬢	JŌ, Miss (used as suffix), girl, unmarried lady, daughter
壌	JŌ earth, soil	憩	KEI to take a rest; *iko(i)*, vacation; *iko(u)*, to take a rest

憲	863 page 173	激	859 page 172
憶	OKU to remember, to keep in mind, to think	濁	DAKU; *nigo(ri)*, turbidity; voiced sound; *nigo(ru)*, to become muddy or cloudy
憾	KAN to regret, to be sorry for	濃	NŌ; *ko(i)*, dark, deep, thick, heavy, strong
懐	KAI one's pocket; to think, to long for; *natsu(kashii)*, beloved, longed for	燃	786 page 158
擁	YŌ; *yō(suru)*, to protect, to embrace, to hold	獲	KAKU; *e(ru)*, to get, to obtain, to gain
操	935 page 188	獣	JŪ; *kemono*, beast, brute
整	345 page 70	磨	MA; *miga(ku)*, to polish, to improve
曇	DON; *kumo(ri)*, cloudy weather, blur; *kumo(ru)*, to become cloudy, to become dim	積	550 page 111
樹	897 page 180	穏	ON; *oda(yaka)*, calm, quiet, peaceful, mild
橋	277 page 56	築	774 page 155
機	476 page 96	篤	TOKU genuine, sincere, hearty, cordial

糖	958 page 192	薫	KUN fragrance; to be fragrant; *kao(ru)*, to be fragrant
緯	I parallels of latitude; cross-threads	薬	420 page 85
縛	BAKU; *shiba(ru)*, to bind, to tie, to arrest	融	YŪ, to melt; to circulate, to ventilate
縫	HŌ; *nu(u)*, to sew, to stitch	衛	646 page 130
縦	903 page 181	衡	KŌ, scale, beam; to measure, to weigh
繁	HAN thick, many, much, thriving; troublesome, busy, mixed	親	166 page 34
膨	BŌ; *fuku(ramu)*, to swell, to expand; *fuku(reru)*, to swell, to expand, to sulk	諭	YU; *sato(su)*, to admonish, to instruct
興	702 page 141	諮	SHI to consult, to ask counsel of; *haka(ru)*, to consult
薄	HAKU; *usu(i)*, thin, light, pale, weak, small (profit, etc.)	謀	BŌ, MU; *haka(ru)*, to scheme, to conspire
薦	SEN to recommend; *susu(meru)*, to recommend	謡	YŌ; *utai*, chanting of a *Noh* drama text
薪	SHIN firewood; *takigi*, firewood	賢	KEN; *kashiko(i)*, wise, intelligent, tactful, smart, shrewd

頼	RAI; *tano(mu)*, to request; *tano(mi)*, a request; *tano(moshii)*, trustworthy; *tayo(ru)*, to rely on	錠	JŌ, lock, padlock; tablet (medical) (used as suffix for counting tablets)
輸	819 page 164	錯	SAKU to be mixed together, to make a mistake
避	HI; *sa(keru)*, to avoid, to keep away from, shirk	錬	REN to temper or forge metal; to train, to cultivate, to polish, to drill morally
還	KAN to return, to come back	隣	RIN; *tonari*, next door house; next to, neighboring
鋼	874 page 175	隷	REI servant, follower
録	640 page 129	頭	203 page 41
錘	SUI weight for scales, sinker for fishing line; *tsumu*, spindle	館	266 page 54

17 STROKES

償	SHŌ; *tsuguna(i)*, indemnity, atonement; *tsuguna(u)*, to make up for, to atone for	厳	865 page 174
優	995 page 200	懇	KON kind, cordial, in love with, intimate
嚇	KAKU to threaten, to menace	擦	SATSU to rub, to scrub, to scratch; *su(reru)*, to rub, to become worn; *su(ru)* to rub, to chafe

擬	GI; gi(suru), to point or aim (an object) at; to imitate; to compare	繊	SEN thin, slender, fine, small
濯	TAKU wash, rinse	翼	YOKU to aid, to assist; tsubasa, wing
燥	SŌ to dry	聴	CHŌ to listen to, to comply with; ki(ku), to listen to, to take notice of
爵	SHAKU peerage, title and court rank	覧	1,001 page 201
矯	KYŌ; ta(meru), to straighten, correct	謄	TŌ to take a copy of, to transcribe
犠	GI sacrifice, victim	謙	KEN to humble oneself, to condescend
環	KAN ring, link; to surround	講	703 page 141
療	RYŌ to cure, to heal	謝	728 page 146
礁	SHŌ submerged rock, unknown reef	謹	KIN to restrain oneself, to be respectful; tsutsushi(mu), to be humble
縮	904 page 181	購	KŌ to purchase, to buy
績	752 page 151	頻	HIN frequent

轄	KATSU control, management	霜	SŌ; *shimo*, frost
醜	SHŪ; *miniku(i)*, ugly, unseemly, ignoble	鮮	SEN fresh, new, clean, Korea, few; *aza(yaka)*, bright, clear, graceful
鍛	TAN; *kita(eru)*, to forge; to train, to cultivate (morally)	齢	REI age, years

18 STROKES

懲	CHŌ; *ko(rasu)*, to punish, to discipline, to chasten; *ko(riru)*, to learn from experience	穫	KAKU to reap, to harvest
曜	236 page 48	簡	843 page 169
濫	RAN at random, wantonly; excessive; to overflow, to float	糧	RYŌ food, provisions
癒	YU heal, cure	織	742 page 149
癖	HEKI; *kuse*, habit, peculiar way, frizz (of hair), weakness	繕	ZEN; *tsukuro(u)*, to patch up, to mend, to trim, to smooth over
瞬	SHUN a short time; to wink, to twinkle, to flicker; *matata(ku)*, to wink, to twinkle, to blink	繭	KEN; *mayu*, silkworm cocoon
礎	SO; *ishizue*, foundation, cornerstone	職	743 page 149

臨	1,004 page 201	題	360 page 73
藩	HAN, Japanese feudal clan or domain	額	665 page 134
襟	KIN; *eri,* neckband, collar	顔	103 page 21
覆	FUKU; *ō(u),* veil, conceal, wrap; *kutsugae(su)* (v.t.), *kutsugae(ru)* (v.i.), overturn	類	632 page 127
観	468 page 94	顕	KEN bright, clear, distinguished, manifest; to show, to manifest
贈	ZŌ; *oku(ru),* to present as a gift	翻	HON; *hirugae(ru),* to flutter; *hirugae(su),* to wave (v.t.); to change (one's mind)
鎖	SA hasp; to shut, to close; *kusari,* chain	騎	KI suffix for counting horsemen; cavalry, saddle horse; to ride, to mount
鎮	CHIN to calm, to quiet, to tranquilize; to suppress; *shizu(meru),* to suppress, to pacify	騒	SŌ; *sawa(gi),* noise, disturbance; *sawa(gu),* to make a noise, to make a disturbance
難	960 page 193	験	500 page 101
離	RI; *hana(reru)* (v.i.), *hana(su)* (v.t.), to separate, to part, to divide, to keep apart	闘	TŌ; *tataka(u),* to fight

19 STROKES

瀬	*se*, shallows, rapids	譜	FU, music, musical score; family record, genealogy
爆	BAKU to burst, to explode	警	857 page 172
璽	JI Imperial seal	鏡	486 page 98
簿	BO notebook	霧	MU; *kiri*, mist, fog, spray
繰	*ku(ru)*, to reel (thread, etc.), to gin (cotton), to turn over (pages, etc.)	韻	IN, rhyme, echo, taste, elegance
羅	RA, silk gauze, thin silk	願	469 page 94
臓	937 page 188	髄	ZUI, marrow, pith
藻	SŌ; *mo*, seaweed	鯨	GEI; *kujira*, whale
覇	HA, supremacy, domination	鶏	KEI; *niwatori*, chicken
識	725 page 146	麗	REI; *uruwa(shii)*, fine, lovely, beautiful, elegant, graceful

20 STROKES

欄	RAN, column (of, a newspaper, etc.); railing	醸	JŌ to brew; *kamo(su)*, to brew, to distil, to bring about
競	487 page 98	鐘	SHŌ; *kane*, bell
籍	SEKI, census, register, membership	響	KYŌ; *hibi(ki)*, sound, echo, vibration; *hibi(ku)*, to echo, to vibrate
議	477 page 96	騰	TŌ to rise, to ascend, to leap
護	696 page 140	懸	KEN, KE to hang, to suspend; to offer a reward; to be anxious; to depend on
譲	JŌ; *yuzu(ru)*, to hand over, to concede to, to yield to, to reserve		

21 STROKES

艦	KAN warship	顧	KO; *kaeri(miru)*, to look back, to reflect upon oneself, to think of, to heed
躍	YAKU; *odo(ru)*, to leap, to jump; to rise, to go up	魔	MA, devil, demon, evil spirit
露	RO to expose, to lay bare; to be exposed, to come to light; Russia; *tsuyu*, dew		

22 STROKES

驚	KYŌ; *odoro(ki)*, surprise; *odoro(ku)*, to be surprised or frightened, to marvel (at)	襲	SHŪ, *oso(u)*, to attack; to succeed to; to make a surprise visit

23 STROKES

鑑	KAN model, pattern, example

SYLLABARY
Katakana and Hiragana

ア *a*	フ ア			あ *a*	一 ナ あ		
イ *i*	ノ イ			い *i*	い い		
ウ *u*	゛ ゛ ウ			う *u*	、 う		
エ *e*	一 丁 エ			え *e*	、 え		
オ *o*	一 ナ オ			お *o*	一 お お		
カ *ka*	フ カ			か *ka*	つ カ か		
キ *ki*	一 二 キ			き *ki*	一 二 き き		
ク *ku*	ノ ク			く *ku*	く		
ケ *ke*	ノ ケ ケ			け *ke*	ι に け		

コ *ko*	フ コ	こ *ko*	⌐ こ
サ *sa*	一 十 サ	さ *sa*	一 き さ
シ *shi*	ヽ ゛ シ	し *shi*	し
ス *su*	フ ス	す *su*	一 す
セ *se*	⌐ セ	せ *se*	一 ナ せ
ソ *so*	ヽ ソ	そ *so*	⌐ ⁊ そ
タ *ta*	ノ ク タ	た *ta*	一 ナ た た
チ *chi*	⌐ 二 チ	ち *chi*	一 ち
ツ *tsu*	ヽ ゛ ツ	つ *tsu*	つ
テ *te*	一 二 テ	て *te*	⌐ て
ト *to*	Ⅰ ト	と *to*	ヽ と

ナ na	一 ナ			な na	一 ナ か な
ニ ni	一 ニ			に ni	し にに
ヌ nu	フ ヌ			ぬ nu	し ぬ
ネ ne	、 ラ イ ネ			ね ne	｜ ね
ノ no	ノ			の no	の
ハ ha	ノ ハ			は ha	し にに は
ヒ hi	一 ヒ			ひ hi	ひ ひ
フ fu	フ			ふ fu	、 う ふ ふ
ヘ he	ヘ			へ he	ヘ
ホ ho	一 ナ オ ホ			ほ ho	し にに にに ほ
マ ma	フ マ			ま ma	一 二 ま

297

ミ *mi*	丶 ミ ミ	み *mi*	ユ み
ム *mu*	∠ ム	む *mu*	ー む む
メ *me*	ノ メ	め *me*	∖ め
モ *mo*	ー ニ モ	も *mo*	し も も
ヤ *ya*	フ ヤ	や *ya*	つ ぅ や
ユ *yu*	フ ユ	ゆ *yu*	い ゆ
ヨ *yo*	フ ヲ ヨ	よ *yo*	ー よ
ラ *ra*	ー ラ	ら *ra*	丶 ら
リ *ri*	ー リ	り *ri*	い り
ル *ru*	ノ ル	る *ru*	る る
レ *re*	レ	れ *re*	ー れ

ロ *ro*	ヽ ノ ロ ロ	ろ *ro*	ろ
ワ *wa*	ヽ ワ	わ *wa*	｜ わ
ヲ *o*	一 ニ ヲ	を *o*	一 ナ を
ン *n*	ヽ ゝ ン	ん *n*	ん

ガ ga	ギ gi	グ gu	ゲ ge	ゴ go
ザ za	ジ ji	ズ zu	ゼ ze	ゾ zo
ダ da	ヂ ji	ヅ zu	デ de	ド do
バ ba	ビ bi	ブ bu	ベ be	ボ bo
パ pa	ピ pi	プ pu	ペ pe	ポ po
キャ kya	キュ kyu	キョ kyo	シャ sha	シュ shu
ショ sho	チャ cha	チュ chu	チョ cho	ニャ nya
ニュ nyu	ニョ nyo	ヒャ hya	ヒュ hyu	ヒョ hyo
ミャ mya	ミュ myu	ミョ myo	リャ rya	リュ ryu
リョ ryo	ギャ gya	ギュ gyu	ギョ gyo	ジャ ja
ジュ ju	ジョ jo	ビャ bya	ビュ byu	ビョ byo
ピャ pya	ピュ pyu	ピョ pyo		

INDEX OF READINGS

This index contains an alphabetical listing of all Japanese readings given in the body of the book. Note that:

1. *On* readings are shown in capital letters and *kun* readings are shown in lower case letters.

2. All Essential characters are referenced by their character number only. For example: *abiru* 浴 625.

3. All General Use characters that are not Essential characters are referenced by their page number. These are preceded by the letter "p" and followed by either "a" or "b" to indicate the left or right column on that page. For example: A 亜 p 218a.

4. When readings include *okurigana,* these are not indicated by parentheses.

INDEX OF READINGS

302

sumi 隅 p *268a*
sumi 墨 p *276a*
sumiyaka 速 *352*
sumu 住 *325*
sumu 済 *881*
sumu 澄 p *282b*
SUN 寸 *920*
suna 砂 *879*
suppai 酸 *715*
sureru, suru 擦 p *288b*
suru 刷 *514*
surudoi 鋭 p *285a*
susumeru 勧 p *269a*
susumeru 薦 p *287a*
susumeru, susumu 進 *343*
sutareru, sutaru 廃 p *261b*
suteru 捨 *894*
suu 吸 *849*
suwaru 座 *880*
suwaru 据 p *253a*
suzu 鈴 p *274b*
suzushii 涼 p *254b*

— T —

TA 多 *180*
TA 太 *181*
TA 他 *354*
ta 田 *60*
taba 束 *561*
taberu 食 *163*
tabi 度 *377*
tabi 旅 *433*
tadachini 直 *192*
tadashi 但 p *218a*
tadashii, tadasu 正 *79*
tadayou 漂 p *277a*
taeru 絶 *756*
taeru 耐 p *239b*
taeru 堪 p *260b*
tagai 互 p *205a*
tagayasu 耕 *699*
TAI 大 *25*
TAI 太 *181*
TAI 体 *182*
TAI 台 *183*
TAI 対 *356*
TAI 待 *357*
TAI 帯 *566*
TAI 隊 *567*
TAI 退 *769*
TAI 貸 *770*
TAI 態 *771*
TAI 息 p *235b*

TAI 耐 p *239b*
TAI 胎 p *239b*
TAI 泰 p *246a*
TAI 袋 p *257b*
TAI 逮 p *258a*
TAI 替 p *263a*
TAI 滞 p *271b*
taira 平 *411*
takai, takamaru, takameru 高 *132*
takara 宝 *983*
take 竹 *71*
take 丈 p *204a*
take 岳 p *227b*
taki 滝 p *271b*
takigi 薪 p *287a*
TAKU 度 *377*
TAKU 宅 *940*
TAKU 択 p *222a*
TAKU 沢 p *222b*
TAKU 卓 p *226a*
TAKU 拓 p *229a*
TAKU 託 p *249a*
TAKU 濯 p *289a*
taku 炊 p *231a*
takumi 巧 p *210b*
takuwaeru 蓄 p *273a*
tama 玉 *48*
tama 球 *275*
tama 弾 p *261b*
tama 霊 p *285a*
tamago 卵 *1,000*
tamashii 魂 p *280b*
tamawaru 賜 p *284a*
tameru 矯 p *289a*
tami 民 *619*
tamotsu 保 *808*
TAN 炭 *361*
TAN 短 *362*
TAN 反 *393*
TAN 単 *569*
TAN 担 *941*
TAN 探 *942*
TAN 誕 *943*
TAN 丹 p *205a*
TAN 胆 p *239b*
TAN 淡 p *254b*
TAN 嘆 p *269b*
TAN 端 p *277b*
TAN 鍛 p *290a*
tana 棚 p *263b*
tane 種 *531*
tani 谷 *135*

tanomi, tanomoshii, tanomu 頼 p *288a*
tanoshii 楽 *98*
taoreru, taosu 倒 p *242a*
tarasu, tareru *918*
tariru 足 *36*
tashika, tashikameru 確 *664*
tassuru 達 *568*
tasu 足 *36*
tasukaru, tasukeru 助 *330*
tatakai, tatakau 戦 *555*
tatakau 闘 p *291b*
tatami, tatamu 畳 p *264b*
tate 縦 *903*
tate 盾 p *238b*
tatematsuru 奉 p *226b*
tateru 立 *37*
tateru 建 *498*
tatoeba, tatoeru 例 *635*
TATSU 達 *568*
tatsu 立 *37*
tatsu 建 *498*
tatsu 絶 *756*
tatsu 断 *773*
tatsu 裁 *882*
tatsu 竜 p *250b*
tattobu, tattoi 貴 *847*
tattobu, tattoi 尊 *939*
tawamureru 戯 p *281b*
tawara 俵 *796*
tayoru 頼 p *288a*
tayori 便 *610*
tazuneru 訪 *984*
tazuneru 尋 p *261a*
tazusaeru 携 p *270b*
te 手 *35*
TEI 体 *182*
TEI 弟 *194*
TEI 丁 *367*
TEI 定 *371*
TEI 庭 *372*
TEI 低 *575*
TEI 底 *576*
TEI 停 *577*
TEI 提 *776*
TEI 程 *777*
TEI 呈 p *219b*
TEI 廷 p *221a*
TEI 抵 p *228b*
TEI 邸 p *232b*
TEI 亭 p *233a*
TEI 帝 p *235a*
TEI 訂 p *240a*

tsukeru, tsuku 付 602
tsuki 月 13
tsukiru 尽 p 216b
tsuku 着 364
tsuku 就 900
tsuku 突 p 231b
tsukue 机 845
tsukuri, tsukuru, 造 761
tsukurou 繕 p 290b
tsukuru 作 141
tsukusu 尽 p 216b
tsuma 妻 708
tsumaranai, tsumari, tsumaru,
    tsumeru 詰 p 273b
tsumetai 冷 634
tsumi 罪 713
tsumori, tsumoru, tsumu 積
    550
tsumu 摘 p 276b
tsumu 錘 p 288a
tsumugu 紡 p 248a
tsuna 綱 p 278a
tsune 常 740
tsuno 角 97
tsunoru 募 p 260a
tsura 面 417
tsuranaru, tsureru, 連 637
tsuranuku 貫 p 258a
tsuri, tsuru 釣 p 258b
tsuru 弦 p 228a
tsurugi 剣 p 242b
tsutaeru, tsutau, tsutawaru 伝
    580
tsutome, tsutomeru 勤 853
tsutomeru 努 582
tsutomeru 務 815
tsutsu 筒 p 265a
tsutsumi 堤 p 260b
tsutsumu 包 611
tsutsushimu 慎 p 270b
tsutsushimu 謹 p 289b
tsuyoi, tsuyomeru 強 111
tsuyu 露 p 293a
tsuzukeru, tsuzuki, tsuzuku 続
    563
tsuzumi 鼓 p 275b

— U —

U 右 22
U 雨 69
U 羽 82
U 有 423
U 宇 829

ubau 奪 p 276a
uchi 内 207
ude 腕 p 266a
ue 上 23
ue, ueru 飢 p 250b
ueru 植 337
ugoku 動 384
uji 氏 522
ukabu, 浮 p 246b
ukagau 伺 p 218a
ukaru, ukeru 受 319
ukeru 請 p 284a
uketamawaru 承 736
uku 浮 p 246b
uma 馬 210
umareru 生 44
umareru 産 518
umaru, umeru 埋 p 243a
ume 梅 592
umi 海 94
umu 生 44
umu 産 518
UN 雲 83
UN 運 251
unagasu 促 p 233b
une 畝 p 247a
uo 魚 109
ura 浦 p 246a
ura 裏 1,002
urameshii, urami, uramu 恨
    p 236a
uranai, uranau 占 p 209b
ureeru, urei 愁 p 270a
ureeru, urei 憂 p 281b
ureru 熟 905
uri, uru 売 211
-uru 得 587
uruoi, uruosu 潤 p 282b
urushi 漆 p 277a
uruwashii 麗 p 292b
ushi 牛 108
ushinau 失 529
ushiro 後 123
usui 薄 p 287a
uta, utau 歌 90
utagai, utagau 疑 848
utai 謡 p 287b
utoi, utomu 疎 p 264b
utsu 打 355
utsu 討 956
utsu 撃 p 281b
utsukushii 美 398
utsuru, utsusu 移 642

utsuru, utsusu 映 830
utsusu 写 313
utsuwa 器 475
uttae, uttaeru 訴 p 266b
uyamau 敬 856
uyauyashii 恭 p 244b
uzu 渦 p 263b

— W —

WA 話 240
WA 和 440
-wa 羽 82
wa 輪 631
WAI 賄 p 274a
wakai 若 896
wakareru, wakaru, wakeru 分
    218
wakareru 別 607
wake 訳 993
WAKU 惑 p 261b
waku 枠 p 230a
waku 沸 p 230b
WAN 湾 p 264a
WAN 腕 p 266a
warau 笑 537
ware 我 833
wari, wareru, waru 割 838
warui 悪 241
wasureru 忘 986
wata 綿 818
watakushi 私 887
wataru, watasu 渡 p 263b
waza 業 278
wazawai 災 707
wazurau, wazurawashii,
    wazurawasu 煩 p 272a

— Y —

YA 夜 232
YA 野 233
ya 家 89
ya 矢 145
ya 屋 256
yabure, yaburu 破 788
yabureru 敗 591
yado, yadoru, yadosu 宿 327
YAKU 役 419
YAKU 薬 420
YAKU 約 621
YAKU 訳 993
YAKU 厄 p 206b
YAKU 躍 p 293a
yaku, yakeru 焼 539